Zen Buddhism

Buddhist Verses
Sutras
and
Teachings

by
Shawn Conners

Translated by
Chen Song

Pagoda Press

Zen Buddhism - Buddhist Verses, Sutras and Teachings
By Shawn Conners
Translations by Chen Song, Barton Williams, et al

First Printing — December 2018

Published by
Pagoda Press

ISBN10: 1-937021-14-9
ISBN13: 978-1-937021-14-6

Table of Contents

Table of Contents (continued)

Table of Contents (continued)

Book 3: Pure Land Sect Teachings
The Threefold Lotus Sutras

Translated from Japanese texts

Introduction
Finding the Buddha along the Silk Road

> *"There is an old saying: 'Keep your mind level. If the mind is level, the whole world will be level.' Consider these words. Realize that all the distinctions of the world are caused by the discriminating views of the mind. There is a path to Enlightenment in those very words. Indeed, the ways to Enlightenment are unlimited."*

Siddhartha Gautama, the great Indian philosopher, is believed to have attained Enlightenment sometime in the middle of the 5th century before the Common Era, while meditating under a Bodhi Tree. From that time of Enlightenment until his death, by which he entered Nirvana, he traveled by foot around the countryside of India, teaching others his philosophy of the Middle Path. The foundations of Buddhist tradition and practice are often called the Three Jewels: the *Buddha*, the *Dharma* (teachings), and the *Sangha* (community). These concepts eventually traveled from India to China, and then to Japan, and became distilled into the movement within the Buddhist faith known as Zen.

The first jewel is the *Buddha*, "The Awakened One"; Buddha Siddhartha Gautama, whose stated goal in *The Four Noble Truths* was to help sentient beings end suffering (*dukkha*), achieve Nirvana, and escape the cycle of suffering and rebirth (*samsara*), caused by our actions and defilements (*karma*).

The Buddha said:

"There are two aims which he who has given up the world ought not to follow after—devotion, on the one hand, to those things whose attractions depend upon the passions, a low and pagan ideal, fit only for the worldly-minded, ignoble, unprofitable; and the practice on the other hand of asceticism, which is painful, ignoble, and unprofitable.

"There is a Middle Path discovered by the Tathāgata— a path which opens the eyes, and bestows understanding, which leads to peace, to insight, to

the higher wisdom, to Nirvāna. Truly! it is this Noble Eightfold Path; that is to say:

> *Right Views*
> *Right Aspirations*
> *Right Speech*
> *Right Conduct*
> *Right Mode of Livelihood*
> *Right Effort*
> *Right Mindfulness*
> *Right Rapture*

"Now this is the Noble Truth as to suffering. Birth is attended with pain, decay is painful, disease is painful, death is painful. Union with the unpleasant is painful, painful is separation from the pleasant; and any craving unsatisfied, that too is painful. In brief, the five aggregates of clinging (that is, the conditions of individuality) are painful.

"Now this is the Noble Truth as to the origin of suffering. Truly! it is the craving thirst that causes the renewal of Becomings, that is accompanied by sensual delights, and seeks satisfaction now here, now there—that is to say, the craving for the gratification of the senses, or the craving for a future life, or the craving for prosperity.

"Now this is the Noble Truth as to the passing away of pain. Truly! it is the passing away so that no passion remains, the giving up, the getting rid of, the being emancipated from, the harboring no longer of this craving thirst.

"Now this is the Noble Truth as to the way that leads to the passing away of pain. Truly! it is this Noble Eightfold Path, that is to say, Right Views, Right Aspirations, Right speech, conduct and mode of livelihood, Right Effort, Right Mindfulness and Right Rapture.

"When a brother has, by himself, known and realized, and continues to abide, here in this visible world, in that Emancipation of mind, in that Emancipation of heart, which is called Arahatship; that is a condition higher still and sweeter still, for the sake of which the brethren lead the religious life under me."

The second jewel, the *Dharma*, or teachings of Buddha Gautama, reached throughout India in a constant and inexorable fashion for several centuries, gaining momentum. As early as the 3rd century before the Common Era, the Maurya Emperor Ashoka the Great, having waged the bloody Kalinga War, ultimately found horror in what had been done in his name during the conquest, and turned to the teachings of the Buddha Gautama. Ashoka also decreed Buddhist teachings to be carved onto stone columns and the polished faces of cliff walls, as monuments to this new way of thinking. He would later send out missionaries to such places as Syria, Egypt, and Macedonia.

Ultimately, it would be through the central Asian countries that China came to learn of Buddhism. The legendary trade route known as the Silk Road passed through boundless territories in the Han dynasty during the 1st and 2nd centuries. Along these "silk routes," the spirit of mercantilism still thrived, as it had since the time of Alexander the Great. Extending 4,000 miles (6,500 km), the Silk Road enabled merchants to transport luxuries such as silk, musk, spices, medicine, as well as serving as a conduit for the spread of knowledge, ideas, and culture between Ancient China, India, Pakistan, Asia Minor and the Mediterranean. Most historians agree that the flow of trade and cultural exchange on the Silk Road was a significant factor in the development of the great civilizations of China, India, Egypt, Persia, Arabia, Rome, and countless others.

Among the trading agents and nomads along these various "silk routes," which became known as the Silk Road, were also missionaries and scholars…with compelling scrolls filled with the teachings of the Buddha Gautama. Many of the scrolls were still in Sanskrit, and thus destined for the literati in China, who were eager to translate them. By the 4th century of the Common Era, most of the *Mahayana* scriptures from India had been successfully translated into Chinese. Among the most cherished were several texts about the Indian yoga practices of breathing and other methods for the attainment of mind control and concentrated meditation, making up the Indian practice of *Dhyāna* (or *Chān* in China and *Zen* in Japan).

The Flower Sermon is often recognized as the symbolic beginning of the movement of Zen Buddhism. *The Flower Sermon* was wordless, encapsulating *tathātā* (one who has arrived at *suchness*): it comprised the purity of direct mental and spiritual communication, wherein Buddha Gautama, (also known as *Śākyamuni*) ascended to a speaking dais and proffered a white flower to his assembly of followers. He was then silent. Among the assembly of followers there was no realization, except by Mahākāśyapa (*Maha Kasho* in Japan*)*, who smiled. According to tradition, the smile signified Mahākāśyapa's direct and complete understanding and cognition of the moment as it was, and Buddha Gautama affirmed this by saying:

"I possess the true Dharma eye, the marvelous mind of Nirvana, the true form of the formless, the subtle Dharma Gate that does not rest on words or letters but is a special transmission outside of the scriptures. This I entrust to Mahākāśyapa."

Thus, a way within the canons of Buddhism developed which concentrated on direct spiritual experience rather than solely on rational creeds or revealed scriptures. Zen is a method of the meditative Buddhist religion which seeks to enlighten people in the manner that Mahākāśyapa experienced.

The Chān sect (in China) and the Zen sect (in Japan) place a great deal of focus on the instructions of Bodhidarma, a teacher in the 5th century of the Common Era, from the southern region of India. After renouncing his status as Prince and becoming a Buddhist monk, Bodhidharma left his kingdom and traveled through Southeast Asia into Southern China, spreading Buddhist teachings and gathering disciples. Later, priests and students spread the teachings of this sect further throughout Northern Asia. Bodhidarma is described biographically in Chān and Zen sect texts in this way:

"Mahākāśyapa was the first, leading the line of transmission;
Twenty-eight Fathers followed him in the West;
The Lamp was then brought over the sea to this country;
And Bodhidharma became the First Father here
His mantle, as we all know, passed over six Fathers,
And by them many minds came to see the Light."

During the 6th century, the King of Paikche (now Korea) dispatched an envoy to present a Buddhist image and scroll of sutras to the Japanese imperial court of Emperor Kinmei. This is generally marked as the first recorded entry of early Buddhism into Japanese culture. The desire for the community of the Enlightened to help others along the Middle Path, through teaching and meditation is known as the third jewel of Buddhism, the *Sangha*.

Presented in this modern special edition is a unique selection of the ancient texts which would follow the path of the Silk Road from India to China to Japan, and then evolve into the school of thought known today as Zen Buddhism. This path follows the Indian *Mahayana* verses from the *Dhammapada*, to a collection of Buddhist sutras (scriptures) culled from Chinese texts, and finally concludes with the *Threefold Lotus*, the three Pure Land sect sutras favored in Japan. The beginning student of Buddhism can therefore seek the Three Jewels: the *Buddha*, the *Dharma*, and the *Sangha,* in the re-telling of the verses and sutras by those missionaries, merchants and scholars who traversed the Silk Road, spreading the word of Buddha Siddhartha Gautama, each on their own path toward Enlightenment.

The editor would like to thank Chen Song, Barton Williams, and the following sources of translation, which were used in the compilation of this edition:

Dhammapada:
1. Friedrich Max Muller
2. K. J. Saunders

Buddhist Sutras:
1. Dwight Goddard
2. Buddhist Text Translation Society

The Pure Land Sect *Threefold Lotus* **Sutras**:
1. The Tripiṭaka Master Kumārajīva
2. J. Takakusu
3. Bukkyo Dendo Kyokai

General Research:
1. His Holiness the 14th Dalai Lama, Tenzin Gyatso
2. T.W. Rhys Davids
3. Teitaro Suzuki
4. Narada Mahathera

Book 1

Buddhist Verses

From
Dhammapada

Transcribed from Sanskrit

Buddhist Verses from the Dhammapada

Chapter I: The Twin-Verses

1 All that we are is the result of what we have thought: it is founded on our thoughts, it is made up of our thoughts. If a man speaks or acts with an evil thought, pain follows him, as the wheel follows the foot of the ox that draws the carriage.

2 All that we are is the result of what we have thought: it is founded on our thoughts, it is made up of our thoughts. If a man speaks or acts with a pure thought, happiness follows him, like a shadow that never leaves him.

3 "He abused me, he beat me, he defeated me, he robbed me,"--in those who harbour such thoughts hatred will never cease.

4 "He abused me, he beat me, he defeated me, he robbed me,"--in those who do not harbour such thoughts hatred will cease.

5 For hatred does not cease by hatred at any time: hatred ceases by love, this is an old rule.

6 The world does not know that we must all come to an end here; but those who know it, their quarrels cease at once.

7 He who lives looking for pleasures only, his senses uncontrolled, immoderate in his food, idle, and weak, Mara (the tempter) will certainly overthrow him, as the wind throws down a weak tree.

8 He who lives without looking for pleasures, his senses well controlled, moderate in his food, faithful and strong, him Mara will certainly not overthrow, any more than the wind throws down a rocky mountain.

9 He who wishes to put on the yellow dress without having cleansed himself from sin, who disregards temperance and truth, is unworthy of the yellow dress.

10 But he who has cleansed himself from sin, is well grounded in all virtues, and regards also temperance and truth, he is indeed worthy of the yellow dress.

11 They who imagine truth in untruth, and see untruth in truth, never arrive at truth, but follow vain desires.

12 They who know truth in truth, and untruth in untruth, arrive at truth, and follow true desires.

13 As rain breaks through an ill-thatched house, passion will break through an unreflecting mind.

14 As rain does not break through a well-thatched house, passion will not break through a well-reflecting mind.

15 The evil-doer mourns in this world, and he mourns in the next; he mourns in both. He mourns and suffers when he sees the evil of his own work.

16 The virtuous man delights in this world, and he delights in the next; he delights in both. He delights and rejoices, when he sees the purity of his own work.

17 The evil-doer suffers in this world, and he suffers in the next; he suffers in both. He suffers when he thinks of the evil he has done; he suffers more when going on the evil path.

18 The virtuous man is happy in this world, and he is happy in the next; he is happy in both. He is happy when he thinks of the good he has done; he is still happier when going on the good path.

19 The thoughtless man, even if he can recite a large portion (of the law), but is not a doer of it, has no share in the priesthood, but is like a cowherd counting the cows of others.

20 The follower of the law, even if he can recite only a small portion (of the law), but, having forsaken passion and hatred and foolishness, possesses true knowledge and serenity of mind, he, caring for nothing in this world or that to come, has indeed a share in the priesthood.

Chapter II: On Earnestness

21 Earnestness is the path of immortality (Nirvana), thoughtlessness the path of death. Those who are in earnest do not die, those who are thoughtless are as if dead already.

22 Those who are advanced in earnestness, having understood this clearly, delight in earnestness, and rejoice in the knowledge of the Ariyas (the elect).

23 These wise people, meditative, steady, always possessed of strong powers, attain to Nirvana, the highest happiness.

24 If an earnest person has roused himself, if he is not forgetful, if his deeds are pure, if he acts with consideration, if he restrains himself, and lives according to law, then his glory will increase.

25 By rousing himself, by earnestness, by restraint and control, the wise man may make for himself an island which no flood can overwhelm.

26 Fools follow after vanity, men of evil wisdom. The wise man keeps earnestness as his best jewel.

27 Follow not after vanity, nor after the enjoyment of love and lust! He who is earnest and meditative, obtains ample joy.

28 When the learned man drives away vanity by earnestness, he, the wise, climbing the terraced heights of wisdom, looks down upon the fools, serene he looks upon the toiling crowd, as one that stands on a mountain looks down upon them that stand upon the plain.

29 Earnest among the thoughtless, awake among the sleepers, the wise man advances like a racer, leaving behind the hack.

30 By earnestness did Maghavan (Indra) rise to the lordship of the gods. People praise earnestness; thoughtlessness is always blamed.

31 A Bhikshu (mendicant) who delights in earnestness, who looks with fear on thoughtlessness, moves about like fire, burning all his fetters, small or large.

32 A Bhikshu (mendicant) who delights in reflection, who looks with fear on thoughtlessness, cannot fall away (from his perfect state)--he is close upon Nirvana.

Chapter III: Thought

33 As a fletcher makes straight his arrow, a wise man makes straight his trembling and unsteady thought, which is difficult to guard, difficult to hold back.

34 As a fish taken from his watery home and thrown on dry ground, our thought trembles all over in order to escape the dominion of Mara (the tempter).

35 It is good to tame the mind, which is difficult to hold in and flighty, rushing wherever it listeth; a tamed mind brings happiness.

36 Let the wise man guard his thoughts, for they are difficult to perceive, very artful, and they rush wherever they list: thoughts well-guarded bring happiness.

37 Those who bridle their mind which travels far, moves about alone, is without a body, and hides in the chamber (of the heart), will be free from the bonds of Mara (the tempter).

38 If a man's thoughts are unsteady, if he does not know the true law, if his peace of mind is troubled, his knowledge will never be perfect.

39 If a man's thoughts are not dissipated, if his mind is not perplexed, if he has ceased to think of good or evil, then there is no fear for him while he is watchful.

40 Knowing that this body is (fragile) like a jar, and making this thought firm like a fortress, one should attack Mara (the tempter) with the weapon of knowledge, one should watch him when conquered, and should never rest.

41 Before long, alas! this body will lie on the earth, despised, without understanding, like a useless log.

42 Whatever a hater may do to a hater, or an enemy to an enemy, a wrongly-directed mind will do us greater mischief.

43 Not a mother, not a father will do so much, nor any other relative; a well-directed mind will do us greater service.

Chapter IV: Flowers

44 Who shall overcome this earth, and the world of Yama (the lord of the departed), and the world of the gods? Who shall find out the plainly shown path of virtue, as a clever man finds out the (right) flower?

45 The disciple will overcome the earth, and the world of Yama, and the world of the gods. The disciple will find out the plainly shown path of virtue, as a clever man finds out the (right) flower.

46 He who knows that this body is like froth, and has learnt that it is as unsubstantial as a mirage, will break the flower-pointed arrow of Mara, and never see the king of death.

47 Death carries off a man who is gathering flowers and whose mind is distracted, as a flood carries off a sleeping village.

48 Death subdues a man who is gathering flowers, and whose mind is distracted, before he is satiated in his pleasures.

49 As the bee collects nectar and departs without injuring the flower, or its colour or scent, so let a sage dwell in his village.

50 Not the perversities of others, not their sins of commission or omission, but his own misdeeds and negligences should a sage take notice of.

51 Like a beautiful flower, full of colour, but without scent, are the fine but fruitless words of him who does not act accordingly.

52 But, like a beautiful flower, full of colour and full of scent, are the fine and fruitful words of him who acts accordingly.

53 As many kinds of wreaths can be made from a heap of flowers, so many good things may be achieved by a mortal when once he is born.

54 The scent of flowers does not travel against the wind, nor (that of) sandal-wood, or of Tagara and Mallika flowers; but the odour of good people travels even against the wind; a good man pervades every place.

55 Sandal-wood or Tagara, a lotus-flower, or a Vassiki, among these sorts of perfumes, the perfume of virtue is unsurpassed.

56 Mean is the scent that comes from Tagara and sandal-wood--the perfume of those who possess virtue rises up to the gods as the highest.

57 Of the people who possess these virtues, who live without thoughtlessness, and who are emancipated through true knowledge, Mara, the tempter, never finds the way.

58, 59. As on a heap of rubbish cast upon the highway the lily will grow full of sweet perfume and delight, thus the disciple of the truly enlightened Buddha shines forth by his knowledge among those who are like rubbish, among the people that walk in darkness.

Chapter V: The Fool

60 Long is the night to him who is awake; long is a mile to him who is tired; long is life to the foolish who do not know the true law.

61 If a traveler does not meet with one who is his better, or his equal, let him firmly keep to his solitary journey; there is no companionship with a fool.

62 "These sons belong to me, and this wealth belongs to me," with such thoughts a fool is tormented. He himself does not belong to himself; how much less sons and wealth?

63 The fool who knows his foolishness, is wise at least so far. But a fool who thinks himself wise, he is called a fool indeed.

64 If a fool be associated with a wise man even all his life, he will perceive the truth as little as a spoon perceives the taste of soup.

65 If an intelligent man be associated for one minute only with a wise man, he will soon perceive the truth, as the tongue perceives the taste of soup.

66 Fools of little understanding have themselves for their greatest enemies, for they do evil deeds which must bear bitter fruits.

67 That deed is not well done of which a man must repent, and the reward of which he receives crying and with a tearful face.

68 No, that deed is well done of which a man does not repent, and the reward of which he receives gladly and cheerfully.

69 As long as the evil deed done does not bear fruit, the fool thinks it is like honey; but when it ripens, then the fool suffers grief.

70 Let a fool month after month eat his food (like an ascetic) with the tip of a blade of Kusa grass, yet he is not worth the sixteenth particle of those who have well weighed the law.

71 An evil deed, like newly-drawn milk, does not turn (suddenly); smouldering, like fire covered by ashes, it follows the fool.

72 And when the evil deed, after it has become known, brings sorrow to the fool, then it destroys his bright lot, nay, it cleaves his head.

73 Let the fool wish for a false reputation, for precedence among the Bhikshus, for lordship in the convents, for worship among other people!

74 "May both the layman and he who has left the world think that this is done by me; may they be subject to me in everything which is to be done or is not to be done," thus is the mind of the fool, and his desire and pride increase.

75 "One is the road that leads to wealth, another the road that leads to Nirvana;" if the Bhikshu, the disciple of Buddha, has learnt this, he will not yearn for honour, he will strive after separation from the world.

Chapter VI: The Wise Man (Pandita)

76 If you see an intelligent man who tells you where true treasures are to be found, who shows what is to be avoided, and administers reproofs, follow that wise man; it will be better, not worse, for those who follow him.

77 Let him admonish, let him teach, let him forbid what is improper- -he will be beloved of the good, by the bad he will be hated.

78 Do not have evil-doers for friends, do not have low people for friends: have virtuous people for friends, have for friends the best of men.

79 He who drinks in the law lives happily with a serene mind: the sage rejoices always in the law, as preached by the elect (Ariyas).

80 Well-makers lead the water (wherever they like); fletchers bend the arrow; carpenters bend a log of wood; wise people fashion themselves.

81 As a solid rock is not shaken by the wind, wise people falter not amidst blame and praise.

82 Wise people, after they have listened to the laws, become serene, like a deep, smooth, and still lake.

83 Good people walk on whatever befall, the good do not prattle, longing for pleasure; whether touched by happiness or sorrow wise people never appear elated or depressed.

84 If, whether for his own sake, or for the sake of others, a man wishes neither for a son, nor for wealth, nor for lordship, and if he does not wish for his own success by unfair means, then he is good, wise, and virtuous.

85 Few are there among men who arrive at the other shore (become Arhats); the other people here run up and down the shore.

86 But those who, when the law has been well preached to them, follow the law, will pass across the dominion of death, however difficult to overcome.

87, 88. A wise man should leave the dark state (of ordinary life), and follow the bright state (of the Bhikshu). After going from his home to a homeless state, he should in his retirement look for enjoyment where there seemed to be no enjoyment. Leaving all pleasures behind, and calling nothing his own, the wise man should purge himself from all the troubles of the mind.

89 Those whose mind is well grounded in the (seven) elements of knowledge, who without clinging to anything, rejoice in freedom from attachment, whose appetites have been conquered, and who are full of light, are free (even) in this world.

Chapter VII: The Venerable (Arhat)

90 There is no suffering for him who has finished his journey, and abandoned grief, who has freed himself on all sides, and thrown off all fetters.

91 They depart with their thoughts well-collected, they are not happy in their abode; like swans who have left their lake, they leave their house and home.

92 Men who have no riches, who live on recognised food, who have perceived void and unconditioned freedom (Nirvana), their path is difficult to understand, like that of birds in the air.

93 He whose appetites are stilled, who is not absorbed in enjoyment, who has perceived void and unconditioned freedom (Nirvana), his path is difficult to understand, like that of birds in the air.

94 The gods even envy him whose senses, like horses well broken in by the driver, have been subdued, who is free from pride, and free from appetites.

95 Such a one who does his duty is tolerant like the earth, like Indra's bolt; he is like a lake without mud; no new births are in store for him.

96 His thought is quiet, quiet are his word and deed, when he has obtained freedom by true knowledge, when he has thus become a quiet man.

97 The man who is free from credulity, but knows the uncreated, who has cut all ties, removed all temptations, renounced all desires, he is the greatest of men.

98 In a hamlet or in a forest, in the deep water or on the dry land, wherever venerable persons (Arhanta) dwell, that place is delightful.

99 Forests are delightful; where the world finds no delight, there the passionless will find delight, for they look not for pleasures.

Chapter VIII: The Thousands

100 Even though a speech be a thousand (of words), but made up of senseless words, one word of sense is better, which if a man hears, he becomes quiet.

101 Even though a Gatha (poem) be a thousand (of words), but made up of senseless words, one word of a Gatha is better, which if a man hears, he becomes quiet.

102 Though a man recite a hundred Gathas made up of senseless words, one word of the law is better, which if a man hears, he becomes quiet.

103 If one man conquers in battle a thousand times thousand men, and if another conquer himself, he is the greatest of conquerors.

104, 105. One's own self conquered is better than all other people; not even a god, a Gandharva, not Mara with Brahman could change into defeat the victory of a man who has vanquished himself, and always lives under restraint.

106 If a man for a hundred years sacrifice month after month with a thousand, and if he but for one moment pay homage to a man whose soul is grounded (in true knowledge), better is that homage than sacrifice for a hundred years.

107 If a man for a hundred years worship Agni (fire) in the forest, and if he but for one moment pay homage to a man whose soul is grounded (in true knowledge), better is that homage than sacrifice for a hundred years.

108 Whatever a man sacrifices in this world as an offering or as an oblation for a whole year in order to gain merit, the whole of it is not worth a quarter (a farthing); reverence shown to the righteous is better.

109 He who always greets and constantly reveres the aged, four things will increase to him, viz. life, beauty, happiness, power.

110 But he who lives a hundred years, vicious and unrestrained, a life of one day is better if a man is virtuous and reflecting.

111 And he who lives a hundred years, ignorant and unrestrained, a life of one day is better if a man is wise and reflecting.

112 And he who lives a hundred years, idle and weak, a life of one day is better if a man has attained firm strength.

113 And he who lives a hundred years, not seeing beginning and end, a life of one day is better if a man sees beginning and end.

114 And he who lives a hundred years, not seeing the immortal place, a life of one day is better if a man sees the immortal place.

115 And he who lives a hundred years, not seeing the highest law, a life of one day is better if a man sees the highest law.

Chapter IX: Evil

116 If a man would hasten towards the good, he should keep his thought away from evil; if a man does what is good slothfully, his mind delights in evil.

117 If a man commits a sin, let him not do it again; let him not delight in sin: pain is the outcome of evil.

118 If a man does what is good, let him do it again; let him delight in it: happiness is the outcome of good.

119 Even an evil-doer sees happiness as long as his evil deed has not ripened; but when his evil deed has ripened, then does the evil-doer see evil.

120 Even a good man sees evil days, as long as his good deed has not ripened; but when his good deed has ripened, then does the good man see happy days.

121 Let no man think lightly of evil, saying in his heart, It will not come nigh unto me. Even by the falling of water-drops a water-pot is filled; the fool becomes full of evil, even if he gathers it little by little.

122 Let no man think lightly of good, saying in his heart, It will not come nigh unto me. Even by the falling of water-drops a water-pot is filled; the wise man becomes full of good, even if he gathers it little by little.

123 Let a man avoid evil deeds, as a merchant, if he has few companions and carries much wealth, avoids a dangerous road; as a man who loves life avoids poison.

124 He who has no wound on his hand, may touch poison with his hand; poison does not affect one who has no wound; nor is there evil for one who does not commit evil.

125 If a man offends a harmless, pure, and innocent person, the evil falls back upon that fool, like light dust thrown up against the wind.

126 Some people are born again; evil-doers go to hell; righteous people go to heaven; those who are free from all worldly desires attain Nirvana.

127 Not in the sky, not in the midst of the sea, not if we enter into the clefts of the mountains, is there known a spot in the whole world where death could not overcome (the mortal).

Chapter X: Punishment

129 All men tremble at punishment, all men fear death; remember that you are like unto them, and do not kill, nor cause slaughter.

130 All men tremble at punishment, all men love life; remember that thou art like unto them, and do not kill, nor cause slaughter.

131 He who seeking his own happiness punishes or kills beings who also long for happiness, will not find happiness after death.

132 He who seeking his own happiness does not punish or kill beings who also long for happiness, will find happiness after death.

133 Do not speak harshly to anybody; those who are spoken to will answer thee in the same way. Angry speech is painful, blows for blows will touch thee.

134 If, like a shattered metal plate (gong), thou utter not, then thou hast reached Nirvana; contention is not known to thee.

135 As a cowherd with his staff drives his cows into the stable, so do Age and Death drive the life of men.

136 A fool does not know when he commits his evil deeds: but the wicked man burns by his own deeds, as if burnt by fire.

137 He who inflicts pain on innocent and harmless persons, will soon come to one of these ten states:

138 He will have cruel suffering, loss, injury of the body, heavy affliction, or loss of mind,

139 Or a misfortune coming from the king, or a fearful accusation, or loss of relations, or destruction of treasures,

140 Or lightning-fire will burn his houses; and when his body is destroyed, the fool will go to hell.

141 Not nakedness, not platted hair, not dirt, not fasting, or lying on the earth, not rubbing with dust, not sitting motionless, can purify a mortal who has not overcome desires.

142 He who, though dressed in fine apparel, exercises tranquility, is quiet, subdued, restrained, chaste, and has ceased to find fault with all other beings, he indeed is a Brahmana, an ascetic (sramana), a friar (bhikshu).

143 Is there in this world any man so restrained by humility that he does not mind reproof, as a well-trained horse the whip?

144 Like a well-trained horse when touched by the whip, be ye active and lively, and by faith, by virtue, by energy, by meditation, by discernment of the law you will overcome this great pain (of reproof), perfect in knowledge and in behaviour, and never forgetful.

145 Well-makers lead the water (wherever they like); fletchers bend the arrow; carpenters bend a log of wood; good people fashion themselves.

Chapter XI: Old Age

146 How is there laughter, how is there joy, as this world is always burning? Why do you not seek a light, ye who are surrounded by darkness?

147 Look at this dressed-up lump, covered with wounds, joined together, sickly, full of many thoughts, which has no strength, no hold!

148 This body is wasted, full of sickness, and frail; this heap of corruption breaks to pieces, life indeed ends in death.

149 Those white bones, like gourds thrown away in the autumn, what pleasure is there in looking at them?

150 After a stronghold has been made of the bones, it is covered with flesh and blood, and there dwell in it old age and death, pride and deceit.

151 The brilliant chariots of kings are destroyed, the body also approaches destruction, but the virtue of good people never approaches destruction, thus do the good say to the good.

152 A man who has learnt little, grows old like an ox, his flesh grows, but his knowledge does not grow.

153, 154. Looking for the maker of this tabernacle, I shall have to run through a course of many births, so long as I do not find (him); and painful is birth again and again. But now, maker of the tabernacle, thou hast been seen; thou shalt not make up this tabernacle again. All thy rafters are broken, thy ridge-pole is sundered; the mind, approaching the Eternal (visankhara, nirvana), has attained to the extinction of all desires.

155 Men who have not observed proper discipline, and have not gained treasure in their youth, perish like old herons in a lake without fish.

156 Men who have not observed proper discipline, and have not gained treasure in their youth, lie, like broken bows, sighing after the past.

Chapter XII: Self

157 If a man hold himself dear, let him watch himself carefully; during one at least out of the three watches a wise man should be watchful.

158 Let each man direct himself first to what is proper, then let him teach others; thus a wise man will not suffer.

159 If a man make himself as he teaches others to be, then, being himself well subdued, he may subdue (others); one's own self is indeed difficult to subdue.

160 Self is the lord of self, who else could be the lord? With self well subdued, a man finds a lord such as few can find.

161 The evil done by oneself, self-begotten, self-bred, crushes the foolish, as a diamond breaks a precious stone.

162 He whose wickedness is very great brings himself down to that state where his enemy wishes him to be, as a creeper does with the tree which it surrounds.

163 Bad deeds, and deeds hurtful to ourselves, are easy to do; what is beneficial and good, that is very difficult to do.

164 The foolish man who scorns the rule of the venerable (Arahat), of the elect (Ariya), of the virtuous, and follows false doctrine, he bears fruit to his own destruction, like the fruits of the Katthaka reed.

165 By oneself the evil is done, by oneself one suffers; by oneself evil is left undone, by oneself one is purified. Purity and impurity belong to oneself, no one can purify another.

166 Let no one forget his own duty for the sake of another's, however great; let a man, after he has discerned his own duty, be always attentive to his duty.

Chapter XIII: The World

167 Do not follow the evil law! Do not live on in thoughtlessness! Do not follow false doctrine! Be not a friend of the world.

168 Rouse thyself! do not be idle! Follow the law of virtue! The virtuous rests in bliss in this world and in the next.

169 Follow the law of virtue; do not follow that of sin. The virtuous rests in bliss in this world and in the next.

170 Look upon the world as a bubble, look upon it as a mirage: the king of death does not see him who thus looks down upon the world.

171 Come, look at this glittering world, like unto a royal chariot; the foolish are immersed in it, but the wise do not touch it.

172 He who formerly was reckless and afterwards became sober, brightens up this world, like the moon when freed from clouds.

173 He whose evil deeds are covered by good deeds, brightens up this world, like the moon when freed from clouds.

174 This world is dark, few only can see here; a few only go to heaven, like birds escaped from the net.

175 The swans go on the path of the sun, they go through the ether by means of their miraculous power; the wise are led out of this world, when they have conquered Mara and his train.

176 If a man has transgressed one law, and speaks lies, and scoffs at another world, there is no evil he will not do.

177 The uncharitable do not go to the world of the gods; fools only do not praise liberality; a wise man rejoices in liberality, and through it becomes blessed in the other world.

178 Better than sovereignty over the earth, better than going to heaven, better than lordship over all worlds, is the reward of the first step in holiness.

Chapter XIV: The Buddha (The Awakened)

179 He whose conquest is not conquered again, into whose conquest no one in this world enters, by what track can you lead him, the Awakened, the Omniscient, the trackless?

180 He whom no desire with its snares and poisons can lead astray, by what track can you lead him, the Awakened, the Omniscient, the trackless?

181 Even the gods envy those who are awakened and not forgetful, who are given to meditation, who are wise, and who delight in the repose of retirement (from the world).

182 Difficult (to obtain) is the conception of men, difficult is the life of mortals, difficult is the hearing of the True Law, difficult is the birth of the Awakened (the attainment of Buddhahood).

183 Not to commit any sin, to do good, and to purify one's mind, that is the teaching of (all) the Awakened.

184 The Awakened call patience the highest penance, long-suffering the highest Nirvana; for he is not an anchorite (pravragita) who strikes others, he is not an ascetic (sramana) who insults others.

185 Not to blame, not to strike, to live restrained under the law, to be moderate in eating, to sleep and sit alone, and to dwell on the highest thoughts, this is the teaching of the Awakened.

186 There is no satisfying lusts, even by a shower of gold pieces; he who knows that lusts have a short taste and cause pain, he is wise;

187 Even in heavenly pleasures he finds no satisfaction, the disciple who is fully awakened delights only in the destruction of all desires.

188 Men, driven by fear, go to many a refuge, to mountains and forests, to groves and sacred trees.

189 But that is not a safe refuge, that is not the best refuge; a man is not delivered from all pains after having gone to that refuge.

190 He who takes refuge with Buddha, the Law, and the Church; he who, with clear understanding, sees the four holy truths:

191 Pain, The origin of pain, The destruction of pain, and The eightfold holy way that leads to the quieting of pain.

192 That is the safe refuge, that is the best refuge; having gone to that refuge, a man is delivered from all pain.

193 A supernatural person (a Buddha) is not easily found, he is not born everywhere. Wherever such a sage is born, that race prospers.

194 Happy is the arising of the awakened, happy is the teaching of the True Law, happy is peace in the church, happy is the devotion of those who are at peace.

195, 196. He who pays homage to those who deserve homage, whether the awakened (Buddha) or their disciples, those who have overcome the host (of evils), and crossed the flood of sorrow, he who pays homage to such as have found deliverance and know no fear, his merit can never be measured by anybody.

Chapter XV: Happiness

197 Let us live happily then, not hating those who hate us! among men who hate us let us dwell free from hatred!

198 Let us live happily then, free from ailments among the ailing! among men who are ailing let us dwell free from ailments!

199 Let us live happily then, free from greed among the greedy! among men who are greedy let us dwell free from greed!

200 Let us live happily then, though we call nothing our own! We shall be like the bright gods, feeding on happiness!

201 Victory breeds hatred, for the conquered is unhappy. He who has given up both victory and defeat, he, the contented, is happy.

202 There is no fire like passion; there is no losing throw like hatred; there is no pain like this body; there is no happiness higher than rest.

203 Hunger is the worst of diseases, the body the greatest of pains; if one knows this truly, that is Nirvana, the highest happiness.

204 Health is the greatest of gifts, contentedness the best riches; trust is the best of relationships, Nirvana the highest happiness.

205 He who has tasted the sweetness of solitude and tranquillity, is free from fear and free from sin, while he tastes the sweetness of drinking in the law.

206 The sight of the elect (Arya) is good, to live with them is always happiness; if a man does not see fools, he will be truly happy.

207 He who walks in the company of fools suffers a long way; company with fools, as with an enemy, is always painful; company with the wise is pleasure, like meeting with kinsfolk.

208 Therefore, one ought to follow the wise, the intelligent, the learned, the much enduring, the dutiful, the elect; one ought to follow a good and wise man, as the moon follows the path of the stars.

Chapter XVI: Pleasure

209 He who gives himself to vanity, and does not give himself to meditation, forgetting the real aim (of life) and grasping at pleasure, will in time envy him who has exerted himself in meditation.

210 Let no man ever look for what is pleasant, or what is unpleasant. Not to see what is pleasant is pain, and it is pain to see what is unpleasant.

211 Let, therefore, no man love anything; loss of the beloved is evil. Those who love nothing and hate nothing, have no fetters.

212 From pleasure comes grief, from pleasure comes fear; he who is free from pleasure knows neither grief nor fear.

213 From affection comes grief, from affection comes fear; he who is free from affection knows neither grief nor fear.

214 From lust comes grief, from lust comes fear; he who is free from lust knows neither grief nor fear.

215 From love comes grief, from love comes fear; he who is free from love knows neither grief nor fear.

216 From greed comes grief, from greed comes fear; he who is free from greed knows neither grief nor fear.

217 He who possesses virtue and intelligence, who is just, speaks the truth, and does what is his own business, him the world will hold dear.

218 He in whom a desire for the Ineffable (Nirvana) has sprung up, who is satisfied in his mind, and whose thoughts are not bewildered by love, he is called urdhvamsrotas (carried upwards by the stream).

219 Kinsmen, friends, and lovers salute a man who has been long away, and returns safe from afar.

220 In like manner his good works receive him who has done good, and has gone from this world to the other, as kinsmen receive a friend on his return.

Chapter XVII: Anger

221 Let a man leave anger, let him forsake pride, let him overcome all bondage! No sufferings befall the man who is not attached to name and form, and who calls nothing his own.

222 He who holds back rising anger like a rolling chariot, him I call a real driver; other people are but holding the reins.

223 Let a man overcome anger by love, let him overcome evil by good; let him overcome the greedy by liberality, the liar by truth!

224 Speak the truth, do not yield to anger; give, if thou art asked for little; by these three steps thou wilt go near the gods.

225 The sages who injure nobody, and who always control their body, they will go to the unchangeable place (Nirvana), where, if they have gone, they will suffer no more.

226 Those who are ever watchful, who study day and night, and who strive after Nirvana, their passions will come to an end.

227 This is an old saying, O Atula, this is not only of to-day: `They blame him who sits silent, they blame him who speaks much, they also blame him who says little; there is no one on earth who is not blamed.'

228 There never was, there never will be, nor is there now, a man who is always blamed, or a man who is always praised.

229, 230. But he whom those who discriminate praise continually day after day, as without blemish, wise, rich in knowledge and virtue, who would dare to blame him, like a coin made of gold from the Gambu river? Even the gods praise him, he is praised even by Brahman.

231 Beware of bodily anger, and control thy body! Leave the sins of the body, and with thy body practise virtue!

232 Beware of the anger of the tongue, and control thy tongue! Leave the sins of the tongue, and practise virtue with thy tongue!

233 Beware of the anger of the mind, and control thy mind! Leave the sins of the mind, and practise virtue with thy mind!

234 The wise who control their body, who control their tongue, the wise who control their mind, are indeed well controlled.

   Buddhist Verses from the Dhammapada

Chapter XVIII: Impurity

235 Thou art now like a sear leaf, the messengers of death (Yama) have come near to thee; thou standest at the door of thy departure, and thou hast no provision for thy journey.

236 Make thyself an island, work hard, be wise! When thy impurities are blown away, and thou art free from guilt, thou wilt enter into the heavenly world of the elect (Ariya).

237 Thy life has come to an end, thou art come near to death (Yama), there is no resting-place for thee on the road, and thou hast no provision for thy journey.

238 Make thyself an island, work hard, be wise! When thy impurities are blown away, and thou art free from guilt, thou wilt not enter again into birth and decay.

239 Let a wise man blow off the impurities of his self, as a smith blows off the impurities of silver one by one, little by little, and from time to time.

240 As the impurity which springs from the iron, when it springs from it, destroys it; thus do a transgressor's own works lead him to the evil path.

241 The taint of prayers is non-repetition; the taint of houses, non- repair; the taint of the body is sloth; the taint of a watchman, thoughtlessness.

242 Bad conduct is the taint of woman, greediness the taint of a benefactor; tainted are all evil ways in this world and in the next.

243 But there is a taint worse than all taints, ignorance is the greatest taint. O mendicants! throw off that taint, and become taintless!

244 Life is easy to live for a man who is without shame, a crow hero, a mischief-maker, an insulting, bold, and wretched fellow.

245 But life is hard to live for a modest man, who always looks for what is pure, who is disinterested, quiet, spotless, and intelligent.

246 He who destroys life, who speaks untruth, who in this world takes what is not given him, who goes to another man's wife;

247 And the man who gives himself to drinking intoxicating liquors, he, even in this world, digs up his own root.

248 O man, know this, that the unrestrained are in a bad state; take care that greediness and vice do not bring thee to grief for a long time!

249 The world gives according to their faith or according to their pleasure: if a man frets about the food and the drink given to others, he will find no rest either by day or by night.

250 He in whom that feeling is destroyed, and taken out with the very root, finds rest by day and by night.

251 There is no fire like passion, there is no shark like hatred, there is no snare like folly, there is no torrent like greed.

252 The fault of others is easily perceived, but that of oneself is difficult to perceive; a man winnows his neighbour's faults like chaff, but his own fault he hides, as a cheat hides the bad die from the gambler.

253 If a man looks after the faults of others, and is always inclined to be offended, his own passions will grow, and he is far from the destruction of passions.

254 There is no path through the air, a man is not a Samana by outward acts. The world delights in vanity, the Tathagatas (the Buddhas) are free from vanity.

255 There is no path through the air, a man is not a Samana by outward acts. No creatures are eternal; but the awakened (Buddha) are never shaken.

Chapter XIX: The Just

256, 257. A man is not just if he carries a matter by violence; no, he who distinguishes both right and wrong, who is learned and leads others, not by violence, but by law and equity, and who is guarded by the law and intelligent, he is called just.

258 A man is not learned because he talks much; he who is patient, free from hatred and fear, he is called learned.

259 A man is not a supporter of the law because he talks much; even if a man has learnt little, but sees the law bodily, he is a supporter of the law, a man who never neglects the law.

260 A man is not an elder because his head is grey; his age may be ripe, but he is called `Old-in-vain.'

261 He in whom there is truth, virtue, love, restraint, moderation, he who is free from impurity and is wise, he is called an elder.

262 An envious greedy, dishonest man does not become respectable by means of much talking only, or by the beauty of his complexion.

263 He in whom all this is destroyed, and taken out with the very root, he, when freed from hatred and wise, is called respectable.

264 Not by tonsure does an undisciplined man who speaks falsehood become a Samana; can a man be a Samana who is still held captive by desire and greediness?

265 He who always quiets the evil, whether small or large, he is called a Samana (a quiet man), because he has quieted all evil.

266 A man is not a mendicant (Bhikshu) simply because he asks others for alms; he who adopts the whole law is a Bhikshu, not he who only begs.

267 He who is above good and evil, who is chaste, who with knowledge passes through the world, he indeed is called a Bhikshu.

268, 269. A man is not a Muni because he observes silence (mona, i.e. mauna), if he is foolish and ignorant; but the wise who, taking the balance, chooses the good and avoids evil, he is a Muni, and is a Muni thereby; he who in this world weighs both sides is called a Muni.

270 A man is not an elect (Ariya) because he injures living creatures; because he has pity on all living creatures, therefore is a man called Ariya.

271, 272. Not only by discipline and vows, not only by much learning, not by entering into a trance, not by sleeping alone, do I earn the happiness of release which no worldling can know. Bhikshu, be not confident as long as thou hast not attained the extinction of desires.

Chapter XX: The Way

273 The best of ways is the eightfold; the best of truths the four words; the best of virtues passionlessness; the best of men he who has eyes to see.

274 This is the way, there is no other that leads to the purifying of intelligence. Go on this way! Everything else is the deceit of Mara (the tempter).

275 If you go on this way, you will make an end of pain! The way was preached by me, when I had understood the removal of the thorns (in the flesh).

276 You yourself must make an effort. The Tathagatas (Buddhas) are only preachers. The thoughtful who enter the way are freed from the bondage of Mara.

277 `All created things perish,' he who knows and sees this becomes passive in pain; this is the way to purity.

278 `All created things are grief and pain,' he who knows and sees this becomes passive in pain; this is the way that leads to purity.

279 `All forms are unreal,' he who knows and sees this becomes passive in pain; this is the way that leads to purity.

280 He who does not rouse himself when it is time to rise, who, though young and strong, is full of sloth, whose will and thought are weak, that lazy and idle man will never find the way to knowledge.

281 Watching his speech, well restrained in mind, let a man never commit any wrong with his body! Let a man but keep these three roads of action clear, and he will achieve the way which is taught by the wise.

282 Through zeal knowledge is gotten, through lack of zeal knowledge is lost; let a man who knows this double path of gain and loss thus place himself that knowledge may grow.

283 Cut down the whole forest (of lust), not a tree only! Danger comes out of the forest (of lust). When you have cut down both the forest (of lust) and its undergrowth, then, Bhikshus, you will be rid of the forest and free!

284 So long as the love of man towards women, even the smallest, is not destroyed, so long is his mind in bondage, as the calf that drinks milk is to its mother.

285 Cut out the love of self, like an autumn lotus, with thy hand! Cherish the road of peace. Nirvana has been shown by Sugata (Buddha).

286 `Here I shall dwell in the rain, here in winter and summer,' thus the fool meditates, and does not think of his death.

287 Death comes and carries off that man, praised for his children and flocks, his mind distracted, as a flood carries off a sleeping village.

288 Sons are no help, nor a father, nor relations; there is no help from kinsfolk for one whom death has seized.

289 A wise and good man who knows the meaning of this, should quickly clear the way that leads to Nirvana.

Chapter XXI: Miscellaneous

290 If by leaving a small pleasure one sees a great pleasure, let a wise man leave the small pleasure, and look to the great.

291 He who, by causing pain to others, wishes to obtain pleasure for himself, he, entangled in the bonds of hatred, will never be free from hatred.

292 What ought to be done is neglected, what ought not to be done is done; the desires of unruly, thoughtless people are always increasing.

293 But they whose whole watchfulness is always directed to their body, who do not follow what ought not to be done, and who steadfastly do what ought to be done, the desires of such watchful and wise people will come to an end.

294 A true Brahmana goes scatheless, though he have killed father and mother, and two valiant kings, though he has destroyed a kingdom with all its subjects.

295 A true Brahmana goes scatheless, though he have killed father and mother, and two holy kings, and an eminent man besides.

296 The disciples of Gotama (Buddha) are always well awake, and their thoughts day and night are always set on Buddha.

297 The disciples of Gotama are always well awake, and their thoughts day and night are always set on the law.

298 The disciples of Gotama are always well awake, and their thoughts day and night are always set on the church.

299 The disciples of Gotama are always well awake, and their thoughts day and night are always set on their body.

300 The disciples of Gotama are always well awake, and their mind day and night always delights in compassion.

301 The disciples of Gotama are always well awake, and their mind day and night always delights in meditation.

302 It is hard to leave the world (to become a friar), it is hard to enjoy the world; hard is the monastery, painful are the houses; painful it is to dwell

with equals (to share everything in common) and the itinerant mendicant is beset with pain. Therefore let no man be an itinerant mendicant and he will not be beset with pain.

303 Whatever place a faithful, virtuous, celebrated, and wealthy man chooses, there he is respected.

304 Good people shine from afar, like the snowy mountains; bad people are not seen, like arrows shot by night.

305 He alone who, without ceasing, practices the duty of sitting alone and sleeping alone, he, subduing himself, will rejoice in the destruction of all desires alone, as if living in a forest.

     Buddhist Verses from the Dhammapada

Chapter XXII: The Downward Course

306 He who says what is not, goes to hell; he also who, having done a thing, says I have not done it. After death both are equal, they are men with evil deeds in the next world.

307 Many men whose shoulders are covered with the yellow gown are ill-conditioned and unrestrained; such evil-doers by their evil deeds go to hell.

308 Better it would be to swallow a heated iron ball, like flaring fire, than that a bad unrestrained fellow should live on the charity of the land.

309 Four things does a wreckless man gain who covets his neighbour's wife, a bad reputation, an uncomfortable bed, thirdly, punishment, and lastly, hell.

310 There is bad reputation, and the evil way (to hell), there is the short pleasure of the frightened in the arms of the frightened, and the king imposes heavy punishment; therefore let no man think of his neighbour's wife.

311 As a grass-blade, if badly grasped, cuts the arm, badly-practised asceticism leads to hell.

312 An act carelessly performed, a broken vow, and hesitating obedience to discipline, all this brings no great reward.

313 If anything is to be done, let a man do it, let him attack it vigorously! A careless pilgrim only scatters the dust of his passions more widely.

314 An evil deed is better left undone, for a man repents of it afterwards; a good deed is better done, for having done it, one does not repent.

315 Like a well-guarded frontier fort, with defences within and without, so let a man guard himself. Not a moment should escape, for they who allow the right moment to pass, suffer pain when they are in hell.

316 They who are ashamed of what they ought not to be ashamed of, and are not ashamed of what they ought to be ashamed of, such men, embracing false doctrines enter the evil path.

317 They who fear when they ought not to fear, and fear not when they ought to fear, such men, embracing false doctrines, enter the evil path.

318 They who forbid when there is nothing to be forbidden, and forbid not when there is something to be forbidden, such men, embracing false doctrines, enter the evil path.

319 They who know what is forbidden as forbidden, and what is not forbidden as not forbidden, such men, embracing the true doctrine, enter the good path.

Chapter XXIII: The Elephant

320 Silently shall I endure abuse as the elephant in battle endures the arrow sent from the bow: for the world is ill-natured.

321 They lead a tamed elephant to battle, the king mounts a tamed elephant; the tamed is the best among men, he who silently endures abuse.

322 Mules are good, if tamed, and noble Sindhu horses, and elephants with large tusks; but he who tames himself is better still.

323 For with these animals does no man reach the untrodden country (Nirvana), where a tamed man goes on a tamed animal, viz. on his own well-tamed self.

324 The elephant called Dhanapalaka, his temples running with sap, and difficult to hold, does not eat a morsel when bound; the elephant longs for the elephant grove.

325 If a man becomes fat and a great eater, if he is sleepy and rolls himself about, that fool, like a hog fed on wash, is born again and again.

326 This mind of mine went formerly wandering about as it liked, as it listed, as it pleased; but I shall now hold it in thoroughly, as the rider who holds the hook holds in the furious elephant.

327 Be not thoughtless, watch your thoughts! Draw yourself out of the evil way, like an elephant sunk in mud.

328 If a man find a prudent companion who walks with him, is wise, and lives soberly, he may walk with him, overcoming all dangers, happy, but considerate.

329 If a man find no prudent companion who walks with him, is wise, and lives soberly, let him walk alone, like a king who has left his conquered country behind,--like an elephant in the forest.

330 It is better to live alone, there is no companionship with a fool; let a man walk alone, let him commit no sin, with few wishes, like an elephant in the forest.

331 If an occasion arises, friends are pleasant; enjoyment is pleasant, whatever be the cause; a good work is pleasant in the hour of death; the giving up of all grief is pleasant.

332 Pleasant in the world is the state of a mother, pleasant the state of a father, pleasant the state of a Samana, pleasant the state of a Brahmana.

333 Pleasant is virtue lasting to old age, pleasant is a faith firmly rooted; pleasant is attainment of intelligence, pleasant is avoiding of sins.

Buddhist Verses from the Dhammapada

Chapter XXIV: Thirst

334 The thirst of a thoughtless man grows like a creeper; he runs from life to life, like a monkey seeking fruit in the forest.

335 Whomsoever this fierce thirst overcomes, full of poison, in this world, his sufferings increase like the abounding Birana grass.

336 He who overcomes this fierce thirst, difficult to be conquered in this world, sufferings fall off from him, like water-drops from a lotus leaf.

337 This salutary word I tell you, `Do ye, as many as are here assembled, dig up the root of thirst, as he who wants the sweet- scented Usira root must dig up the Birana grass, that Mara (the tempter) may not crush you again and again, as the stream crushes the reeds.'

338 As a tree, even though it has been cut down, is firm so long as its root is safe, and grows again, thus, unless the feeders of thirst are destroyed, the pain (of life) will return again and again.

339 He whose thirst running towards pleasure is exceeding strong in the thirty-six channels, the waves will carry away that misguided man, viz. his desires which are set on passion.

340 The channels run everywhere, the creeper (of passion) stands sprouting; if you see the creeper springing up, cut its root by means of knowledge.

341 A creature's pleasures are extravagant and luxurious; sunk in lust and looking for pleasure, men undergo (again and again) birth and decay.

342 Men, driven on by thirst, run about like a snared hare; held in fetters and bonds, they undergo pain for a long time, again and again.

343 Men, driven on by thirst, run about like a snared hare; let therefore the mendicant drive out thirst, by striving after passionlessness for himself.

344 He who having got rid of the forest (of lust) (i.e. after having reached Nirvana) gives himself over to forest-life (i.e. to lust), and who, when removed from the forest (i.e. from lust), runs to the forest (i.e. to lust), look at that man! though free, he runs into bondage.

345 Wise people do not call that a strong fetter which is made of iron, wood, or hemp; far stronger is the care for precious stones and rings, for sons and a wife.

346 That fetter wise people call strong which drags down, yields, but is difficult to undo; after having cut this at last, people leave the world, free from cares, and leaving desires and pleasures behind.

347 Those who are slaves to passions, run down with the stream (of desires), as a spider runs down the web which he has made himself; when they have cut this, at last, wise people leave the world free from cares, leaving all affection behind.

348 Give up what is before, give up what is behind, give up what is in the middle, when thou goest to the other shore of existence; if thy mind is altogether free, thou wilt not again enter into birth and decay.

349 If a man is tossed about by doubts, full of strong passions, and yearning only for what is delightful, his thirst will grow more and more, and he will indeed make his fetters strong.

350 If a man delights in quieting doubts, and, always reflecting, dwells on what is not delightful (the impurity of the body, &c.), he certainly will remove, nay, he will cut the fetter of Mara.

351 He who has reached the consummation, who does not tremble, who is without thirst and without sin, he has broken all the thorns of life: this will be his last body.

352 He who is without thirst and without affection, who understands the words and their interpretation, who knows the order of letters (those which are before and which are after), he has received his last body, he is called the great sage, the great man.

353 `I have conquered all, I know all, in all conditions of life I am free from taint; I have left all, and through the destruction of thirst I am free; having learnt myself, whom shall I teach?'

354 The gift of the law exceeds all gifts; the sweetness of the law exceeds all sweetness; the delight in the law exceeds all delights; the extinction of thirst overcomes all pain.

355 Pleasures destroy the foolish, if they look not for the other shore; the foolish by his thirst for pleasures destroys himself, as if he were his own enemy.

356 The fields are damaged by weeds, mankind is damaged by passion: therefore a gift bestowed on the passionless brings great reward.

357 The fields are damaged by weeds, mankind is damaged by hatred: therefore a gift bestowed on those who do not hate brings great reward.

358 The fields are damaged by weeds, mankind is damaged by vanity: therefore a gift bestowed on those who are free from vanity brings great reward.

359 The fields are damaged by weeds, mankind is damaged by lust: therefore a gift bestowed on those who are free from lust brings great reward.

Chapter XXV: The Bhikshu (Mendicant)

360 Restraint in the eye is good, good is restraint in the ear, in the nose restraint is good, good is restraint in the tongue.

361 In the body restraint is good, good is restraint in speech, in thought restraint is good, good is restraint in all things. A Bhikshu, restrained in all things, is freed from all pain.

362 He who controls his hand, he who controls his feet, he who controls his speech, he who is well controlled, he who delights inwardly, who is collected, who is solitary and content, him they call Bhikshu.

363 The Bhikshu who controls his mouth, who speaks wisely and calmly, who teaches the meaning and the law, his word is sweet.

364 He who dwells in the law, delights in the law, meditates on the law, follows the law, that Bhikshu will never fall away from the true law.

365 Let him not despise what he has received, nor ever envy others: a mendicant who envies others does not obtain peace of mind.

366 A Bhikshu who, though he receives little, does not despise what he has received, even the gods will praise him, if his life is pure, and if he is not slothful.

367 He who never identifies himself with name and form, and does not grieve over what is no more, he indeed is called a Bhikshu.

368 The Bhikshu who acts with kindness, who is calm in the doctrine of Buddha, will reach the quiet place (Nirvana), cessation of natural desires, and happiness.

369 O Bhikshu, empty this boat! if emptied, it will go quickly; having cut off passion and hatred thou wilt go to Nirvana.

370 Cut off the five (senses), leave the five, rise above the five. A Bhikshu, who has escaped from the five fetters, he is called Oghatinna, 'saved from the flood.'

371 Meditate, O Bhikshu, and be not heedless! Do not direct thy thought to what gives pleasure that thou mayest not for thy heedlessness have to swallow the iron ball (in hell), and that thou mayest not cry out when burning, 'This is pain.'

     Buddhist Verses from the Dhammapada

372 Without knowledge there is no meditation, without meditation there is no knowledge: he who has knowledge and meditation is near unto Nirvana.

373 A Bhikshu who has entered his empty house, and whose mind is tranquil, feels a more than human delight when he sees the law clearly.

374 As soon as he has considered the origin and destruction of the elements (khandha) of the body, he finds happiness and joy which belong to those who know the immortal (Nirvana).

375 And this is the beginning here for a wise Bhikshu: watchfulness over the senses, contentedness, restraint under the law; keep noble friends whose life is pure, and who are not slothful.

376 Let him live in charity, let him be perfect in his duties; then in the fulness of delight he will make an end of suffering.

377 As the Vassika plant sheds its withered flowers, men should shed passion and hatred, O ye Bhikshus!

378 The Bhikshu whose body and tongue and mind are quieted, who is collected, and has rejected the baits of the world, he is called quiet.

379 Rouse thyself by thyself, examine thyself by thyself, thus self-protected and attentive wilt thou live happily, O Bhikshu!

380 For self is the lord of self, self is the refuge of self; therefore curb thyself as the merchant curbs a good horse.

381 The Bhikshu, full of delight, who is calm in the doctrine of Buddha will reach the quiet place (Nirvana), cessation of natural desires, and happiness.

382 He who, even as a young Bhikshu, applies himself to the doctrine of Buddha, brightens up this world, like the moon when free from clouds.

Chapter XXVI - The Brahmana (Arhat)

383 Stop the stream valiantly, drive away the desires, O Brahmana! When you have understood the destruction of all that was made, you will understand that which was not made.

384 If the Brahmana has reached the other shore in both laws (in restraint and contemplation), all bonds vanish from him who has obtained knowledge.

385 He for whom there is neither this nor that shore, nor both, him, the fearless and unshackled, I call indeed a Brahmana.

386 He who is thoughtful, blameless, settled, dutiful, without passions, and who has attained the highest end, him I call indeed a Brahmana.

387 The sun is bright by day, the moon shines by night, the warrior is bright in his armour, the Brahmana is bright in his meditation; but Buddha, the Awakened, is bright with splendour day and night.

388 Because a man is rid of evil, therefore he is called Brahmana; because he walks quietly, therefore he is called Samana; because he has sent away his own impurities, therefore he is called Pravragita (Pabbagita, a pilgrim).

389 No one should attack a Brahmana, but no Brahmana (if attacked) should let himself fly at his aggressor! Woe to him who strikes a Brahmana, more woe to him who flies at his aggressor!

390 It advantages a Brahmana not a little if he holds his mind back from the pleasures of life; when all wish to injure has vanished, pain will cease.

391 Him I call indeed a Brahmana who does not offend by body, word, or thought, and is controlled on these three points.

392 After a man has once understood the law as taught by the Well-awakened (Buddha), let him worship it carefully, as the Brahmana worships the sacrificial fire.

393 A man does not become a Brahmana by his platted hair, by his family, or by birth; in whom there is truth and righteousness, he is blessed, he is a Brahmana.

394 What is the use of platted hair, O fool! what of the raiment of goat-skins? Within thee there is ravening, but the outside thou makest clean.

395 The man who wears dirty raiments, who is emaciated and covered with veins, who lives alone in the forest, and meditates, him I call indeed a Brahmana.

396 I do not call a man a Brahmana because of his origin or of his mother. He is indeed arrogant, and he is wealthy: but the poor, who is free from all attachments, him I call indeed a Brahmana.

397 Him I call indeed a Brahmana who has cut all fetters, who never trembles, is independent and unshackled.

398 Him I call indeed a Brahmana who has cut the strap and the thong, the chain with all that pertains to it, who has burst the bar, and is awakened.

399 Him I call indeed a Brahmana who, though he has committed no offence, endures reproach, bonds, and stripes, who has endurance for his force, and strength for his army.

400 Him I call indeed a Brahmana who is free from anger, dutiful, virtuous, without appetite, who is subdued, and has received his last body.

401 Him I call indeed a Brahmana who does not cling to pleasures, like water on a lotus leaf, like a mustard seed on the point of a needle.

402 Him I call indeed a Brahmana who, even here, knows the end of his suffering, has put down his burden, and is unshackled.

403 Him I call indeed a Brahmana whose knowledge is deep, who possesses wisdom, who knows the right way and the wrong, and has attained the highest end.

404 Him I call indeed a Brahmana who keeps aloof both from laymen and from mendicants, who frequents no houses, and has but few desires.

405 Him I call indeed a Brahmana who finds no fault with other beings, whether feeble or strong, and does not kill nor cause slaughter.

406 Him I call indeed a Brahmana who is tolerant with the intolerant, mild with fault-finders, and free from passion among the passionate.

407 Him I call indeed a Brahmana from whom anger and hatred, pride and envy have dropt like a mustard seed from the point of a needle.

408 Him I call indeed a Brahmana who utters true speech, instructive and free from harshness, so that he offend no one.

409 Him I call indeed a Brahmana who takes nothing in the world that is not given him, be it long or short, small or large, good or bad.

410 Him I call indeed a Brahmana who fosters no desires for this world or for the next, has no inclinations, and is unshackled.

411 Him I call indeed a Brahmana who has no interests, and when he has understood (the truth), does not say How, how? and who has reached the depth of the Immortal.

412 Him I call indeed a Brahmana who in this world is above good and evil, above the bondage of both, free from grief from sin, and from impurity.

413 Him I call indeed a Brahmana who is bright like the moon, pure, serene, undisturbed, and in whom all gaiety is extinct.

414 Him I call indeed a Brahmana who has traversed this miry road, the impassable world and its vanity, who has gone through, and reached the other shore, is thoughtful, guileless, free from doubts, free from attachment, and content.

415 Him I call indeed a Brahmana who in this world, leaving all desires, travels about without a home, and in whom all concupiscence is extinct.

416 Him I call indeed a Brahmana who, leaving all longings, travels about without a home, and in whom all covetousness is extinct.

417 Him I call indeed a Brahmana who, after leaving all bondage to men, has risen above all bondage to the gods, and is free from all and every bondage.

418 Him I call indeed a Brahmana who has left what gives pleasure and what gives pain, who is cold, and free from all germs (of renewed life), the hero who has conquered all the worlds.

419 Him I call indeed a Brahmana who knows the destruction and the return of beings everywhere, who is free from bondage, welfaring (Sugata), and awakened (Buddha).

420 Him I call indeed a Brahmana whose path the gods do not know, nor spirits (Gandharvas), nor men, whose passions are extinct, and who is an Arhat (venerable).

421 Him I call indeed a Brahmana who calls nothing his own, whether it be before, behind, or between, who is poor, and free from the love of the world.

422 Him I call indeed a Brahmana, the manly, the noble, the hero, the great sage, the conqueror, the impassible, the accomplished, the awakened.

423 Him I call indeed a Brahmana who knows his former abodes, who sees heaven and hell, has reached the end of births, is perfect in knowledge, a sage, and whose perfections are all perfect.

Book 2

Buddhist Sutras

The Lankavatara Sutra
(Self-Realisation of Noble Wisdom)

The Brarahmajala Sutra
(The Brahma Net Sutra)

Translated from
Chinese scrolls

A Brief Essay on the Introduction of Buddhism from India to China

The Traffic between India and China in early times was considerable, in spite of the tremendous difficulties and dangers of the passes over the high Himalayas, the Tibetan deserts and the tempests of the Southern seas. But in spite of the difficulties, intimations of Buddhism began to percolate into China certainly as early as the 1st century before the Common Era and by the 1st century after, eminent Indian scholars were finding it worth their trouble to make the arduous journey for the sake of the welcome and the honor they received at the Imperial Court and by the literati, so that by the 2nd century, Buddhist scriptures were being rapidly translated into Chinese.

When Buddhism reached China it found two main currents of cultural conditions with which it had to contend and make terms, namely, Confucianism and Taoism, neither of which, strictly speaking, were religions. The teachings of Confucius were intellectual and were almost wholly devoted to inculcating habits of ethical idealism among all classes of people. By its presentation of an ideal "superior man" and its emphasis on "propriety" and "obedience" it appealed principally to the educated and official classes and tended toward conservatism and the perpetuation of ancient customs and intellectual ideas.

The teachings of Taoism on the other hand had many things in common with Buddhism; it can be truly said that Lao Tsu by his doctrines of Tao and Wu-wei had prepared the way and made ready a welcome for the coming of Buddhism. Nevertheless, there was something in the easy-going laissez-faire naturalism of Lao Tsu that was diametrically opposed to the austere restraint and discipline of Buddhism. They both loved the quiet of solitude, but the Taoist sage wanted a little congenial company with whom to play checkers and drink wine and quote poetry; while the Buddhist saint sought real solitude that he might be less hindered in his strenuous concentration of mind in the attainment of a self-realization of ultimate truth.

The doctrines of Tao and Buddha could be harmonized without strain in both their active aspect and their essence of mingled wisdom and beneficence. As the Sanskrit terms of Indian Buddhism slowly gave way to Chinese, the term Tao was freely used for Buddhahood both by itself and in many compounds. The words Tao and Buddha are often used almost synonymously, but still there remains a shade of distinction between the active and passive sides of reality. One of the early Chán Masters said:

"Buddha is Tao, Tao is dhyana." The common use of Tao in Buddhist names is also very significant.

The first name that emerges in this connection is Tao-an. He was a notable monk, learned in both Confucian and Taoist lore and books of his are still extant dealing with these yoga practices of dhyana and commenting upon them. It is easy to see from them that he looked upon these Indian practices as good working methods for attaining Taoist ideals of non-activity and non-desire.

Tao-an left a disciple, Hui-yuan (333-416 BCE), who was also a great scholar and learned in Taoist mysticism. He is most remembered as the founder of a Buddhist center or fraternity near Kuling, known as the White Lotus Society, whose characteristic was their concentration on the Divine Name, in consequence of which he is commonly looked upon as the founder of the Pure Land sects of China and Japan.

As it appeared in China it was at first largely a practice of Indian yoga methods as an aid to meditation. The characteristic that now began to emerge in the teachings and interest of Tao-an and Hui-yuan was the more definite focusing of mind and its more energetic character.

After Hui-yuan there came into prominence one of his disciples, Tao-seng (434 BCE), who with his disciple, Tao-you, developed the doctrine of "Sudden Awakening," as against the almost universal belief in the "Gradual Attainment," that thereafter entered into Chinese Buddhism to condition its distinctive characteristic. By this teaching the old conception of the gradual attainment of Buddhahood through myriads of kotis of re-births was challenged and in its place was offered, through the right concentration of dhyana, the possibility of sudden and perfect enlightenment. The Chinese Chán Buddhism that came to monopolise the religious field was the mingling of these two distinctively Chinese elements: A more strenuous *dhyana*, and the possibility of a sudden awakening and attainment of enlightenment, with the Indian philosophy of the Mahayana.

The next outstanding name, and the one to whom is usually given the chief credit for being the founder of Chán Buddhism in China, is Bodhidharma. He was an Indian monk of princely family who must have arrived in South China about 470 CE., and who lived and travelled in China for fifty years until about 520.

In the following sutras there are certain Sanskrit words that are of great importance to the understanding of the teaching that are difficult to translate in single words.

DHARMA: Law, Truth. specifically Dharma has come to be used for the Buddha's teaching as a whole, and also as Truth in its universal aspect.

DHARMAKAYA: Truth-body, Truth-principle, Truth-essence. It is used synonymously with such terms as: Buddhahood, Tathagatahood, Nirvana, Noble Wisdom, Universal or Divine Mind, to refer to Ultimate Reality as being universal, undifferentiated, harmonious, inscrutable.

BUDDHA: The Perfectly Enlightened One; the One who has fully attained the goal of spiritual unification.

TATHAGATA: The One who has "thus come." It is used synonymously with Buddha to express the highest personification of Reality. The two terms may be differentiated in the sense that Buddha is the "ingoing" aspect of spiritual attainment, while Tathagata is the "forth-going" aspect of spiritual self-giving and service, both being manifestations of Dharmakaya.

PRAJNA: the active aspect of Dharmakaya; Ultimate Principle of unified Love and Wisdom. It is commonly translated Wisdom but it means far more than that as it includes both the differentiating principle of intellection and the integrating principle of Love. In significance it resembles the Chinese Tao.

ARYA-PRAJNA: Noble Wisdom, synonymous with all other terms denoting Ultimate Reality.

TATHAGATA-GARBHA: The Womb from which emerge all manifestations and all individuations. It is used synonymously with Universal or Divine Mind. Dharmakaya refers to the universal, or pure essence, or "such-ness" of Reality, in contrast to the transformations of the Tathagata.

ALAYA-VIJNANA: Universal, or Divine Mind, or all-conserving Mind. It is used synonymously with Tathagata-garbha and Noble Wisdom.

ARYA-JNANA: that which transcends knowledge, or Transcendental Intelligence. It is used synonymously with Arya-prajna, but signifies the realisation-aspect of Noble Wisdom.

BODHI: is the wisdom content of Prajna.

KARUNA: is the love or compassion content of Prajna.

JNANA: is the knowledge, or cognition, or thinking content of Prajna.

MANAS: the intuitive mind; the connecting link between Universal Mind and the individual, or conscious, or discriminating, mind.

MANO-VIJNANA: the conscious, perceiving, discriminating, thinking, intellectual, mind.

VIJNANA: the principle of discrimination; the sense-minds.

CITTA: mind in general.

Translated by Dwight Goddard

The Lankavatara Sutra

Self-Realisation of Noble Wisdom

Chapter 1

Discrimination

THUS HAVE I HEARD: The Blessed One once appeared in the Castle of Lanka which is on the summit of Mt. Malaya in the midst of the great Ocean. A great many Bodhisattva-Mahasattvas had miraculously assembled from all the Buddha-lands, and a large number of bhikshus were gathered there. The Bodhisattva-Mahasattvas with Mahamati at their head were all perfect masters of the various Samadhis, the tenfold Self-mastery, the ten Powers, and the six Psychic Faculties. Having been anointed by the Buddha's own hands, they all well understood the significance of the objective world; they all knew how to apply the various means, teachings and disciplinary measures according to the various mentalities and behaviors of beings; they were all thoroughly versed in the five Dharmas, the three Svabhavas, the eight Vijnanas, and the twofold Egolessness.

The Blessed One, knowing of the mental agitations going on in the minds of those assembled (like the surface of the ocean stirred into waves by the passing winds), and his great heart moved by compassion, smiled and said: In the days of old the Tathagatas of the past who were Arhats and fully-enlightened Ones came to the Castle of Lanka on Mount Malaya and discoursed on the Truth of Noble Wisdom that is beyond the reasoning knowledge of the philosophers as well as being beyond the understanding of ordinary disciples and masters; and which is realizable only within the inmost consciousness; for your sakes, I too, would discourse on the same Truth. All that is seen in the world is devoid of effort and action because all things in the world are like a dream, or like an image miraculously projected. This is not comprehended by the philosophers and the ignorant, but those who thus see things see them truthfully. Those who see things otherwise walk in discrimination and, as they depend upon discrimination, they cling to dualism. The world as seen by discrimination is like seeing one's own image reflected in a mirror, or one's shadow, or the moon reflected in water, or an echo heard in the valley. People grasping their own shadows of discrimination become attached to this thing and that thing and failing to abandon dualism they go on forever discriminating and thus never attain tranquility. By tranquility is meant Oneness, and Oneness gives birth to the highest Samadhi which is gained by entering into the realm of Noble Wisdom that is realizable only within one's inmost consciousness.

Then all the Bodhisattva-Mahasattvas rose from their seats and respectfully paid him homage and Mahamati the Bodhisattva-Mahasattva sustained by the power of the Buddhas drew his upper garment over one shoulder, knelt and pressing his hands together, praised him in the following verses:

As thou reviewest the world with thy perfect intelligence and compassion, it must seem to thee like an ethereal flower of which one cannot say: it is born, it is destroyed, for the terms being and non-being do not apply to it.

As thou reviewest the world with thy perfect intelligence and compassion, it must seem to thee like a dream of which it cannot be said: it is permanent or it is destructible, for being and non-being do not apply to it.

As thou reviewest all things by thy perfect intelligence and compassion, they must seem to thee like visions beyond the reach of the human mind, as being and non-being do not apply to them.

With thy perfect intelligence and compassion which are beyond all limit, thou comprehendest the egolessness of things and persons, and art free and clear from the hindrances of passion and learning and egotism.

Thou dost not vanish into Nirvana. nor does Nirvana abide in thee, for Nirvana transcends all duality of knowing and known, of being and non-being.

Those who see thee thus, serene and beyond conception, will be emancipated from attachment, will be cleansed of all defilement, both in this world and in the spiritual world beyond.

In this world whose nature is like a dream, there is place for praise and blame, but in the ultimate Reality of Dharmakaya which is far beyond the senses and the discriminating mind, what is there to praise? O thou most Wise!

THEN SAID MAHAMATI the Bodhisattva-Mahasattva: O blessed One, Sugata, Arhat and Fully-enlightened One, pray tell us about the realisation of Noble Wisdom which is beyond the path and usage of the philosophers; which is devoid of all predicates such as being and non-being, oneness and otherness, duality and singularity, existence and non-existence, eternity and non-eternity; which has nothing to do with individuality and generality, nor false-imagination, nor any illusions arising from the mind itself; but which manifests itself as the Truth of Highest Reality. By which, going up continuously by the stages of purification, one enters at last upon the stage of Tathagatahood, whereby, by the power of his original vows unattended by any striving, one will radiate its influence to infinite worlds, like a gem reflecting its variegated colors, whereby I and other Bodhisattva-Mahasattvas, will be enabled to bring all beings to the same perfection of virtue.

Said the Blessed One: Well done, well done, Mahamati! And again, well done, indeed! It is because of your compassion for the world, because of the benefit it will bring to many people both human kind and celestial, that you have presented yourself before us to make this request. Therefore, Mahamati, listen well and truly reflect upon what I shall say, for I will instruct you.

Then Mahamati and the other Bodhisattva-Mahasattvas gave devout attention to the teaching of the Blessed One.

Mahamati, since the ignorant and simple-minded, not knowing that the world is only something seen of the mind itself, cling to the complexness of external objects, cling to the notions of being and nonbeing, oneness and otherness, duality and singularity, existence and non-existence, eternity and non-eternity, and think that they have a self-nature of their own, all of which rises from the discriminations of the mind and is perpetuated by habit-energy, and from which they are given over to false imagination. It is all like a mirage in which springs of water are seen as if they were real. They are thus imagined by animals who, made thirsty by the heat of the season, run after them. Animals, not knowing that the springs are an hallucination of their own minds, do not realise that there are no such springs. In the same way, Mahamati, the ignorant and simple-minded, their minds burning with the fires of greed, anger and folly, finding delight in a world of multitudinous forms, their thoughts obsessed with ideas of birth, growth and destruction, not well understanding what is meant by existent and non-existent, and being impressed by the erroneous discriminations and speculations since time without beginning, fall into the habit of grasping this and that and thereby becoming attached to them.

It is like the city of the Gandharvas which the unwitting take to be a real city though it is not so in fact. The city appears as in a vision owing to their attachment to the memory of a city preserved in the mind as a seed; the city can thus be said to be both existent and non-existent. In the same way, clinging to the memory of erroneous speculations and doctrines accumulated since time without beginning, they hold fast to such ideas as oneness and otherness, being and nonbeing, and their thoughts are not at all clear as to what after all is only seen of the mind. It is like a man dreaming in his sleep of a country that seems to be filled with various men, women, elephants, horses, cars, pedestrians, villages, towns, hamlets, cows, buffalos, mansions, woods, mountains, rivers and lakes, and who moves about in that city until he is awakened. As he lies half awake, he recalls the city of his dreams and reviews his experiences there; what do you think, Mahamati, is this dreamer who is letting his mind dwell upon the various unrealities he has seen in his dream: is he to be considered wise or foolish? In the same way, the ignorant and simple-minded who are favorably influenced by the erroneous views of the philosophers do not recognize that the views that are influencing them are only dream-like ideas originating in the mind itself, and consequently they are held fast by their notions of oneness and otherness, of being and non-being. It is like a painter's canvas on which the ignorant imagine they see the elevations and depressions of mountains and valleys.

In the same way there are people today being brought up under the influence of similar erroneous views of oneness and otherness, of duality and singularity, whose mentality is being conditioned by the habit-energy of these false-imaginings and who later on will declare those who hold the true doctrine of no-birth which is free from the alternatives of being and non-being, to be nihilists and by so doing will bring themselves and others to ruin. By the natural law of cause and effect these followers of pernicious views uproot meritorious causes that otherwise would lead to unstained purity. They are to be shunned by those whose desires are for more excellent things.

It is like the dim-eyed ones who seeing a hairnet exclaim to one another: "It is wonderful! Look, Honorable Sirs, it is wonderful!" But the hairnet has never existed; in fact, it is neither an entity, nor a nonentity, for it has both been seen and has not been seen. in the same manner those whose minds have been addicted to the discriminations of the erroneous views cherished by the philosophers which are given over to the realistic views of being and non-being, will contradict the good Dharma and will end in the destruction of themselves and others.

It is like a wheel of fire made by a revolving firebrand which is no wheel but which is imagined to be one by the ignorant. Nor is it not-a-wheel because it has not been seen by some. By the same reasoning, those who are in the habit of listening to the discriminations and views of the philosophers will regard things born as non-existent and those destroyed by causation as existent. It is like a mirror reflecting colors and images as determined by conditions but without any partiality. It is like the echo of the wind that gives the sound of a human voice. It is like a mirage of moving water seen in a desert. In the same way the discriminating mind of the ignorant which has been heated by false-imaginations and speculations is stirred into mirage-like waves by the winds of birth, growth and destruction. It is like the magician Pisaca, who by means of his spells makes a wooden image or a dead body to throb with life, though it has no power of its own. In the same way the ignorant and the simpleminded, committing themselves to erroneous philosophical views become thoroughly devoted to the ideas of oneness and otherness, but their confidence is not well grounded. For this reason, Mahamati, you and other Bodhisattva-Mahasattvas should cast off all discriminations leading to the notions of birth, abiding and destructions, of oneness and otherness, of duality and singularity, of being and non-being and thus getting free of the bondage of habit-energy become able to attain the reality realizable within yourselves of Noble Wisdom.

THEN SAID MAHAMATI to the Blessed One: Why is it that the ignorant are given up to discrimination and the wise are not?

The Blessed One replied: It is because the ignorant cling to names, signs and ideas; as their minds move along these channels they feed on multiplicities of objects and fall into the notion of an ego-soul and what belongs to it; they make discriminations of good and bad among appearances and cling to the agreeable. As they thus cling there is a reversion to ignorance, and karma born of greed, anger and folly, is accumulated. As the accumulation of karma goes on they become imprisoned in a cocoon of discrimination and are thenceforth unable to free themselves from the round of birth and death.

Because of folly they do not understand that all things are like maya, like the reflection of the moon in water, that there is no self-substance to be imagined as an ego-soul and its belongings, and that all their definitive ideas rise from their false discriminations of what exists only as it is seen of the mind itself. They do not realise that things have nothing to do with qualified and qualifying, nor with the course of birth, abiding and destruction, and instead they assert that they are born of a creator, of time, of atoms, of some celestial spirit. It is because the ignorant are given up to discrimination that they move along with the stream of appearances, but it is not so with the wise.

Chapter 2

False-Imagination and Knowledge of Appearances

THEN MAHAMATI the Bodhisattva-Mahasattva spoke to the Blessed One, saying: You speak of the erroneous views of the philosophers, will you please tell us of them, that we may be on our guard against them?

The Blessed One replied, saying: Mahamati, the error in these erroneous teachings that are generally held by the philosophers lies in this: they do not recognise that the objective world rises from the mind itself; they do not understand that the whole mind-system also rises from the mind itself; but depending upon these manifestations of the mind as being real they go on discriminating them, like the simple-minded ones that they are, cherishing the dualism of this and that, of being and non-being, ignorant of the fact that there is but one common Essence.

On the contrary my teaching is based upon the recognition that the objective world, like a vision, is a manifestation of the mind itself; it teaches the cessation of ignorance, desire, deed and causality; it teaches the cessation of suffering that arises from the discriminations of the triple world.

There are some Brahman scholars who, assuming something out of nothing, assert that there is a substance bound up with causation which abides in time, and that the elements that make up personality and its environment have their genesis and continuation in causation and after thus existing, pass away. Then there are other scholars who hold a destructive and nihilistic view concerning such subjects as continuation, activity, breaking-up, existence, Nirvana, the Path, karma, fruition and Truth. Why? Because they have not attained an intuitive understanding of Truth itself and therefore they have no clear insight into the fundamentals of things. They are like a jar broken into pieces which is no longer able to function as a jar; they are like a burnt seed which is no longer capable of sprouting. But the elements that make up personality and its environment which they regard as subject to change are really incapable of uninterrupted transformations. Their views are based upon erroneous discriminations of the objective world; they are not based upon the true conception.

Again, if it is true that something comes out of nothing and there is the rise of the mind-system by reason of the combination of the three effect-producing causes, we could say the same of any non-existing thing: for instance, that a tortoise could grow hair, or sand produce oil. This proposition is of no avail; it ends in affirming nothing. It follows that the deed, work and cause of which they speak is of no use, and so also is their reference to being and non-being. If they argue that there is a combination of the three effect-producing causes, they must do it on the principle of cause and effect, that is, that something comes out of something and not out of nothing. As long as a world of relativity is asserted, there is an ever recurring chain of causation which cannot be denied under any circumstance, therefore we cannot talk of anything coming to an end or of cessation. As long as these scholars remain on their philosophical ground their demonstration must conform to logic and their textbooks, and the memory-habit of erroneous intellection will ever cling to them. To make the matter worse, the simple-minded ones, poisoned by this erroneous view, will declare this incorrect way of thinking taught by the ignorant, to be the same as that presented by the All-knowing One.

But the way of instruction presented by the Tathagatas is not based on assertions and refutations by means of words and logic. There are four forms of assertion that can be made concerning things not in existence, namely, assertions made about individual marks that are not in existence; about objects that are not in existence; about a cause that is non-existent; and about philosophical views that are erroneous. By refutation is meant that one, because of ignorance, has not examined properly the error that lies at the base of these assertions.

The assertion about individual marks that really have no existence, concerns the distinctive marks as perceived by the eye, ear, nose, etc., as indicating individuality and generality in the elements that make up personality and its external world; and then, taking these marks for reality and getting attached to them, to get into the habit of affirming that things are just so and not otherwise.

The assertion about objects that are non-existent is an assertion that rises from attachment to these associated marks of individuality and generality. Objects in themselves are neither in existence nor in non-existence and are quite devoid of the alternative of being and non-being, and should only be thought of as one thinks of the horns of a hare, a horse, or a camel, which never existed. Objects are discriminated by the ignorant who are addicted to assertion and negation, because their intelligence has not been acute enough to penetrate into the truth that there is nothing but what is seen of the mind itself.

The assertion of a cause that is non-existent assumes the causeless birth of the first element of the mind-system which later on comes to have only a maya-like non-existence. That is to say, there are philosophers who assert that an originally un-born mind-system begins to function under the conditions of eye, form, light and memory, which functioning goes on for a time and then ceases. This is an example of a cause that is non-existent.

The assertion of philosophical views concerning the elements that make up personality and its environing world that are non-existent, assume the existence of an ego, a being, a soul, a living being, a "nourisher," or a spirit. This is an example of philosophical views that are not true. It is this combination of discrimination of imaginary marks of individuality, grouping them and giving them a name and becoming attached to them as objects, by reason of habit-energy that has been accumulating since beginningless time, that one builds up erroneous views whose only basis is false-imagination. For this reason Bodhisattvas should avoid all discussions relating to assertions and negations whose only basis is words and logic.

Word-discrimination goes on by the coordination of brain, chest, nose, throat, palate, lips, tongue, teeth and lips. Words are neither different nor not-different from discrimination. Words rise from discrimination as their cause; if words were different from discrimination they could not have discrimination for their cause; then again, if words are not different, they could not carry and express meaning. Words, therefore, are produced by causation and are mutually conditioning and shifting and, just like things, are subject to birth and destruction.

There are four kinds of word discrimination, all of which are to be avoided because they are alike unreal. First there are the words indicating individual marks which rise from discriminating forms and signs as being real in themselves and, then, becoming attached to them. There are memory-words which rise from the unreal surroundings which come before the mind when it recalls some previous experience. Then there are words growing out of attachment to the erroneous distinctions and speculations of the mental processes. And finally, there are words growing out of inherited prejudices as seeds of habit-energy have accumulated since beginningless time, or which had their origin in some long forgotten clinging to false-imagination and erroneous speculations.

Then there are words where there are no corresponding objects, as for instance, the hare's horns, a barren woman's child, etc.--there are no such things but we have the words, just the same. Words are an artificial creation; there are Buddha-lands where there are no words. In some Buddha-lands ideas are indicated by looking steadily, in others by gestures, in still others by a frown, by a movement of the eyes, by laughing, by yawning, by the clearing of the throat, or by trembling. For instance, in the Buddha-land of the Tathagata Samantabhadra, Bodhisattvas, by a dhyana transcending words and ideas, attain the recognition of all things as un-born and they, also, experience various most excellent Samadhis that transcend words. Even in this world such specialised beings as ants and bees carry on their activities very well without recourse to words. No, Mahamati, the validity of things is independent of the validity of words.

Moreover, there are other things that belong to words, namely, the syllable-body of words, the name-body of words, and the sentence-body of words. By. syllable-body is meant that by which words and sentences are set up or indicated: there is a reason for some syllables, some are mnemonic, and some are chosen arbitrarily. By name-body is meant the object depending upon which a name-word obtains its significance, or in other words, name-body is the "substance" of a name-word. By sentence-body is meant the completion of the meaning by expressing the word more fully in a sentence. The name for this sentence-body is suggested by the footprints left in the road by elephants, horses, people, deer, cattle, goats, etc. But neither words nor sentences can exactly express meanings, for words are only sweet sounds that are arbitrarily chosen to represent things, they are not the things themselves, which in turn are only manifestations of mind. Discrimination of meaning is based upon the false-imagination that these sweet sounds which we call words and which are dependent upon whatever subjects they are supposed to stand for, and which subjects are supposed to be self-existent, all of which is based on error. Disciples should be on their guard against the seductions of words and sentences and their illusive meanings, for by them the ignorant and the dull-witted become entangled and helpless as an elephant floundering about in the deep mud.

Words and sentences are produced by the law of causation and are mutually conditioning, they cannot express highest Reality. Moreover, in highest Reality there are no differentiations to be discriminated and there is nothing to be predicated in regard to it. Highest Reality is an exalted state of bliss, it is not a state of word-discrimination and it cannot be entered into by mere statements concerning it. The Tathagatas have a better way of teaching, namely, through self-realisation of Noble Wisdom.

MAHAMATI ASKED the Blessed One: Pray tell us about the causation of all things whereby I and other Bodhisattvas may see into the nature of causation and may no more discriminate it as to the gradual or simultaneous rising of all things?

The Blessed One replied: There are two factors of causation by reason of which all things come into seeming existence, external and internal factors. The external factors are a lump of clay, a stick, a wheel, a thread, water, a worker, and his labor, the combination of all of which produces a jar. As with a jar which is made from a lump of clay, or a piece of cloth made from thread, or matting made from fragrant grass, or a sprout growing out of a seed, or fresh butter made from sour milk by a man churning it; so it is with all things which appear one after another in continuous succession. As regards the inner factors of causation, they are of such kinds as ignorance, desire, purpose, all of which enter into the idea of causation. Born of these two factors there is the manifestation of personality and the individual things that make up its environment, but they are not individual and distinctive things: they are only so discriminated by the ignorant.

Causation may be divided into six elements: indifference-cause, dependence-cause, possibility-cause, agency-cause, objectivity-cause, manifesting-cause. Indifference-cause means that if there is no discrimination present, there is no power of combination present and so no combination takes place, or if present there is dissolution. Dependence-cause means that the elements must be present. Possibility-cause means that when a cause is to become effective there must be a suitable meeting of conditions both internal and external. Agency-cause means that there must be a principle vested with supreme authority like a sovereign king present and asserting itself. Objectivity-cause means that to be a part of the objective world the mind-system must be in existence and must be keeping up its continuous activity. Manifesting-cause means that as the discriminating faculty of the mind-system becomes busy individual marks will be revealed as forms are revealed by the light of a lamp.

All causes are thus seen to be the outcome of discrimination carried on by the ignorant and simple-minded, and there is, therefore, no such thing as gradual or simultaneous rising of existence. If such a thing as the gradual rising of existence is asserted, it can be disproved by showing that there is no basic substance to hold the individual signs together which makes a gradual rising impossible. If simultaneous rising of existence is asserted, there would be no distinction between cause and effect and there will be nothing to characterise a cause as such. While a child is not yet born, the term father has no significance. Logicians argue that there is that which is born and that which gives birth by the mutual functioning of such causal factors as cause, substance, continuity, acceleration, etc., and so they conclude that there is a gradual rising of existence; but this gradual rising does not obtain except by reason of attachment to the notion of self-nature.

When ideas of body, property and abode are seen, discriminated and cherished in what after all is nothing but what is conceived by the mind itself, an external world is perceived under the aspects of individuality and generality which, however, are not realities, and, therefore, neither a gradual nor a simultaneous rising of things is possible. It is only when the mind-system comes into activity and discriminates the manifestations of mind that existence can be said to come into view. For these reasons, Mahamati, you must get rid of notions of gradation and simultaneity in the combination of causal activities.

MAHAMATI SAID: Blessed One, To what kind of discrimination and to what kind of thoughts should the term, false-imagination, be applied?

The Blessed One replied: So long as people do not understand the true nature of the objective world, they fall into the dualistic view of things. They imagine the multiplicity of external objects to be real and become attached to them and are nourished by their habit-energy. Because of this a system of mentation--mind and what belongs to it--is discriminated and is thought of as real; this leads to the assertion of an ego-soul and its belongings, and thus the mind-system goes on functioning. Depending upon and attaching itself to the dualistic habit of mind, they accept the views of the philosophers founded upon these erroneous distinctions, of being and non-being, existence and non-existence, and there evolves what we call, false-imaginations.

But, Mahamati, discrimination does not evolve nor is it put away because, when all that is seen is truly recognised to be nothing but the manifestation of mind, how can discrimination as regards being and non-being evolve? It is for the sake of the ignorant who are addicted to the discrimination of the multiplicity of things which are of their own mind, that it is said by me that discrimination takes its rise owing to attachment to the aspect of multiplicity which is characteristic of objects. How otherwise can the ignorant and simple-minded recognize that there is nothing but what is seen of the mind itself, and how otherwise can they gain an insight into the true nature of mind and be able to free themselves from wrong conceptions of cause and effect? How otherwise can they gain a clear conception of the Bodhisattva stages, and attain a "turning-about" in the deepest seat of their consciousness, and finally attain an inner self-realisation of Noble Wisdom which transcends the five Dharmas, the three Self-natures, and the whole idea of a discriminated Reality? For this reason is it said by me that discrimination takes its rise from the mind becoming attached to the multiplicities of things which in themselves are not real, and that emancipation comes from thoroughly understanding the meaning of Reality as it truly is.

False-imaginations rise from the consideration of appearances: things are discriminated as to form, signs and shape; as to having color, warmth, humidity, motility or rigidity. False-imagination consists in becoming attached to these appearances and their names. By attachment to objects is meant, the getting attached to inner and outer things as if they were real. By attachment to names is meant, the recognition in these inner and outer things of the characteristic marks of individuation and generality, and to regard them as definitely belonging to the names of the objects.

False-imagination teaches that because all things are bound up with causes and conditions of habit-energy that has been accumulating since beginningless time by not recognising that the external world is of mind itself, all things are comprehensible under the aspects of individuality and generality. By reason of clinging to these false-imaginations there is multitudinousness of appearances which are imagined to be real but which are only imaginary. To illustrate: when a magician depending on grass, wood, shrubs and creepers, exercises his art, many shapes and beings take form that are only magically created; sometimes they even make figures that have bodies and that move and act like human beings; they are variously and fancifully discriminated but there is no reality in them; everyone but children and the simple-minded know that they are not real. Likewise based upon the notion of relativity false-imagination perceives a variety of appearances which the discriminating mind proceeds to objectify and name and become attached to, and memory and habit-energy perpetuate. Here is all that is necessary to constitute the self-nature of false-imagination.

The various features of false-imagination can be distinguished as follows: as regards words, meaning, individual marks, property, self-nature, cause, philosophical views, reasoning, birth, no-birth, dependence, bondage and emancipation. Discrimination of words is the becoming attached to various sounds carrying familiar meanings. Discrimination of meaning comes when one imagines that words rise depending upon whatever subjects they express, and which subjects are regarded as self-existent. Discrimination of individual marks is to imagine that whatever is denoted in words concerning the multiplicities of individual marks (which in themselves are like a mirage) is true, and clinging tenaciously to them, to discriminate all things according to such categories as, warmth, fluidity, motility, and solidity. Discrimination of property is to desire a state of wealth, such as gold, silver, and various precious stories.

Discrimination of self-nature is to make discriminations according to the views of the philosophers in reference to the self-nature of all things which they imagine and stoutly maintain to be true, saying: "This is just what it is and it cannot be otherwise." Discrimination of cause is to distinguish the notion of causation in reference to being and non-being and to imagine that there are such things as "cause-signs." Discrimination of philosophical views means considering different views relating to the notions of being and nonbeing, oneness and otherness, duality and not-duality, existence and non-existence, all of which are erroneous, and becoming attached to particular views. Discrimination of reasoning means the teaching whose reasoning is based on the grasping of the notion of an ego-substance and what belongs to it. Discrimination of birth means getting attached to the notion that things come into existence and pass out of existence according to causation. Discrimination of no-birth is to see that causeless substances which were not, come into existence by reason of causation. Discrimination of dependence means the mutual dependence of gold and the filament made of it. Discrimination of bondage and imagination is like imagining that there is something bound because of something binding, as in the case of a man who ties a knot and loosens one.

These are the various features of false-imagination to which all the ignorant and simple-minded cling. Those attached to the notion of relativity are attached to the notion of the multitudinousness of things which arises from false-imagination. It is like seeing varieties of objects depending upon maya, but these varieties thus revealing themselves are discriminated by the ignorant as something other than maya itself, according to their way of thinking. Now the truth is, maya and varieties of objects are neither different nor not different; if they were different, varieties of objects would not have maya for their characteristic; if they are not different there would be no distinction between them. But as there is a distinction these two-- maya and varieties of objects-are neither different nor not-different, for the very good reason: they are one thing.

MAHAMATI SAID to the Blessed One: Is error an entity or not? The Blessed One replied: Error has no character in it making for attachment; if error had such a character no liberation would be possible from its attachment to existence, and the chain of origination would only be understood in the sense of creation as upheld by the philosophers. Error is like maya, also, and as maya is incapable from producing other maya, so error in itself cannot produce error; it is discrimination and attachment that produce evil thoughts and faults. Moreover, maya has no power of discrimination in itself; it only rises when invoked by the charm of the magician. Error has in itself no habit-energy; habit-energy only rises from discrimination and attachment. Error in itself has no faults; faults are due to the confused discriminations fondly cherished by the ignorant concerning the ego-soul and its mind. The wise have nothing to do either with maya or error.

Maya, however, is not an unreality because it only has the appearance of reality; all things have the nature of maya. It is not because all things are imagined and clung to because of the multitudinous of individual signs, that they are like maya; it is because they are alike unreal and as quickly appearing and disappearing. Being attached to erroneous thoughts they confuse and contradict themselves and others. As they do not clearly grasp the fact that the world is no more than mind itself, they imagine and cling to causation, work, birth and individual signs, and their thoughts are characterised by error and false-imaginations. The teaching that all things are characterised by the self-nature of maya and a dream is meant to make the ignorant and simple-minded cast aside the idea of self-nature in anything.

False-imagination teaches that such things as light and shade, long and short, black and white are different and are to be discriminated; but they are not independent of each other; they are only different aspects of the same thing, they are terms of relation not of reality. Conditions of existence are not of a mutually exclusive character; in essence things are not two but one. Even Nirvana and Samsara's world of life and death are aspects of the same thing, for there is no Nirvana except where is Samasara, and no Samsara except where is Nirvana. All duality is falsely imagined.

Mahamati, you and all the Bodhisattvas should discipline yourselves in the realisation and patient acceptance of the truths of the emptiness, un-bornness, no self-natureness, and the non-duality of all things. This teaching is found in all the sutras of all the Buddhas and is presented to meet the varied dispositions of all beings, but it is not the Truth itself. These teachings are only a finger pointing toward Noble Wisdom. They are like a mirage with its springs of water which the deer take to be real and chase after. So with the teachings in all the sutras: They are intended for the consideration and guidance of the discriminating minds of all people, but they are not the Truth itself, which can only be self-realised within one's deepest consciousness.

Mahamati, you and all the Bodhisattvas must seek for this inner self-realisation of Noble Wisdom, and be not captivated by word-teaching.

Chapter 3

Right Knowledge or Knowledge of Relations

THEN MAHAMATI SAID: Pray tell us, Blessed One, about the being and the non-being of all things?

The Blessed One replied: People of this world are dependent in their thinking on one of two things: on the notion of being whereby they take pleasure in realism, or in the notion of non-being whereby they take pleasure in nihilism; in either case they imagine emancipation where there is no emancipation. Those who are dependent upon the notion of being, regard the world as rising from a causation that is really existent, and that this actually existing and becoming world does not take its rise from a causation that is non-existent. This is the realistic view as held by some people. Then there are other people who are dependent on the notion of the non-being of all things. These people admit the existence of greed, anger and folly, and at the same time they deny the existence of the things that produce greed, anger and folly. This is not rational, for greed, anger and folly are no more to be taken hold of as real than are things; they neither have substance nor individual marks. Where there is a state of bondage, there is binding and means for binding; but where there is emancipation, as in the case of Buddhas, Bodhisattvas, masters and disciples, who have ceased to believe in both being and non-being, there is neither bondage, binding nor means for binding.

It is better to cherish the notion of an ego-substance than to entertain the notion of emptiness derived from the view of being and non-being, for those who so believe fail to understand the, fundamental fact that the external world is nothing but a manifestation of mind. Because they see things as, transient, as rising from cause and passing away from cause, now dividing, now combining into the elements which make up the aggregates of personality and its external world and now passing away, they are doomed to suffer every moment from the changes that follow one after another, and finally are doomed to ruin.

THEN MAHAMATI ASKED the Blessed One, saying: Tell us, Blessed One, how all things can be empty, un-born, and have no self-nature, so that we may be awakened and quickly realise highest enlightenment?

The Blessed One replied: What is emptiness, indeed! It is a term whose very self-nature is false-imagination, but because of one's attachment to false-imagination we are obliged to talk of emptiness, no-birth, and no-self-nature. There are seven kinds of emptiness: emptiness of mutuality which is non-existence; emptiness of individual marks; emptiness of self-nature; emptiness of no-work; emptiness of work; emptiness of all things in the sense that they are unpredicable; and emptiness in its highest sense of Ultimate Reality.

By the emptiness of mutuality which is non-existence is meant that when a thing is missing here, one speaks of its being empty here. For instance: in the lecture hall of Mrigarama there are no elephants present, nor bulls, nor sheep; but as to monks there are many present. We can rightly speak of the hall as being empty as far as animals are concerned. It is not asserted that the lecture hall is empty of its own characteristics, or that the monks are empty of that which makes up their monkhood, nor that in some other place there are no elephants, bulls, nor sheep to be found. In this case we are speaking of things in their aspect of individuality and generality, but from the point of view of mutuality some things do not exist somewhere. This is the lowest form of emptiness and is to be sedulously put away.

By emptiness of individual marks is meant that all things have no distinguishing marks of individuality and generality. Because of mutual relations and interactions things are superficially discriminated but when they are further and more carefully investigated and analysed they are seen to be non-existent and nothing as to individuality and generality can be predicated of them. Thus when individual marks can no longer be seen, ideas of self, otherness and duality, no longer hold good. So it must be said that all things are empty of self-marks.

By emptiness of self-nature is meant that all things in their self-nature are un-born; therefore, is it said that things are empty as to self-nature. By emptiness of no-work is meant that the aggregate of elements that makes up personality and its external world is Nirvana itself and from the beginning there is no activity in them; therefore, one speaks of the emptiness of no-work. By emptiness of work is meant that the aggregates being devoid of an ego and its belongings, go on functioning automatically as there is mutual conjunction of. causes and conditions; thus one speaks of the emptiness of work. By emptiness of all things in the sense that they are unpredicable is meant that, as the very nature of false-imagination is inexpressible, so all things are unpredicable, and, therefore, are empty in that sense. By emptiness in its highest sense of the emptiness of Ultimate Reality is meant that in the attainment of inner self-realisation of Noble Wisdom there is no trace of habit-energy generated by erroneous conceptions; thus one speaks of the highest emptiness of Ultimate Reality.

When things are examined by right knowledge there are no signs obtainable which would characterise them with marks of individuality and generality, therefore, they are said to have no self-nature. Because these signs of individuality and generality are seen both as existing and yet are known to be non-existent, are seen as going out and yet are known not to be going out, they are never annihilated. Why is this true? For this reason; because the individual signs that should make up the self-nature of all things are non-existent. Again in their self-nature things are both eternal and non-eternal. Things are not eternal because the marks of individuality appear and disappear, that is, the marks of self-nature are characterised by non-eternality. On the other hand, because things are un-born and are only mind-made, they are in a deep sense eternal. That is, things are eternal because of their very non-eternality.

Further, besides understanding the emptiness of all things both in regard to substance and self-nature, it is necessary for Bodhisattvas to clearly understand that all things are un-born. It is not asserted that things are not born in a superficial sense, but that in a deep sense they are not born of themselves. All that can be said, is this, that relatively speaking, there is a constant stream of becoming, a momentary and uninterrupted change from one state of appearance to another. When it is recognised that the world as it presents itself is no more than a manifestation of mind, then birth is seen as no-birth and all existing objects, concerning which discrimination asserts that they are and are not, are non-existent and, therefore, un-born; being devoid of agent and action things are un-born.

If things are not born of being and non-being, but are simply manifestations of mind itself, they have no reality, no self-nature, they are like the horns of a hare, a horse, a donkey, a camel. But the ignorant and the simple-minded, who are given over to their false and erroneous imaginings, discriminate things where they are not. To the ignorant the characteristic marks of the self-nature of body-property-and-abode seem to be fundamental and rooted in the very nature of the mind itself, so they discriminate their multitudinousness and become attached to them.

There are two kinds of attachment: attachment to objects as having self-nature, and attachment to words as having self-nature. The first takes place by not knowing that the external world is only a manifestation of the mind itself; and the second arises from one's clinging to words and names by reason of habit-energy. in the teaching of no-birth, causation is out of place because, seeing that all things are like maya and a dream, one does not discriminate individual signs. That all things are un-born and have no self-nature be-cause they are like maya is asserted to meet the thesis of the philosophers that birth is by causation. They foster the notion that the birth of all things is derived from the concept of being and non-being, and fail to regard it as it truly is, as caused by attachment to the multitudinousness which arises from discriminations of the mind itself.

Those who believe in the birth of something that has never been in existence and, coming into existence, vanishes away, are obliged to assert that things come to exist and vanish away by causation--such people find no foothold in my teachings. When it is realised that there is nothing born, and nothing passes away, then there is no way to admit being and non-being, and the mind becomes quiescent.

THEN MAHAMATI SAID to the Blessed One: The philosophers declare that the world rises from causal agencies according to a law of causation; they state that their cause is unborn and is not to be annihilated. They mention nine primary elements: Ishvara the Creator, the Creation, atoms, etc., which being elementary are unborn and not to be annihilated. The Blessed One, while teaching that all things are un-born and that there is no annihilation, also declares that the world takes its rise from ignorance, discrimination, attachment, deed, etc., working according to a law of causation. Though the two sets of elements may differ in form and name, there does not appear to be any essential difference between the two positions. If there is anything that is distinctive and superior in the Blessed One's teaching, pray tell us, Blessed One, what it is?

The Blessed One replied: My teaching of no-birth and no-annihilation is not like that of the philosophers, nor is it like their doctrine of birth and impermanency. That to which the philosophers ascribe the characteristic of no-birth and no-annihilation is the self-nature of all things, which causes them to fall into the dualism of being and non-being. My teaching transcends the whole conception of being and non-being; it has nothing to do with birth, abiding and destruction; nor with existence and non-existence. I teach that the multitudinousness of objects have no reality in themselves but are only seen of the mind and, therefore, are of the nature of maya and a dream. I teach the non-existence of things because they carry no signs of any inherent self-nature. It is true that in one sense they are seen and discriminated by the senses as individualised objects; but in another sense, because of the absence of any characteristic marks of self-nature, they are not seen but are only imagined. In one sense they are graspable, but in another sense, they are not graspable. When it is clearly understood that there is nothing in the world but what is seen of the mind itself, discrimination no more rises, and the wise are established in their true abode which is the realm of quietude. The ignorant discriminate and work trying to adjust themselves to external conditions, and are constantly perturbed in mind; unrealities are imagined and discriminated, while realities are unseen and ignored. It is not so with the wise. To illustrate: What the ignorant see is like the magically-created city of the Gandharvas, where children are shown streets and houses, and phantom merchants, and people going in and coming out. This imaginary city with its streets and houses and people going in and coming out, are not thought of as being born or being annihilated, because in their case there is no question as to their existence or non-existence. In like manner, I teach, that there is nothing made nor un-made; that there is nothing that has connection with birth and destruction except as the ignorant cherish falsely imagined notions as to the reality of the external world. When objects are not seen and judged as they truly are in themselves, there is discrimination and clinging to the notions of being and non-being, and individualised self-nature, and. as long as these notions of individuality and self-nature persist, the philosophers are bound to explain the external world by a law of causation. This position raises the question of a first cause which the philosophers meet by asserting that their first cause, Ishvara and the primal elements, are un-born and un-annihilate; which position is without evidence and is irrational.

Ignorant people and worldly philosophers cherish a kind of no-birth, but it is not the no-birth which I teach. I teach the un-bornness of the un-born essence of all things which teaching is established in the minds of the wise by their self-realisation of Noble Wisdom. A ladle, clay, a vessel, a wheel, or seeds, or elements--these are external conditions; ignorance discrimination, attachment, habit, karma, these are inner conditions. When this entire universe is regarded as concatenation and as nothing else but concatenation, then the mind, by its patient acceptance of the truth that all things are un-born, gains tranquillity.

Chapter 4

Perfect Knowledge, or Knowledge of Reality

THEN MAHAMATI ASKED the Blessed one: Pray tell us, Blessed One, about the five Dharmas, so that we may fully understand Perfect Knowledge?

The Blessed One replied: The five Dharmas are: appearance, name, discrimination, right-knowledge and Reality. By appearance is meant that which reveals itself to the senses and to the discriminating-mind and is perceived as form, sound, odour, taste, and touch. Out of these appearances ideas are formed, such as clay, water, jar, etc., by which one says: this is such and such a thing and is no other, this is name. When appearances are contrasted and names compared, as when we say: this is an elephant, this is a horse, a cart, a pedestrian, a man, a woman, or, this is mind and what belongs to it,--the things thus named are said to be discriminated. As these discriminations come to be seen as mutually conditioning, as empty of self-substance, as un-born, and thus come to be seen as they truly are, that is, as manifestations of the mind itself, this is right-knowledge. By it the wise cease to regard appearances and names as realities.

When appearances and names are put away and all discrimination ceases, that which remains is the true and essential nature of things and, as nothing can be predicated as to the nature of essence, it is called the "Suchness" of Reality. This universal, undifferentiated, inscrutable, "Suchness" is the only Reality, but it is variously characterised as Truth, Mind-essence, Transcendental Intelligence, Noble Wisdom, etc. This Dharma of the imagelessness of the Essence-nature of Ultimate Reality is the Dharma which has been proclaimed by all the Buddhas, and when all things are understood in full agreement with it, one is in possession of Perfect Knowledge, and is on his way to the attainment of the Transcendental Intelligence of the Tathagatas.

THEN MAHAMATI SAID to the Blessed One: Are the three self-natures, of things, ideas, and Reality, to be considered as included in the Five Dharmas, or as having their own characteristics complete in themselves.

The Blessed One replied: The three self-natures, the eightfold mind-system, and the twofold egolessness are all included in the Five Dharmas. The self-natures of things, of ideas, and of the sixfold mind-system, correspond with the Dharmas of appearance, name and discrimination; the self-nature of Universal Mind and Reality corresponds to the Dharmas of right-knowledge and "Suchness."

By becoming attached to what is seen of the mind itself, there is an activity awakened which is perpetuated by habit-energy that becomes manifest in the mind-system. From the activities of the mind-system there rises the notion of an ego-soul and its belongings; the discriminations, attachments, and notion of an ego-soul, rising simultaneously like the sun and its rays of light.

By the egolessness of things is meant that the elements that make up the aggregates of personality and its objective world being characterised by the nature of maya and destitute of anything that can be called ego-substance, are therefore un-born and have no self-nature. How can things be said to have an ego-soul? By the egolessness of persons is meant that in the aggregates that make up personality there is no ego-substance, nor anything that is like ego-substance nor that belongs to it. The mind-system, which is the most characteristic mark of personality, originated in ignorance, discrimination, desire and deed; and its activities are perpetuated by perceiving, grasping and becoming attached to objects as if they were real. The memory of these discriminations, desires, attachments and deeds is stored in Universal Mind since beginningless time, and is still being accumulated where it conditions the appearance of personality and its environment and brings about constant change and destruction from moment to moment. The manifestations are like a river, a seed, a lamp, a cloud, the wind; Universal mind in its voraciousness to store up everything, is like a monkey never at rest, like a fly ever in search of food and without partiality, like a fire that is never satisfied, like a water-lifting machine that goes on rolling. Universal mind as defiled by habit-energy is like a magician that causes phantom things and people to appear and move about. A thorough understanding of these things is necessary to an understanding of the egolessness of persons.

There are four kinds of Knowledge: Appearance-knowledge, relative-knowledge, perfect-knowledge, and Transcendental Intelligence. Appearance-knowledge belongs to the ignorant and simple-minded who are addicted to the notion of being and non-being, and who are frightened at the thought of being unborn. It is produced by the concordance of the triple combination and attaches itself to the multiplicities of objects; it is characterised by attainability and accumulation; it is subject to birth and destruction. Appearance-knowledge belongs to word-mongers who revel in discriminations, assertions and negations.

Relative-knowledge belongs to the mind-world of the philosophers. It rises from the mind's ability to consider the relations which appearances bear to each other and to the mind considering them, it rises from the mind's ability to arrange, combine and analyse these relations by its powers of discursive logic and imagination, by reason of which it is able to peer into the meaning and significance of things.

Perfect-knowledge belongs to the world of the Bodhisattvas who recognise that all things are but manifestations of mind; who clearly understand the emptiness, the un-bornness, the egolessness of all things; and who have entered into an understanding of the Five Dharmas, the twofold egolessness, and into the truth of imagelessness. Perfect-knowledge differentiates the Bodhisattva stages, and is the pathway and the entrance into the exalted state of self-realisation of Noble Wisdom.

Perfect-knowledge (jnana) belongs to the Bodhisattvas who are entirely free from the dualisms of being and non-being, no-birth and no-annihilation, all assertions and negations, and who, by reason of self-realisation, have gained an insight into the truths of egolessness and imagelessness. They no longer discriminate the world as subject to causation: they regard the causation that rules the world as something like the fabled city of the Gandharvas. To them the world is like a vision and a dream, it is like the birth and death of a barren-woman's child; to them there is nothing evolving and nothing disappearing.

The wise who cherish Perfect-knowledge, may be divided into three classes: disciples, masters and Arhats. Common disciples are separated from masters as common disciples continue to cherish the notion of individuality and generality; masters rise from common disciples when, forsaking the error of individuality and generality, they still cling to the notion of an ego-soul by reason of which they go off by themselves into retirement and solitude. Arhats rise when the error of all discrimination is realised. Error being discriminated by the wise turns into Truth by virtue of the "turning-about" that takes place within the deepest consciousness. Mind, thus emancipated, enters into perfect self-realisation of Noble Wisdom.

But, Mahamati, if you assert that there is such a thing as Noble Wisdom, it no longer holds good, because anything of which something is asserted thereby partakes of the nature of being and is thus characterised with the quality of birth. The very assertion: "All things are un-born" destroys the truthfulness of it. The same is true of the statements: "All things are empty," and "All things have no self-nature,"—both are untenable when put in the form of assertions. But when it is pointed out that all things are like a dream and a vision, it means that in one way things are perceived, and in another way they are not perceived; that is, in ignorance they are perceived but in Perfect-knowledge they are not perceived. All assertions and negations being thought-constructions are un-born. Even the assertion that Universal Mind and Noble Wisdom are Ultimate Reality, is thought construction and, therefore, is un-born. As "things" there is no Universal Mind, there is no Noble Wisdom, there is no Ultimate Reality. The insight of the wise who move about in the realm of imagelessness and its solitude is pure. That is, for the wise all "things" are wiped away and even the state of imagelessness ceases to exist.

Chapter 5

The Mind System

THEN MAHAMATI SAID to the Blessed One: Pray tell us, Blessed One, what is meant by the mind (citta)?

The Blessed One replied: All things of this world, be they seemingly good or bad, faulty or faultless, effect-producing or not effect-producing, receptive or non-receptive, may be divided into two classes: evil out-flowings and the non out-flowing good. The five grasping elements that make up the aggregates of personality, namely, form, sensation, perception, discrimination, and consciousness, and that are imagined to be good and bad, have their rise in the habit-energy of the mind-system,-- they are the evil out-flowings of life. The spiritual attainments and the joys of the Samadhis and the fruitage of the Samapattis that come to the wise through their self-realisation of Noble Wisdom and that culminate in their return and participation in the relations of the triple world are called the non out-flowing good.

The mind-system which is the source of the evil out-flowings consists of the five sense-organs and their accompanying sense-minds (vijnanas) all of which are unified in the discriminating-mind (manovijnana). There is an unending succession of sense-concepts flowing into this discriminating or thinking-mind which combines them and discriminates them and passes judgment upon them as to their goodness or badness. Then follows aversion to or desire for them and attachment and deed; thus the entire system moves on continuously and closely bound together. But it fails to see and understand that what it sees and discriminates and grasps is only a manifestation of its own activity and has no other basis, and so the mind goes on erroneously perceiving and discriminating differences of forms and qualities, not remaining still even for a minute.

In the mind-system there are three modes of activity distinguishable: the sense-minds functioning while remaining in their original nature, the sense-minds as producing effects, and the sense-minds as evolving. By normal functioning the sense-minds grasp appropriate elements of their external world, by which sensation and perception arise at once and by degrees in every sense-organ and every sense-mind, in the pores of the skin, and even in the atoms that make up the body, by which the whole field is apprehended like a mirror reflecting objects, and not realising that the external world itself is only a manifestation of mind. The second mode of activity produces effects by which these sensations react on the discriminating mind to produce perceptions, attractions, aversions, grasping, deed and habit. The third mode of activity has to do with the growth, development and passing of the mind-system, that is, the mind-system is in subjection to its own habit-energy accumulated from beginningless time, as for instance: the "eyeness" in the eye that predisposes it to grasp and become attached to multiple forms and appearances. In this way the activities of the evolving mind-system by reason of its habit-energy stirs up waves of objectivity on the face of Universal Mind which in turn conditions the activities and evolvement of the mind-system. Appearances, perception, attraction, grasping, deed, habit, reaction, condition one another incessantly, and the functioning sense-minds, the discriminating-mind and Universal Mind are thus bound up together. Thus, by reason of discrimination of that which by nature is maya-like and unreal false-imagination and erroneous reasoning takes place, action follows and its habit-energy accumulates thereby defiling the pure face of Universal Mind, and as a result the mind-system comes into functioning and the physical body has its genesis. But the discriminating-mind has no thought that by its discriminations and attachments it is conditioning the whole body and so the sense-minds and the discriminating-mind go on mutually related and mutually conditioned in a most intimate manner and building up a world of representations out of the activities of its own imagination. As a mirror reflects forms, the perceiving senses perceive appearances which the discriminating-mind gathers together and proceeds to discriminate, to name and become attached to. Between these two functions there is no gap, nevertheless, they are mutually conditioning. The perceiving senses grasp that for which they have an affinity, and there is a transformation takes place in their structure by reason of which the mind proceeds to combine, discriminate, apprise, and act; then follows habit-energy and the establishing of the mind and its continuance.

The discriminating-mind because of its capacity to discriminate, judge, select and reason about, is also called the thinking, or intellectual-mind. There are three divisions of its mental activity: mentation which functions in connection with attachment to objects and ideas, mentation that functions in connection with general ideas, and mentation that examines into the validity of these general ideas. The mentation which functions in connection with attachment to objects and ideas derived from discrimination, discriminates the mind from its mental processes and accepts the ideas from it as being real and becomes attached to them. A variety of false judgements are thus arrived at as to being, multiplicity, individuality, value, etc., a strong grasping takes place which is perpetuated by habit-energy and thus discrimination goes on asserting itself.

These mental processes give rise to general conceptions of warmth, fluidity, motility, and solidity, as characterising the objects of discrimination, while the tenacious holding to these general ideas gives rise to proposition, reason, definition, and illustration, all of which lead to the assertions of relative knowledge and the establishment of confidence in birth, self-nature, and an ego-soul.

By mentation as an examining function is meant the intellectual act of examining into these general conclusions as to their validity, significance, and truthfulness. This is the faculty that leads to understanding, right-knowledge and points the way to self-realisation.

THEN MAHAMATI SAID to the Blessed One: Pray tell us, Blessed One, what relation ego-personality bears to the mind-system?

The Blessed One replied: To explain it, it is first necessary to speak of the self-nature of the five grasping aggregates that make up personality, although as I have already shown they are empty, un-born, and without self-nature. These five grasping aggregates are: form, sensation, perception, discrimination, consciousness. Of these, form belongs to what is made of the so-called primary elements, whatever they may be. The four remaining aggregates are without form and ought not to be reckoned as four, because they merge imperceptibly into one another. They are like space which cannot be numbered; it is only due to imagination that they are discriminated and likened to space. Because things are endowed with appearances of being, characteristic-marks, perceivableness, abode, work, one can say that they are born of effect-producing causes, but this cannot be said of these four intangible aggregates for they are without form and marks. These four mental aggregates that make up personality are beyond calculability, they are beyond the four propositions, they are not to be predicated as existing nor as not existing, but together they constitute what is known as mortal-mind. They are even more maya-like and dream-like than are things, nevertheless, as discriminating mortal-mind they obstruct the self-realisation of Noble Wisdom. But it is only by the ignorant that they are enumerated and thought of as an ego-personality; the wise do not do so. This discrimination of the five aggregates that make up personality and that serve as a basis for an ego-soul and ground for its desires and self-interests must be given up, and in its place the truth of imagelessness and solitude should be established.

THEN SAID MAHAMATI to the Blessed One: Pray tell us, Blessed One, about Universal Mind and its relation to the lower mind-system?

The Blessed One replied: The sense-minds and their centralised discriminating-mind are related to the external world which is a manifestation of itself and is given over to perceiving, discriminating, and grasping its maya-like appearances. Universal Mind (Alaya-vijnana) transcends all individuation and limits. Universal Mind is thoroughly pure in its essential nature, subsisting unchanged and free from faults of impermanence, undisturbed by egoism, unruffled by distinctions, desires and aversions. Universal Mind is like a great ocean, its surface ruffled by waves and surges but its depths remaining forever unmoved. In itself it is devoid of personality and all that belongs to it, but by reason of the defilement upon its face it is like an actor and plays a variety of parts, among which a mutual functioning takes place and the mind-system arises. The principle of intellection becomes divided and mind, the functions of mind, the evil out-flowings of mind, take on individuation. The sevenfold gradation of mind appears: namely, intuitive self-realisation, thinking-desiring-discriminating, seeing, hearing, tasting, smelling, touching, and all their interactions and reactions take their rise.

The discriminating-mind is the cause of the sense-minds and is their support and with them is kept functioning as it describes and becomes attached to a world of objects, and then, by means of its habit-energy, it defiles the face of Universal Mind. Thus Universal Mind becomes the storage and clearing house of all the accumulated products of mentation and action since beginningless time.

Between Universal Mind and the individual discriminating-mind is the intuitive-mind (manas) which is dependent upon Universal Mind for its cause and support and enters into relations with both. It partakes of the universality of Universal Mind, shares its purity, and like it, is above form and momentariness. It is through the intuitive-mind that the good non out-flowings emerge, are manifested and are realised. Fortunate it is that intuition is not momentary for if the enlightenment which comes by intuition were momentary the wise would lose their wisdom which they do not. But the intuitive-mind enters into relations with the lower mind-system, shares its experiences and reflects upon its activities.

Intuitive-mind is one with Universal Mind by reason of its participation in Transcendental Intelligence (Arya-jnana), and is one with the mind-system by its comprehension of differentiated knowledge (vijnana). Intuitive-mind has no body of its own nor any marks by which it can be differentiated. Universal Mind is its cause and support but it is evolved along with the notion of an ego and what belongs to it, to which it clings and upon which it reflects. Through intuitive-mind, by the faculty of intuition which is a mingling of both identity and perceiving, the inconceivable wisdom of Universal Mind is revealed and made realisable. Like Universal Mind it cannot be the source of error.

The discriminating-mind is a dancer and a magician with the objective world as his stage. Intuitive-mind is the wise jester who travels with the magician and reflects upon his emptiness and transiency. Universal Mind keeps the record and knows what must be and what may be. It is because of the activities of the discriminating-mind that error rises and an objective world evolves and the notion of an ego-soul becomes established. If and when the discriminating-mind can be gotten rid of, the whole mind-system will cease to function and Universal Mind will alone remain. Getting rid of the discriminating-mind removes the cause of all error.

THEN SAID MAHAMATI to the Blessed One: Pray tell us, Blessed One, what is meant by the cessation of the mind-system?

The Blessed One replied: The five sense-functions and their discriminating and thinking function have their risings and complete endings from moment to moment. They are born with discrimination as cause, with form and appearance and objectivity closely linked together as condition. The will-to-live is the mother, ignorance is the father. By setting up names and forms greed is multiplied and thus the mind goes mutually conditioning and being conditioned. By becoming attached to names and forms, not realising that they have no more basis than the activities of the mind itself, error rises, false-imagination as-to pleasure and pain rises, and the way to emancipation is blocked. The lower system of sense-minds and the discriminating-mind do not really suffer pleasure and pain-they only imagine they do. Pleasure and pain are the deceptive reactions of mortal-mind as it grasps an imaginary objective world.

There are two ways in which the ceasing of the mind-system may take place: as regards form, and as regards continuation. The sense-organs function as regards form by the interaction of form, contact and grasping; and they cease to function when this contact is broken. As regards continuation,--when these interactions of form, contact and grasping cease, there is no more continuation of the seeing, hearing and other sense functions; with the ceasing of these sense functions, the discriminations, graspings and attachments of the discriminating-mind cease; and with their ceasing act and deed and their habit-energy cease, and there is no more accumulation of karma-defilement on the face of Universal Mind.

If the evolving mortal-mind were of the same nature as Universal Mind the cessation of the lower mind-system would mean the cessation of Universal Mind, but they are different for Universal Mind is not the cause of mortal-mind. There is no cessation of Universal Mind in its pure and essence-nature. What ceases to function is not Universal Mind in its essence-nature, but is the cessation of the effect-producing defilements upon its face that have been caused by the accumulation of the habit-energy of the activities of the discriminating and thinking mortal-mind. There is no cessation of Divine Mind which, in itself, is the abode of Reality and the Womb of Truth.

By the cessation of the sense-minds is meant, not the cessation of their perceiving functions, but the cessation of their discriminating and naming activities which are centralised in the discriminating mortal-mind. By the cessation of the mind-system as a whole is meant, the cessation of discrimination, the clearing away of the various attachments, and, therefore, the clearing away of the defilements of habit-energy on the face of Universal Mind which have been accumulating since beginningless time by reason of these discriminations, attachments, erroneous reasonings, and following acts. The cessation of the continuation aspect of the mind-system as a whole, takes place when there is the cessation of that which supports the mind-system, namely, the discriminating mortal-mind. With the cessation of mortal-mind the entire world of maya and desire disappears. Getting rid of the discriminating mortal-mind is Nirvana.

But the cessation of the discriminating-mind cannot take place until there has been a "turning-about" in the deepest seat of consciousness. The mental habit of looking outward by the discriminating-mind upon an external objective world must be given up, and a new habit if realising Truth within the intuitive-mind by becoming one with Truth itself must be established. Until this intuitive self-realisation of Noble Wisdom is attained, the evolving mind-system will go on. But when an insight into the five Dharmas, the three self-natures, and the twofold egolessness is attained, then the way will be opened for this "turning-about" to take place. With the ending of pleasure and pain, of conflicting ideas, of the disturbing interests of egoism, a state of tranquillisation will be attained in which the truths of emancipation will be fully understood and there will be no further evil outflowings of the mind-system to interfere with the perfect self-realisation of Noble Wisdom.

Chapter 6

Transcendental Intelligence

THEN SAID MAHAMATI: Pray tell us, Blessed One, what constitutes Transcendental Intelligence?

The Blessed One replied: Transcendental Intelligence is the inner state of self-realisation of Noble Wisdom. It is realised suddenly and intuitively as the "turning-about" takes place in the deepest seat of consciousness; it neither enters nor goes out-it is like the moon seen in water. Transcendental Intelligence is not subject to birth nor destruction; it has nothing to do with combination nor concordance; it is devoid of attachment and accumulation; it transcends all dualistic conceptions.

When Transcendental Intelligence is considered, four things must be kept in mind: words, meanings, teachings and Noble Wisdom (Arya-prajna). Words are employed to express meanings but they are dependent upon discriminations and memory as cause, and upon the employment of sounds or letters by which a mutual transference of meaning is possible. Words are only symbols and may or may not clearly and fully express the meaning intended and, moreover, words may be understood quite differently from what was intended by the speaker. Words are neither different nor not different from meaning and meaning stands in the same relation to words.

If meaning is different from words, it could not be made manifest by means of words; but meaning is illumined by words as things are by a lamp. Words are just like a man carrying a lamp to look for his property, by which he can say: this is my property. Just so, by means of words and speech originating in discrimination, the Bodhisattva can enter into the meaning of the teachings of the Tathagatas and through the meaning he can enter into the exalted state of self-realisation of Noble Wisdom, which, in itself, is free from word discrimination. But if a man becomes attached to the literal meaning of words and holds fast to the illusion that words and meaning are in agreement, especially in such things as Nirvana which is un-born and un-dying, or as to distinctions of the Vehicles, the five Dharmas, the three self-natures, then he will fail to understand the true meaning and will become entangled in assertions and refutations. Just as varieties of objects are seen and discriminated in dreams and in visions, so ideas and statements are discriminated erroneously, and error goes on multiplying.

The ignorant and simple-minded declare that meaning is not otherwise than words, that as words are, so is meaning. They think that as meaning has no body of its own that it cannot be different from words and, therefore, declare meaning to be identical with words. In this they are ignorant of the nature of words, which are subject to birth and death, whereas meaning is not; words are dependent upon letters and meaning is not; meaning is apart from existence and non-existence, it has no substratum, it is un-born. The Tathagatas do not teach a Dharma that is dependent upon letters. Anyone who teaches a doctrine that is dependent upon letters and words is a mere prattler, because Truth is beyond letters and words and books.

This does not mean that words and books never declare what is in conformity with meaning and truth, but it means that words and books are dependent upon discriminations, while meaning and truth are not; moreover, words and books are subject to the interpretation of individual minds, while meaning and truth are not. But if Truth is not expressed in words and books, the scriptures which contain the meaning of Truth would disappear, and when the scriptures disappear there will be no more disciples and masters and Bodhisattvas and Buddhas, and there will be nothing to teach. But no one must become attached to the words of the scriptures because even the canonical texts sometimes deviate from their straightforward course owing to the imperfect functioning of sentient minds. Religious discourses are given by myself and other Tathagatas in response to the varying needs and faiths of all manner of beings, in order to free them from dependence upon the thinking function of the mind-system, but they are not given to take the place of self-realisation of Noble Wisdom. When there is recognition that there is nothing in the world but what is seen of the mind itself, all dualistic discriminations will be discarded and the truth of imagelessness will be understood, and will be seen to be in conformity with meaning rather than with words and letters.

The ignorant and simple-minded being fascinated with their self-imaginations and erroneous reasonings, keep on dancing and leaping about, but are unable to understand the discourse by words about the truth of self-realisation, much less are they able to understand the Truth itself. Clinging to the external world, they cling to the study of books which are a means only, and do not know properly how to ascertain the truth of self-realisation, which is Truth unspoiled by the four propositions. Self-realisation is an exalted state of inner attainment which transcends all dualistic thinking and which is above the mind-system with its logic, reasoning, theorising, and illustrations. The Tathagatas discourse to the ignorant, but sustain the Bodhisattvas as they seek self-realisation of Noble Wisdom.

Therefore, let every disciple take good heed not to become attached to words as being in perfect conformity with meaning, because

Truth is not in the letters. When a man with his finger-tip points to something to somebody, the finger-tip may be mistaken for the thing pointed at; in like manner the ignorant and simple-minded, like children, are unable even to the day of their death to abandon the idea that in the finger-tip of words there is the meaning itself. They cannot realise Ultimate Reality because of their intent clinging to words which were intended to be no more than a pointing finger. Words and their discrimination bind one to the dreary round of rebirths into the world of birth-and-death; meaning stands alone and is a guide to Nirvana. Meaning is attained by much learning, and much learning is attained by becoming conversant with meaning and not with words; therefore, let seekers for truth reverently approach those who are wise and avoid the sticklers for particular words.

As for teachings: there are priests and popular preachers who are given to ritual and ceremony and who are skilled in various incantations and in the art of eloquence; they should not be honored nor reverently attended upon, for what one gains from them is emotional excitement and worldly enjoyment; it is not the Dharma. Such preachers, by their clever manipulation of words and phrases and various reasonings and incantations, being the mere prattle of a child, as far as one can make out and not at all in accordance with truth nor in unison with meaning, only serves to awaken sentiment and emotion, while it stupifies the mind. As he himself does not understand the meaning of all things, he only confuses the minds of his hearers with his dualistic views. Not understanding himself, that there is nothing but what is seen of the mind, and himself attached to the notion of self-nature in external things, and unable to know one path from another, he has no deliverance to offer others. Thus these priests and popular preachers who are clever in various incantations and skilled in the art of eloquence, themselves never being emancipated from such calamities as birth, old age, disease, sorrow, lamentation, pain and despair, lead the ignorant into bewilderment by means of their various words, phrases, examples, and conclusions.

Then there are the materialistic philosophers. No respect nor service is to be shown them because their teachings, though they may be explained by using hundreds of thousands of words and phrases, do not go beyond the concerns of this world and this body and in the end they lead to suffering. As the materialists recognise no truth as existing by itself, they are split up into many schools, each of which clings to its own way of reasoning.

But there is that which does not belong to materialism and which is not reached by the knowledge of the philosophers who cling to false-discriminations and erroneous reasonings because they fail to see that, fundamentally, there is no reality in external objects. When it is recognised that there is nothing beyond what is seen of the mind itself, the discrimination of being and non-being ceases and, as there is thus no external world as the object of perception, nothing remains but the solitude of Reality. This does not belong to the materialistic philosophers, it is the domain of the Tathagatas. If such things are imagined as the coming and going of the mind-system, vanishing and appearing, solicitation, attachment, intense affection, a philosophic hypothesis, a theory, an abode, a sense-concept, atomic attraction, organism, growth, thirst, grasping, these things belong to materialism, they are not mine. These are things that are the object of worldly interest, to be sensed, handled and tasted; these are the things that attract one, that bind one to the external world; these are the things that appear in the elements that make up the aggregates of personality where, owing to the procreative force of lust, there arise all kinds of disaster, birth, sorrow, lamentation, pain, despair, disease, old age, death. All these things concern worldly interests and enjoyment; they lie along the path of the philosophers, which is not the path of the Dharma. When the true egolessness of things and persons is understood, discrimination ceases to assert itself; the lower mind-system ceases to function; the various Bodhisattva stages are followed one after another; the Bodhisattva is able to utter his ten inexhaustible vows and is anointed by all the Buddhas. The Bodhisattva becomes master of himself and of all things by virtue of a life of spontaneous and radiant effortlessness. Thus the Dharma, which is Transcendental Intelligence, transcends all discriminations, all false-reasonings, all philosophical systems, all dualism.

THEN MAHAMATI SAID to the Blessed One: In the Scriptures mention is made of the Womb of Tathagatahood and it is taught that that which is born of it is by nature bright and pure, originally unspotted and endowed with the thirty-two marks of excellence. As it is described it is a precious gem but wrapped in a dirty garment soiled by greed, anger, folly and false-imagination. We are taught that this Buddha-nature immanent in every one is eternal, unchanging, auspicious. Is not this which is born of the Womb of Tathagatahood the same as the soul-substance that is taught by the philosophers? The Divine Atman as taught by them is also claimed to be eternal, inscrutable, unchanging, imperishable. Is there, or is there not a difference?

The Blessed One replied: No, Mahamati, my Womb of Tathagatahood is not the same as the Divine Atman as taught by the philosophers. What I teach is Tathagatahood in the sense of Dharmakaya, Ultimate Oneness, Nirvana, emptiness, unbornness, unqualifiedness, devoid of will-effort. The reason why I teach the doctrine of Tathagatahood is to cause the ignorant and simple-minded to lay aside their fears as they listen to the teaching of egolessness and come to understand the state of non-discrimination and imagelessness. The religious teachings of the Tathagatas are just like a potter making various vessels by his own skill of hand with the aid of rod, water and thread, out of the one mass of clay, so the Tathagatas by their command of skillful means issuing from Noble Wisdom, by various terms, expressions, and symbols, preach the twofold egolessness in order to remove the last trace of discrimination that is preventing disciples from attaining a self-realisation of Noble Wisdom. The doctrine of the Tathagata-womb is disclosed in order to awaken philosophers from their clinging to the notion of a Divine Atman as transcendental personality, so that their minds that have become attached to the imaginary notion of "soul" as being something self-existent, may be quickly awakened to a state of perfect enlightenment. All such notions as causation, succession, atoms, primary elements, that make up personality, personal soul, Supreme Spirit, Sovereign God, Creator, are all figments of the imagination and manifestations of mind. No, Mahamati, the Tathagata*s doctrine of the Womb of Tathagatahood is not the same as the philosopher's Atman.

The Bodhisattva is said to have well grasped the teachings of the Tathagatas when, all alone in a lonely place, by means of his Transcendental Intelligence, he walks the path leading to Nirvana. Thereon his mind will unfold by perceiving, thinking, meditating, and, abiding in the practise of concentration until he attains the "turning about" at the source of habit-energy, he will thereafter lead a life of excellent deeds. His mind concentrated on the state of Buddhahood, he will become thoroughly conversant with the noble truth of self-realisation; he will become perfect master of his own mind; he will be like a gem radiating many colors; he will be able to assume bodies of transformation; he will be able to enter into the minds of all to help them; and, finally, by gradually ascending the stages he will become established in the perfect Transcendental Intelligence of the Tathagatas.

Nevertheless, Transcendental Intelligence (Arya-jnana) is not Noble Wisdom (Arya-prajna) itself; it is only an intuitive awareness of it. Noble Wisdom is a perfect state of imagelessness; it is the Womb of "Suchness"; it is the all-conserving Divine Mind (Alaya-vijnana) which in its pure Essence forever abides in perfect patience and undisturbed tranquility.

Chapter 7

Self-Realisation

THEN SAID MAHAMATI: Pray tell us, Blessed One, what is the nature of self-realisation by reason of which we shall be able to attain Transcendental Intelligence?

The Blessed One replied: Transcendental Intelligence rises when the intellectual-mind reaches its limit and, if things are to be realised in their true and essence nature, its processes of mentation, which are based on particularised ideas, discriminations and judgments, must be transcended by an appeal to some higher faculty of cognition, if there be such a higher faculty. There is such a faculty in the intuitive-mind (Manas), which as we have seen is the link between the intellectual-mind and Universal Mind. While it is not an individualised organ like the intellectual-mind, it has that which is much better, direct dependence upon Universal Mind. While intuition does not give information that can be analysed and discriminated, it gives that which is far superior, self-realisation through identification.

MAHAMATI THEN ASKED the Blessed One, saying: Pray tell us, Blessed One, what clear understandings an earnest disciple should have if he is to be successful in the discipline that leads to self-realisation?

The Blessed One replied: There are four things by the fulfilling of which an earnest disciple may gain self-realisation of Noble Wisdom and become a Bodhisattva-Mahasattva: First, he must have a clear understanding that all things are only manifestations of the mind itself; second, he must discard the notion of birth, abiding and disappearance; third, he must clearly understand the egolessness of both things and persons; and fourth, he must have a true conception of what constitutes self-realisation of Noble Wisdom. Provided with these four understandings, earnest disciples may become Bodhisattvas and attain Transcendental Intelligence.

As to the first; he must recognise and be fully convinced that this triple world is nothing but a complex manifestation of one's mental activities; that it is devoid of selfness and its belongings; that there are no strivings, no comings, no goings. He must recognise and accept the fact that this triple world is manifested and imagined as real only under the influence of habit-energy that has been accumulated since the beginning less past by reason of memory, false-imagination, false-reasoning, and attachments to the multiplicities of objects and reactions in close relationship and in conformity to ideas of body-property-and-abode.

As to the second; he must recognise and be convinced that all things are to be regarded as forms seen in a vision and a dream, empty of substance, un-born and without self-nature; that all things exist only by reason of a complicated network of causation which owes its rise to discrimination and attachment and which eventuates in the rise of the mind-system and its belongings and evolvements.

As to the third; he must recognise and patiently accept the fact that his own mind and personality is also mind-constructed, that it is empty of substance, unborn and egoless. With these three things clearly in mind, the Bodhisattva will be able to enter into the truth of imagelessness.

As to the fourth; he must have a true conception of what constitutes self-realisation of Noble Wisdom. First, it is not comparable to the perceptions attained by the sense-mind, neither is it comparable to the cognition of the discriminating and intellectual-mind. Both of these presuppose a difference between self and not-self and the knowledge so attained is characterised by individuality and generality. Self-realisation is based on identity and oneness; there is nothing to be discriminated nor predicated concerning it. But to enter into it the Bodhisattva must be free from all presuppositions and attachments to things, ideas and selfness.

THEN SAID MAHAMATI to the Blessed One: Pray tell us, Blessed One, concerning the characteristics of deep attachments to existence and as to how we may become detached from existence?

The Blessed One replied: When one tries to understand the significance of things by means of words and discriminations, there follow immeasurably deep-seated attachments to existence. For instance: there are the deep-seated attachments to signs of individuality, to causation, to the notion of being and non-being, to the discrimination of birth and death, of doing and not-doing, to the habit of discrimination itself upon which the philosophers are so dependent.

There are three attachments that are especially deep-seated in the minds of all: greed, anger and infatuation, which are based on lust, fear and pride. Back of these lies discrimination and desire which is procreative and is accompanied with excitement and avariciousness and love of comfort and desire for eternal life; and, following, is a succession of rebirths on the five paths of existence and a continuation of attachments. But if these attachments are broken off, no signs of attachment nor of detachment will remain because they are based on things that are non-existent; when this truth is clearly understood the net of attachment is cleared away.

But depending upon and attaching itself to the triple combination which works in unison there is the rising and the continuation of the mind-system incessantly functioning, and because of it there is the deeply-felt and continuous assertion of the will-to-live. When the triple combination that causes the functioning of the mind-system ceases to exist, there is the triple emancipation and there is no further rising of any combination. When the existence and the non-existence of the external world are recognised as rising from the mind itself, then the Bodhisattva is prepared to enter into the state of imagelessness and therein to see into the emptiness which characterises all discrimination and all the deep-seated attachments resulting therefrom. Therein he will see no signs of deep-rooted attachment nor detachment; therein he will see no one in bondage and no one in emancipation, except those who themselves cherish bondage and emancipation, because in all things there is no "substance" to be taken hold of.

But so long as these discriminations are cherished by the ignorant and simple-minded they go on attaching themselves to them and, like the silkworm, go on spinning their thread of discrimination and enwrapping themselves and others, and are charmed with their prison. But to the wise there are no signs of attachment nor of detachment; all things are seen as abiding in solitude where there is no evolving of discrimination. Mahamati, you and all the Bodhisattvas should have your abode where you can see all things from the view-point of solitude.

Mahamati, when you and other Bodhisattvas understand well the distinction between attachment and detachment, you will be in possession of skillful means for avoiding becoming attached to words according to which one proceeds to grasp meanings. Free from the domination of words you will be able to establish yourselves where there will be a "turning about" in the deepest seat of consciousness by means of which you will attain self-realisation of Noble Wisdom and be able to enter into all the Buddha-lands and assemblies. There you will be stamped with the stamp of the powers, self-command, the psychic faculties, and will be endowed with the wisdom and the power of the ten inexhaustible vows, and will become radiant with the variegated rays of the Transformation Bodies. Therewith you will shine without effort like the moon, the sun, the magic wishing-jewel, and at every stage will view things as being of perfect oneness with yourself, uncontaminated by any self-consciousness. Seeing that all things are like a dream, you will be able to enter into the stage of the Tathagatas and be able to deliver discourses on the Dharma to the world of beings in accordance with their needs and be able to free them from all dualistic notions and false discriminations.

Mahamati, there are two ways of considering self-realisation: namely, the teachings about it, and the realisation itself. The teachings as variously given in the nine divisions of the doctrinal works, for the instructions of those who are inclined toward it, by making use of skillful means and expedients, are intended to awaken in all beings a true perception of the Dharma. The teachings are designed to keep one away from all the dualistic notions of being and non-being and oneness and otherness.

Realisation itself is within the inner consciousness. It is an inner experience that has no connection with the lower mind-system and its discriminations of words, ideas and philosophical speculations. It shines out with its own clear light to reveal the error and foolishness of mind-constructed teachings, to render impotent evil influences from without, and to guide one unerringly to the realm of the good non-outflowings. Mahamati, when the earnest disciple and Bodhisattva is provided with these requirements, the way is open to his perfect attainment of self-realisation of Noble Wisdom, and to the full enjoyment of the fruits that arise therefrom.

THEN MAHAMATI ASKED the Blessed One, saying: Pray tell us, Blessed One, about the One Vehicle which the Blessed One has said characterises the attainment of the inner self-realisation of Noble Wisdom?

The Blessed One replied: In order to discard more easily discriminations and erroneous reasonings, the Bodhisattva should retire by himself to a quiet, secluded place where he may reflect within himself without relying on anyone else, and there let him exert himself to make successive advances along the stages; this solitude is the characteristic feature of the inner attainment of self-realisation of Noble Wisdom.

I call this the One Vehicle, not because it is the One Vehicle, but because it is only in solitude that one is able to recognise and realise the path of the One Vehicle. So long as the mind is distracted and is making conscious effort, there can be no culmination as regards the various vehicles; it is only when the mind is alone and quiet that it is able to forsake the discriminations of the external world and seek realisation of an inner realm where there is neither vehicle nor one who rides in it. I speak of the three vehicles in order to carry the ignorant. I do not speak much about the One Vehicle because there is no way by which earnest disciples and masters can realise Nirvana, unaided. According to the discourses of the

Tathagatas earnest disciples should be segregated and disciplined and trained in meditation and dhyana whereby they are aided by many devices and expedients to realise emancipation. It is because earnest disciples and masters have not fully destroyed the habit-energy of karma and the hindrances of discriminative knowledge and human passion that they are often unable to accept the twofold egolessness and the inconceivable transformation death, that I preach the triple vehicle and not the One Vehicle. When earnest disciples have gotten rid of all their evil habit-energy and been able to realise the twofold egolessness, then they will not be intoxicated by the bliss of the Samadhis and will be awakened into the super-realm of the good non-outflowings. Being awakened into the realm of the good non-outflowings, they will be able to gather up all the requisites for the attainment of Noble Wisdom which is beyond conception and is of sovereign power. But really, Mahamati, there are no vehicles, and so I speak of the One Vehicle. Mahamati, the full recognition of the One Vehicle has never been attained by either earnest disciples, masters, or even by the great Brahma; it has been attained only by the Tathagatas themselves. That is the reason that it is known as the One Vehicle. I do not, speak much about it because there is no way by which earnest disciples can realise Nirvana unaided.

THEN MAHAMATI ASKED the Blessed One, saying: What are the steps that will lead an awakened disciple toward the self-realisation of Noble Wisdom?

The Blessed One replied: The beginning lies in the recognition that the external world is only a manifestation of the activities of the mind itself, and that the mind grasps it as an external world simply because of its habit of discrimination and false-reasoning. The disciple must get into the habit of looking at things truthfully. He must recognise the fact that the world has no self-nature, that it is un-born, that it is like a passing cloud, like an imaginary wheel made by a revolving firebrand, like the castle of the Gandharvas, like the moon reflected in the ocean, like a vision, a mirage, a dream. He must come to understand that mind in its essence-nature has nothing to do with discrimination nor causation; he must not listen to discourses based on the imaginary terms of qualifications; he must understand that Universal Mind in its pure essence is a state of imagelessness, that it is only because of the accumulated defilements on its face that body-property-and-abode appear to be its manifestations, that in its own pure nature it is unaffected and unaffecting by such changes as rising, abiding and destruction; he must fully understand that all these things come with the awakening of the notion of an ego-soul and its conscious mind. Therefore, Mahamati, let those disciples who wish to realise Noble Wisdom by following the Tathagata Vehicle desist from all discrimination and erroneous reasoning about such notions as the elements that make up the aggregates of personality and its sense-world or about such ideas as causation, rising, abiding and destruction, and exercise themselves in the discipline of dhyana that leads to the realisation of Noble Wisdom.

To practice dhyana, the earnest disciple should retire to a quiet and solitary place, remembering that life-long habits of discriminative thinking cannot be broken off easily nor quickly. There are four kinds of concentrative meditation (dhyana): The dhyana practised by the ignorant; the dhyana devoted to the examination of meaning; the dhyana with "suchness" (tathata) for its object; and the dhyana of the Tathagatas.

The dhyana practised by the ignorant is the one resorted to by those who are following the example of the disciples and masters but who do not understand its purpose and, therefore, it becomes "still-sitting" with vacant minds. This dhyana is practised, also, by those who, despising the body, see it as a shadow and a skeleton full of suffering and impurity, and yet who cling to the notion of an ego, seek to attain emancipation by the mere cessation of thought.

The dhyana devoted to the examination of meaning, is the one practised by those who, perceiving the untenability of such ideas as self, other and both, which are held by the philosophers, and who have passed beyond the twofold-egolessness, devote dhyana to an examination of the significance of egolessness and the' differentiations of the Bodhisattva stages.

The dhyana with Tathata, or "Suchness," or Oneness, or the Divine Name, for its object is practised by those earnest disciples and masters who, while fully recognising the twofold egolessness and the imagelessness of Tathata, yet cling to the notion of an ultimate Tathata.

The dhyana of the Tathagatas is the dhyana of those who are entering upon the stage of Tathagatahood and who, abiding in the triple bliss which characterises the self-realisation of Noble Wisdom, are devoting themselves for the sake of all beings to the accomplishment of incomprehensible works for their emancipation. This is the pure dhyana of the Tathagatas. When all lesser things and ideas are transcended and forgotten, and there remains only a perfect state of imagelessness where Tathagata and Tathata are merged into perfect Oneness, then the Buddhas will come together from all their Buddha-lands and with shining hands resting on his forehead will welcome a new Tathagata.

Chapter 8

The Attainment of Self- Realisation

THEN SAID MAHAMATI to the Blessed One: Pray tell us more as to what constitutes the state of self-realisation?

The Blessed One replied: In the life of an earnest disciple there are two aspects that are to be distinguished: namely, the state of attachment to the self-natures arising from discrimination of himself and his field of consciousness to which he is related; and second, the excellent and exalted state of self-realisation of Noble Wisdom. The state of attachment to the discriminations of the self-natures of things, ideas and selfhood is accompanied by emotions of pleasure or aversion according to experience or as laid down in books of logic. Conforming himself to the egolessness of things and holding back wrong views as to his own egoness, he should abandon these thoughts and hold himself firmly to the continuously ascending journey of the stages.

The exalted state of self-realisation as it relates to an earnest disciple is a state of mental concentration in which he seeks to identify himself with Noble Wisdom. In that effort he must seek to annihilate all vagrant thoughts and notions belonging to the externality of things, and all ideas of individuality and generality, of suffering and impermanence, and cultivate the noblest ideas of egolessness and emptiness and imagelessness; thus will he attain a realisation of truth that is free from passion and is ever serene. When this active effort at mental concentration is successful it is followed by a more passive, receptive state of Samadhi in which the earnest disciple will enter into the blissful abode of Noble Wisdom and experience its consummations in the transformations of Samapatti. This is an earnest disciple's first experience of the exalted state of realisation, but as yet there is no discarding of habit-energy nor escaping from the transformation of death.

Having attained this exalted and blissful state of realisation as far as it can be attained by disciples, the Bodhisattva must not give himself up to the enjoyment of its bliss, for that would mean cessation, but should think compassionately of other beings and keep ever fresh his original vows; he should never let himself rest in nor exert himself in the bliss of the Samadhis.

But, Mahamati, as earnest disciples go on trying to advance on the path that leads to full realisation, there is one danger against which they must be on their guard. Disciples may not appreciate that the mind-system, because of its accumulated habit-energy, goes on functioning, more or less unconsciously, as long as they live. They may sometimes think that they can expedite the attainment of their goal of tranquillisation by entirely suppressing the activities of the mind-system. This is a mistake, for even if the activities of the mind are suppressed, the mind will still go on functioning because the seeds of habit-energy will still remain in it. What they think is extinction of mind, is really the non-functioning of the mind's external world to which they are no longer attached. That is, the goal of tranquillisation is to be reached not by suppressing all mind activity but by getting rid of discriminations and attachments.

Then there are others who, afraid of the suffering incident to the discriminations of life and death, unwisely seek Nirvana. They have come to see that all things subject to discrimination have no reality and so imagine that Nirvana must consist in the annihilation of the senses and their fields of sensation; they do not appreciate that birth-and-death and Nirvana are not separate one from the other. They do not know that Nirvana is Universal Mind in its purity. Therefore, these stupid ones who cling to the notion that Nirvana is a world by itself that is outside what is seen by the mind, ignoring all the teachings of the Tathagatas concerning the external world, go on rolling themselves along the wheel of birth-and-death. But when they experience the "turning-about" in their deepest consciousness which will bring with it the perfect self-realisation of Noble Wisdom, then they will understand.

The true functioning of the mind is very subtle and difficult to be understood by young disciples, even masters with all their powers of right-knowledge and Samadhis often find it baffling. It is only the Tathagatas and the Bodhisattvas who are firmly established on the seventh stage who can fully understand its workings. Those earnest disciples and masters who wish to fully understand all the aspects of the different stages of Bodhisattvahood by the aid of their right-knowledge must do so by becoming thoroughly convinced that objects of discrimination are only seen to be so by the mind and, thus, by keeping themselves away from all discriminations and false reasonings which are also of the mind itself, by ever seeking to see things truly (yathabhutam), and by planting roots of goodness in Buddha-lands that know no limits made by differentiations.

To do all this the Bodhisattva should keep himself away from all turmoil, social excitements and sleepiness; let him keep away from the treatises and writings of worldly philosophers, and from the ritual and ceremonies of professional priestcraft. Let him retire to a secluded place in the forest and there devote himself to the practise of the various spiritual disciplines, because it is only by so doing that he will become capable of attaining in this world of multiplicities a true insight into the workings of

Universal Mind in its Essence. There surrounded by his good friends the Buddhas, earnest disciples will become capable of understanding the significance of the mind-system and its place as a mediating agent between the external world and Universal Mind and he will become capable of crossing the ocean of birth-and-death which rises from ignorance, desire and deed.

Having gained a thorough understanding of the mind-system, the three self-natures, the twofold egolessness, and established himself in the measure of self-realisation that goes with that attainment, all of which may be gained by his right-knowledge, the way will be clear for the Bodhisattva's further advance along the stages of Bodhisattvahood. The disciple should then abandon the understanding of mind which he has gained by right-knowledge, which in comparison with Noble Wisdom is like a lame donkey, and entering on the eighth stage of Bodhisattvahood, he should then discipline himself in Noble Wisdom according to its three aspects.

These aspects are: First, imagelessness which comes forth when all things belonging to discipleship, mastership, and philosophy are thoroughly mastered. Second, the power added by all the Buddhas by reason of their original vows including the identification of their lives and the sharing of their merit with all sentient lives. Third, the perfect self-realisation that thus far has only been realised in a measure. As the Bodhisattva succeeds in detaching himself from viewing all things, including his own imagined egoness, in their phenomenality, and realises the states of Samadhi and Samapatti whereby he surveys the world as a vision and a dream, and being sustained by all the Buddhas, he will be able to pass on to the full attainment of the Tathagata stage, which is Noble Wisdom itself. This is the triplicity of the noble life and being furnished with this triplicity the perfect self-realisation of Noble Wisdom has been attained.

THEN MAHAMATI ASKED the Blessed One, saying: Blessed One, is the purification of the evil outflowings of the mind which come from clinging to the notions of an objective world and an empirical soul, gradual or instantaneous?

The Blessed One replied: There are three characteristic out-flows of the mind, namely, the evil outflowings that rise from thirst, grasping and attachment; the evil out-flowings that arise from the illusions of the mind and the infatuations of egoism; and the good non-outflowings that arise from Noble Wisdom. The evil out-flowings that take place from recognising an external world, which in truth is only a manifestation of mind, and from becoming attached to it, are gradually purified and not instantaneously.

Good behavior can only come by the path of restraint and effort. It is like a potter making pots that is done gradually and with attention and effort. It is like the mastery of comedy, dancing, singing, lute-playing, writing, and any other art; it must be acquired gradually and laboriously. Its reward will be a clearing insight into the emptiness and transiency of all things.

The evil out-flowings that arise from the illusions of the mind and the infatuations of egoism, concern the mental life more directly and are such things as fear, anger, hatred and pride; these are purified by study and meditation and that, too, must be attained gradually and not instantaneously. It is like the amra fruit that ripens slowly; it is like grass, shrubs, herbs and trees that grow up from the earth gradually. Each must follow the path of study and meditation by himself gradually and with effort, but because of the original vows of the Bodhisattvas and all the Tathagatas who have devoted their merits and identified their lives with all animate life that all may be emancipated, they are not without aid and encouragement; but even with the aid of the Tathagatas, the purification of the evil out-flowings of the mind are at best slow and gradual, requiring both zeal and patience. Its reward is the gradual understanding of the twofold egolessness and its patient acceptance, and the feet well set on the stages of Bodhisattvahood.

But the good non-outflowings that come with self-realisation of Noble Wisdom, is a purification that comes instantaneously by the grace of the Tathagatas. It is like a mirror reflecting all forms and images instantaneously and without discrimination; it is like the sun or the moon revealing all forms instantaneously and illuminating them dispassionately with its light. In the same way the Tathagatas lead earnest disciples to a state of imagelessness; all the accumulations of habit-energy and karma that had been collecting since beginningless time because of attachment to erroneous views which have been entertained regarding an ego-soul and its external world, are cleared away, revealing instantaneously the realm of Transcendental Intelligence that belongs to Buddahood. Just as Universal Mind defiled by accumulations of habit-energy and karma reveals multiplicities of ego-souls and their external worlds of false-imagination, so Universal Mind cleared of its defilements through the gradual purifications of the evil out-flowings that come by effort, study and meditation, and by the gradual self-realisation of Noble Wisdom, at the long last, like the Dharmata Buddha shining forth spontaneously with the rays that issue from its pure Self-nature, shines forth instantaneously. By it the mentality of all Bodhisattvas is matured instantaneously: they find themselves in the palatial abodes of the Akanistha heavens, themselves spontaneously radiating the various treasures of its spiritual abundance.

Chapter 9

The Fruit of Self- Realisation

MAHAMATI ASKED the Blessed One: Pray tell us, Blessed One, what is the fruitage that comes with self -realisation of Noble Wisdom?

The Blessed One replied: First, there will come a clearing insight into the meaning and significance of things and following that will come an unfolding insight into the significance of the spiritual ideals (Paramitas) by reason of which the Bodhisattvas will be able to enter more deeply into the abode of imagelessness and be able to experience the higher Samadhis and gradually to pass through the higher stages of Bodhisattvahood.

After experiencing the "turning-about" in the deepest seat of consciousness, they will experience other Samadhis even to the highest, the Vajravimbopama, which belongs to the Tathagatas and their transformations. They will be able to enter into the realm of consciousness that lies beyond the consciousness of the mind-system, even the consciousness of Tathagatahood. They will become endowed with all the powers, psychic faculties, self-mastery, loving compassion, skillful means, and ability to enter into other Buddha-lands. Before they had attained self-realisation of Noble Wisdom they had been influenced by the self-interests of egoism, but after they attain self-realisation they will find themselves reacting spontaneously to the impulses of a great and compassionate heart endowed with skillful and boundless means and sincerely and wholly devoted to the emancipation of all beings.

MAHAMATI SAID: Blessed One, tell us about the sustaining power of the Tathagatas by which the Bodhisattvas are aided to attain self-realisation of Noble Wisdom?

The Blessed One replied: There are two kinds of sustaining power, which issue from the Tathagatas and are at the service of the Bodhisattvas, sustained by which the Bodhisattvas should prostrate themselves before them and show their appreciation by asking questions. The first kind of sustaining power is the Bodhisattva's own adoration and faith in the Buddhas by reason of which the Buddhas are able to manifest themselves and render their aid and to ordain them with their own hands. The second kind of sustaining power is the power radiating from the Tathagatas that enables the Bodhisattvas to attain and to pass through the various Samadhis and Samapattis without becoming intoxicated by their bliss.

Being sustained by the power of the Buddhas, the Bodhisattva even at the first stage will be able to attain the Samadhi known as the Light of Mahayana. in that Samadhi Bodhisattvas will become conscious of the presence of the Tathagatas coming from all their different abodes in the ten quarters to impart to the Bodhisattvas their sustaining power in various ways. As the Bodhisattva Vajragarbha was sustained in his Samadhis and as many other Bodhisattvas of like degree and virtue have been sustained, so all earnest disciples and masters and Bodhisattvas may experience this sustaining power of the Buddhas in their Samadhis and Samapattis. The disciple's faith and the Tathagata's merit are two aspects of the same sustaining power and by it alone are the Bodhisattvas enabled to become one with the company of the Buddhas.

Whatever Samadhis, psychic faculties and teachings are realised by the Bodhisattvas, they are made possible only by the sustaining power of the Buddhas; if it were otherwise, the ignorant and the simpleminded might attain the same fruitage. Wherever the Tathagatas enter with their sustaining power there will be music, not only music made by human lips and played by human hands on various instruments, but there will be music among the grass and shrubs and trees, and in mountains and towns and palaces and hovels; much more will there be music in the hearts of those endowed with sentiency. The deaf, dumb and blind will be cured of their deficiencies and will rejoice in their emancipation. Such is the extraordinary virtue of the sustaining power imparted by the Tathagatas.

By the bestowal of this sustaining power, the Bodhisattvas are enabled to avoid the evils of passion, hatred and enslaving karma; they are enabled to transcend the dhyana of the beginners and to advance beyond the experience and truth already attained; they are enabled to demonstrate the Paramitas; and finally, to attain the stage of Tathagatahood. Mahamati, if it were not for this sustaining power, they would relapse into the ways and thoughts of the philosophers, easygoing disciples and the evil-minded, and would thus fall short of the highest attainment. For these reasons, earnest disciples and sincere Bodhisattvas are sustained by the power of all the Tathagatas.

THEN SAID MAHAMATI: It has been said by the Blessed One that by fulfilling the six Paramitas, Buddhahood is realised. Pray tell us what the Paramitas are, and how they are to be fulfilled?

The Blessed One replied: The Paramitas are ideals of spiritual perfection that are to be the guide of the Bodhisattvas on the path to self-realisation. There are six of them but they are to be considered in three different ways according to the progress of the Bodhisattva on the stages.

At first they are to be considered as ideals for the worldly life; next as ideals for the mental life; and, lastly, as ideals of the spiritual and unitive life.

In the worldly life where one is still holding tenaciously to the notions of an ego-soul and what concerns it and holding fast to discriminations of dualism, if only for worldly benefits, one should cherish ideals of charity, good behavior, patience, zeal, thoughtfulness and wisdom. Even in the worldly life the practice of these virtues will bring rewards of happiness and success.

Much more in the mind-world of earnest disciples and masters will their practice bring joys of emancipation, enlightenment and peace of mind, because the Paramitas are grounded on right-knowledge and lead to thoughts of Nirvana, even if the Nirvana of their thoughts is for themselves. In the mind-world the Paramitas become more ideal and more sympathetic; charity can no longer be expressed in the giving of impersonal gifts but will call for the more costly gifts of sympathy and understanding; good behavior will call for something more than outward conformity to the five precepts because in the light of the Paramitas they must practise humility, simplicity, restraint and self-giving. Patience will call for something more than forbearance with external circumstances and the temperaments of other people: it will now call for patience with one's self. Zeal will call for something more than industry and outward show of earnestness: it will call for more self-control in the task of following the Noble Path and in manifestating the Dharma in one's own life. Thoughtfulness will give way to mindfulness wherein discriminated meanings and logical deductions and rationalisations will give way to intuitions of significance and spirit. The Paramita of Wisdom (Prajna) will no longer be concerned with pragmatic wisdom and erudition, but will reveal itself in its true perfectness of All-inclusive Truth which is Love.

The third aspect of the Paramitas as seen in the ideal perfections of the Tathagatas can only be fully understood by the Bodhisattva-Mahasattvas who are devoted to the highest spiritual discipline and have fully understood that there is nothing to be seen in the world but that which issues from the mind itself; in whose minds the discriminations of dualities has ceased to function; and seizing and clinging has become non-existent.

Thus free from all attachments to individual objects and ideas, their minds are free to consider ways of benefitting and giving happiness to others, even to all sentient beings To the Bodhisattva-Mahasattvas the ideal of charity is shown in the self-yielding of the Tathagata's hope of Nirvana that all may enjoy it together. While having relations with an objective world there is no rising in the minds of the Tathagatas of discriminations between the interests of self and the interests of others, between good and evil, there is just the spontaneity and effortless actuality of perfect behavior. To practise patience with full knowledge of this and that, of grasp and grasping, but with no thought of discrimination nor of attachment, that is the Tathagatas Paramita of Patience. To exert oneself with energy from the first part of the night to its end in conformity with the disciplinary measures with no rising of discrimination as to comfort or discomfort, that is the Tathagata's Paramita of Zeal. Not to discriminate between self and others in thoughts of Nirvana, but to keep the mind fixed on Nirvana, that is the Paramita of Mindfulness. As to the Prajna-Paramita, which is Noble Wisdom, who can predicate it? When in Samadhi the mind ceases to discriminate and there is only perfect and love-filled imagelessness, then an inscrutable "turning-about" will take place in the inmost consciousness and one will have attained self-realisation of Noble Wisdom, that is the highest Prajna-Paramita.

THEN MAHAMATI SAID to the Blessed One: You have spoken of an astral-body, a "mind-vision-body" (manomayakaya) which the Bodhisattvas are able to assume, as being one of the fruits of self-realisation of Noble Wisdom: pray tell us, Blessed One, what is meant by such a transcendental body?

The Blessed One replied: There are three kinds of such transcendental bodies: First, there is the one In which the Bodhisattva attains enjoyment of the Samadhis and Samapattis. Second, there is the one which is assumed by the Tathagatas according to the class of beings to be sustained, and which achieves and perfects spontaneously with no attachment and no effort. Third, there is the one in which the Tathagatas receive their intuition of Dharmakaya.

The transcendental personality that enters into the enjoyment of the Samadhis comes with the third, fourth and fifth stages as the mentations of the mindsystem become quieted and waves of consciousness are no more stirred on the face of Universal Mind. In this state, the conscious-mind is still aware, in a measure, of the bliss being experienced by this cessation of the mind's activities.

The second kind of transcendental personality is the kind assumed by the Bodhisattvas and Tathagatas as bodies of transformation by which they demonstrate their original vows in the work of achieving and perfecting; it comes with the eighth stage of Bodhisattvahood. When the Bodhisattva has a thorough-going penetration into the maya-like nature of things and understands the dharma of imagelessness, he will experience the "turning-about" in his deepest consciousness and will become able to experience the higher Samadhis even to the highest. By entering into these exalted Samadhis he attains a personality that transcends the conscious-mind, by reason of which he obtains supernatural powers of self-mastery and activities because of which he is able to move as he wishes, as quickly as a dream changes, as quickly as an image changes in a mirror. This transcendental body is not a product of the elements and yet there is something in it that is analogous to what is so produced; it is furnished with all the differences appertaining to the world of form but without their limitations; possessed of this "mind-vision-body" he is able to be present in all the assemblages in all the Buddha-lands. Just as his thoughts move instantly and without hindrance over walls and rivers and trees and mountains, and just as in memory he recalls and visits the scenes of his past experiences, so, while his mind keeps functioning in the body, his thoughts May be a hundred thousand yojanas away. In the same fashion the transcendental personality that experiences the Samadhi Vajravimbopama will be endowed with supernatural powers and psychic faculties and self-mastery by reason of which he will be able to follow the noble paths that lead to the assemblages of the Buddhas, moving about as freely as he may wish. But his wishes will no longer be self-centered nor tainted by discrimination and attachment, for this transcendental personality is not his old body, but is the transcendental embodiment of his original vows of self-yielding in order to bring all beings to maturity.

The third kind of transcendental personality is so ineffable that it is able to attain intuitions of the Dharmakaya, that is, it attains intuitions of the boundless and inscrutable cognition of Universal Mind. As Bodhisattva-Mahasattvas attain the highest of the stages and become conversant with all the treasures to be realised in Noble Wisdom, they will attain this inconceivable transformation-body which is the true nature of all the Tathagatas past, present and future, and will participate in the blissful peace which pervades the Dharma of all the Buddhas.

Chapter 10

Discipleship: Lineage of the Arhats

THEN MAHAMATI ASKED the Blessed One: Pray tell us how many kinds of disciples there are?

The Blessed One replied: There are as many kinds of disciples as there are individuals, but for convenience they may be divided into two groups: disciples of the lineage of the Arhats, and disciples known as Bodhisattvas. Disciples of the lineage of the Arhats may be considered under two aspects: First, according to the number of times they will return to this life of birth-and-death; and second, according to their spiritual progress. Under the first aspect, they may be subdivided into three groups: The "Stream-entered," the "Once-returning," and the "Never-returning."

The Stream-entered are those disciples, who having freed themselves from the attachments to the lower discriminations and who have cleansed themselves from the twofold hindrances and who clearly understand the meaning of the twofold egolessness, yet who still cling to the notions of individuality and generality and to their own egoness. They will advance along the stages to the sixth only to succumb to the entrancing bliss of the Samadhis. They will be reborn seven times, or five times, or three times, before they will be able to pass the sixth stage. The Once-returning are the Arhats, and the Never-returning are the Bodhisattvas who have reached the seventh stage.

The reason for these gradations is because of their attachment to the three degrees of false-imagination: namely, faith in moral practices, doubt, and the view of their individual personality. When these three hindrances are overcome, they will be able to attain the higher stages. As to moral practices: the ignorant, simple-minded disciples obey the rules of morality, piety and penance, because they desire thereby to gain worldly advancement and happiness, with the added hope of being reborn in more favorable conditions. The Stream-entered ones do not cling to moral practices for any hope of reward for their minds are fixed on the exalted state of self-realisation; the reason they devote themselves to the details of morality is that they wish to master such truths as are in conformity with the undefiled out-flowings. As regards the hindrance of doubt in the Buddha's teachings, that will continue so long as any of the notions of discriminations are cherished and will disappear when they disappear. Attachment to the view of individual personality will be gotten rid of as the disciple gains a more thorough understanding of the notions of being and non-being, self-nature and egolessness, thereby getting rid of the attachments to his own selfness that goes with those discriminations. By breaking up and clearing away these three hindrances the Stream-entered ones will be able to discard all greed, anger and folly.

As for the Once-returning Arhats; there was once in them the discrimination of forms, signs, and appearances, but as they gradually learned by right knowledge not to view individual objects under the aspect of quality and qualifying, and as they became acquainted with what marks the attainment of the practice of dhyana, they have reached a stage of enlightenment where in one more rebirth they will be able to put an end to the clinging to their own self-interests. Free of this burden of error and its attachments, the passions will no more assert themselves and the hindrances will be cleared away forever.

Under the second aspect disciples may be grouped according to the spiritual progress they have attained, into four classes, namely, disciples (sravaka), masters (pratyekabuddha), Arhats, and Bodhisattvas.

The first class of disciples mean well but they find it difficult to understand unfamiliar ideas. Their minds are joyful when studying about and practising the things belonging to appearances that can be discriminated, but they become confused by the notion of an uninterrupted chain of causation, and they become fearful when they consider the aggregates that make up personality and its object world as being maya-like, empty and egoless. They are able to advance to the fifth or sixth stage where they are able to do away with the rising of passions, but not with the notions that give rise to passion and, therefore, they are unable to get rid of the clinging to an ego-soul and its accompanying attachments, habits and habit-energy. In this same class of disciples are the earnest disciples of other faiths, who clinging to the notions of such things as, the soul as an eternal entity, Supreme Atman, Personal God, seek a Nirvana that is in harmony with them. There are others, more materialistic in their ideas, who think that all things exist in dependence upon causation and, therefore, that Nirvana must be in like dependence. But none of these, earnest though they be, have gained an insight into the truth of the twofold egolessness and are, therefore, of limited spiritual insight as regards deliverance and non-deliverance; for them there is no emancipation. They have great self-confidence but they can never gain a true knowledge of Nirvana until they have learned to discipline themselves in the patient acceptance of the twofold egolessness.

The second class of masters are those who have gained a high degree of intellectual understanding of the truths concerning the aggregates that make up personality and its external world but who are filled with fear when they face the significance and consequences of these truths, and the demands which their learning makes upon them, that is, not to become attached to the external world and its manifold forms making for comfort and power, and to keep away from the entanglements of its social relations. They are attracted by the possibilities that are attainable by so doing, namely, the possession of miraculous powers such as dividing the personality and appearing in different places at the same time, or manifesting bodies of transformation. To gain these powers they even resort to the solitary life, but this class of masters never get beyond the seductions of their learning and egoism, and their discourses are always in conformity with that characteristic and limitation. Among them are many earnest disciples who show a degree of spiritual insight that is characterised by sincerity and undismayed willingness to meet all the demands that the stages make upon them. When they see that all that makes up the objective world is only manifestation of mind, that it is without self-nature, un-born and egoless, they accept it without fear, and when they see that their own ego-soul is also empty, un-born and egoless, they are untroubled and undismayed, with earnest purpose they seek to adjust their lives to the full demands of these truths, but they cannot forget the notions that lie back of these facts, especially the notion of their own conscious ego-self and its relation to Nirvana. They are of the Stream-entered class.

The class known as Arhats are those earnest masters who belong to the once-returning class. By their spiritual insight they have reached the sixth and seventh stages. They have thoroughly understood the truth of the twofold egolessness and the imagelessness. of Reality; with them there is no more discrimination, nor passions, nor pride of egoism; they have gained an exalted insight and seen into the immensity of the Buddha-lands. By attaining an inner perception of the true nature of Universal Mind they are steadily purifying their habit-energy. The Arhat has attained emancipation, enlightenment, the Dhyanas, the Samadhis, and his whole attention is given to the attainment of Nirvana, but the idea of Nirvana causes mental perturbations because he has a wrong idea of Nirvana. The notion of Nirvana in his mind is divided: he discriminates Nirvana from self, and self from others. He has attained some of the fruits of self-realisation but he still thinks and discourses on the Dhyanas, subjects for meditation, the Samadhis, the fruits. He pridefully says: "There are fetters, but I am disengaged from them." His is a double fault: he both denounces the vices of the ego, and still clings to its fetters. So long as he continues to discriminate notions of dhyana, dhyana practice, subjects for dhyana, right-knowledge and truth, there is a bewildered state of mind, he has not attained perfect emancipation. Emancipation comes with the acceptance of imagelessness.

He is master of the Dhyanas and enters into the Samadhis, but to reach the higher stages one must pass beyond the Dhyanas, the immeasurables, the world of no-form, and the bliss of the Samadhis into the Samapattis leading to the cessation of thought itself. The dhyana-practiser, dhyana, the subject of dhyana, the cessation of thought, once-returning, never-returning, all these are divided and bewildering states of mind. Not until all discrimination is abandoned is their perfect emancipation. Thus the Arhat, master of the dhyanas, participating in the Samadhis, but unsupported by the Buddhas yields to the entrancing bliss of the Samadhis- and passes to his Nirvana. The Arhat is in the class of the Once-returning.

Disciples and masters and Arhats may ascend the stages up to the sixth. They perceive that the triple world is no more than mind itself; they perceive that there is no becoming attached to the multiplicities of external objects except through the discriminations and activities of the mind itself; they perceive that there is no ego-soul; and, therefore, they attain a measure of tranquillisation. But their tranquillisation is not perfect every minute of their lives, for with them there is something effect-producing, some grasped and grasping, some lingering trace of dualism and egoism.

Though disengaged from the actively functioning passions, they are still bound in with the habit-energy of passion and, becoming intoxicated with the wine of the Samadhis, they still have their abode in the realm of the out-flowings. Perfect tranquillisation is possible only with the seventh stage. So long as their minds are in confusion, they cannot attain to a clear conviction as to the cessation of all multiplicity and the actuality of the perfect oneness of all things. In their minds the self-nature of things is still discriminated as good and bad, therefore, their minds are in confusion and they cannot pass beyond the sixth stage. But at the sixth stage all discrimination ceases as they become engrossed in the bliss of the Samadhis wherein they cherish the thought of Nirvana and, as Nirvana is possible at the sixth stage, they pass into their Nirvana, but it is not the Nirvana of the Buddhas.

Chapter 11

Bodhisattvahood and Its Stages

THEN SAID MAHAMATI to the Blessed One: Will you tell us now about the disciples who are Bodhisattvas?

The Blessed One replied: The Bodhisattvas are those earnest disciples who are enlightened by reason of their efforts to attain self-realisation of Noble Wisdom and who have taken upon themselves the task to enlighten others. They have gained a clear understanding of the truth that all things are empty, un-born, and of a maya-like nature; they have ceased from viewing things discriminatively and from considering them in their relations; they thoroughly understand the truth of twofold egolessness and have adjusted themselves to it with patient acceptance; they have attained a definite realisation of imagelessness; and they are abiding in the perfect-knowledge that they have gained by self-realisation of Noble Wisdom.

Well stamped by the seal of "Suchness" they entered upon the first of the Bodhisattva stages. The first stage is called the Stage of joy (Pramudita). Entering this stage is like passing out of the glare and shadows into a realm of "no-shadows"; it is like passing out of the noise and tumult of the crowded city into the quietness of solitude. The Bodhisattva feels within himself the awakening of a great heart of compassion and he utters his ten original vows: To honor and serve all Buddhas; to spread the knowledge and practice of the Dharma; to welcome all coming Buddhas; to practice the six Paramitas; to persuade all beings to embrace the Dharma; to attain a perfect understanding of the universe; to attain a perfect understanding of tile mutuality of all beings; to attain perfect self-realisation of the oneness of all the Buddhas and Tathagatas n self-nature, purpose and resources; to become acquainted with all skillful means for the carrying out of these vows for the emancipation of all beings; to realise supreme enlightenment through the perfect self-realisation of Noble Wisdom, ascending the stages and entering Tathagatahood.

In the spirit of these vows the Bodhisattva gradually ascends the stages to the sixth. All earnest disciples, masters and Arhats have ascended thus far, but being enchanted by the bliss of the Samadhis and not being supported by the powers of the Buddhas, they pass to their Nirvana. The same fate would befall the Bodhisattvas except for the sustaining power of the Buddhas, by that they are enabled to refuse to enter Nirvana until all beings can enter Nirvana with them. The Tathagatas point out to them the virtues of Buddahood which are beyond the conception of the intellectual-mind, and they encourage and strengthen the Bodhisattvas not to give in to the enchantment of the bliss of the Samadhis, but to press on to further advancement along the stages. If the Bodhisattvas had entered Nirvana at this stage, and they would have done so without the sustaining power of the Buddhas, there would have been the cessation of all things and the family of the Tathagatas would have become extinct.

Strengthened by the new strength that comes to them from the Buddhas and with the more perfect insight that is theirs by reason of their advance in self-realisation of Noble Wisdom, they re-examine the nature of the mind-system, the egolessness of personality, and the part that grasping and attachment and habit-energy play in the unfolding drama of life; they re-examine the illusions of the fourfold logical analysis, and the various elements that enter into enlightenment and self-realisation, and, in the thrill of their new powers of self-mastery, the Bodhisattvas enter upon the seventh stage of Far-going (Duramgama).

Supported by the sustaining power of the Buddhas, the Bodhisattvas at this stage enter into the bliss of the Samadhi of perfect tranquillisation. Owing to their original vows they are transported by emotions of love and compassion as they become aware of the part they are to perform in the carrying out of their vows for the emancipation of all beings. Thus they do not enter into Nirvana, but, in truth, they too are already in Nirvana because in their emotions of love and compassion there is no rising of discrimination; henceforth, with them, discrimination no more takes place. Because of Transcendental Intelligence only one conception is present-the promotion of the realisation of Noble Wisdom. Their insight issues from the Womb of Tathagatahood and they enter into their task with spontaneity and radiancy because it is of the self-nature of Noble Wisdom. This is called the Bodhisattva's Nirvana-the losing oneself in the bliss of perfect self-yielding. This is the seventh stage, the stage of Far-going.

The eighth stage, is the stage of No-recession (Acala). Up to this stage, because of the defilements upon the face of Universal Mind caused by the accumulation of habit-energy since beginningless time, the mindsystem and all that pertains to it has been evolved and sustained. The mind-system functioned by the discriminations of an external and objective world to which it became attached and by which it was perpetuated. But with the Bodhisattva's attainment of the eighth stage there comes the "turning-about" within his deepest consciousness from self-centered egoism to universal compassion for all beings, by which he attains perfect self-realisation of Noble Wisdom. There is an instant cessation of the delusive activities of the whole mind-system; the dancing of the waves of habit-energy on the face of Universal Mind are forever stilled, revealing its own inherent quietness and solitude, the inconceivable Oneness of the Womb of Tathagatahood.

Henceforth there is no more looking outward upon an external world by senses and sense-minds, nor a discrimination of particularised concepts and ideas and propositions by an intellectual-mind, no more grasping, nor attachment, nor pride of egoism, nor habit-energy. Henceforth there is only the inner experience of Noble Wisdom which has been attained by entering into its perfect Oneness.

Thus establishing himself at the eighth stage of No-recession, the Bodhisattva enters into the bliss of the ten Samadhis, but avoiding the path of the disciples and masters who yielded themselves up to their entrancing bliss and who passed to their Nirvanas, and supported by his vows and the Transcendental Intelligence which now is his and being sustained by the power of the Buddhas, he enters upon the higher paths that lead to Tathagatahood. He passes through the bliss of the Samadhis to assume the transformation body of a Tathagata that through him all beings may be emancipated. Mahamati, If there had been no Tathagata-womb and no Divine Mind then there would have been no rising and disappearance of the aggregates that make up personality and its external world, no rising and disappearance of ignorant people nor holy people, and no task for Bodhisattvas; therefore, while walking in the path of self-realisation and entering into the enjoyments of the Samadhis, you must never abandon working hard for the emancipation of all beings and your self-yielding love will never be in vain. To philosophers the conception of Tathagata-womb seems devoid of purity and soiled by these external manifestations, but it is not so understood by the Tathagatas,--to them it is not a proposition of philosophy but is an intuitive experience as real as though it was an amalaka fruit held in the palm of the hand.

With the cessation of the mind-system and all its evolving discriminations, there is cessation of all strain and effort. It is like a man in a dream who imagines he is crossing a river and who exerts himself to the utmost to do so, who is suddenly awakened. Being awake, he thinks: "Is this real or is it unreal?" Being now enlightened, he knows that it is neither real nor unreal. Thus when the Bodhisattva arrives at the eighth stage, he is able to see all things truthfully and, more than that, he is able to thoroughly understand the significance of all the dream-like things of his life as to how they came to pass and as to how they pass away. Ever since beginningless time the mind-system has perceived multiplicities of forms and conditions and ideas which the thinking-mind has discriminated and the empirical-mind has experienced and grasped and clung to. From this has risen habit-energy that by its accumulation has conditioned the illusions of existence and non-existence, individuality and generality, and has thus perpetuated the dream-state of false-imagination. But now, to the Bodhisattvas of the eighth stage, life is past and is remembered as it truly was--a passing dream.

As long as the Bodhisattva had not passed the seventh stage, even though he had attained an intuitive understanding of the true meaning of life and its maya-like nature, and as to how the mind carried on its discriminations and attachments yet, nevertheless, the cherishing of the notions of these things had continued and, although he no longer experienced within himself any ardent desire for things nor any impulse to grasp them yet, nevertheless, the notions concerning them persisted and perfumed his efforts to practise the teachings of the Buddhas and to labor for the emancipation of all beings. Now, in the eighth stage, even the notions have passed away, and all effort and striving is seen to be unnecessary. The Bodhisattva's Nirvana is perfect tranquillisation, but it is not extinction nor inertness; while there is an entire absence of discrimination and purpose, there is the freedom and spontaneity of potentiality that has come with the attainment and patient acceptance of the truths of egolessness and imagelessness. Here is perfect solitude, undisturbed by any gradation or continuous succession, but radiant with the potency and freedom of its self-nature which is the self-nature of Noble Wisdom, blissfully peaceful with the serenity of Perfect Love.

Entering upon the eighth stage, with the turning-about at the deepest seat of consciousness, the Bodhisattva will become conscious that he has received the second kind of Transcendental-body (Manomayakaya). The transition from mortal-body to Transcendental-body has nothing to do with mortal death, for the old body continues to function and the old mind serves the needs of the old body, but now it is free from the control of mortal mind. There has been an inconceivable transformation-death (acintya-parinama-cyuti) by which the false-imagination of his particularised individual personality has been transcended by a realisation of his oneness with the universalised mind of Tathagatahood, from which realisation there will be no recession. With that realisation he finds himself amply endowed with all the Tathagata's powers, psychic faculties, and self-mastery, and, just as the good earth is the support of all beings in the world of desire (karmadhatu), so the Tathagatas become the support of all beings in the Transcendental World of No-form.

The first seven of the Bodhisattva stages were in the realm of mind and the eighth, while transcending mind, was still in touch with it; but in the ninth stage of Transcendental Intelligence (Sadhumati), by reason of his perfect intelligence and insight into the imagelessness of Divine Mind which he had attained by self-realisation of Noble Wisdom, he is in the realm of Tathagatahood. Gradually the Bodhisattva will realise his Tathagata-nature and the possession of all its powers and psychic faculties, self-mastery, loving compassion, and skillful means, and by means of them will enter into all the Buddha-lands. Making use of these new powers, the Bodhisattva will assume various transformation-bodies and personalities for the sake of benefiting others. Just as in the former mental life, imagination had risen from relative-knowledge, so now skillful-means rise spontaneously from Transcendental Intelligence. It is like the magical gem that reflects instantaneously appropriate responses to one's wishes. The Bodhisattva passes over to all the assemblages of the Buddhas and listens to them as they discourse on the dream-like nature of all things and concerning the truths that transcend all notions of being and nonbeing, that have no relation to birth and death, nor to eternality nor extinction. Thus facing the Tathagatas as they discourse on Noble Wisdom that is far beyond the mental capacity of disciples and masters, he will attain a hundred thousand Samadhis, indeed, a hundred thousand nyutas of kotis of Samadhis, and in the spirit of these Samadhis he will instantly pass from one Buddha-land to another, paying homage to all the Buddhas, being born into all the celestial mansions, manifesting Buddha-bodies, and himself discoursing on the Triple Treasure to lesser Bodhisattvas that they too may partake of the fruits of self-realisation of Noble Wisdom.

Thus passing beyond the last stage of Bodhisattvahood, he becomes a Tathagata himself endowed with all the freedom of the Dharmakaya. The tenth stage belongs to the Tathagatas. Here the Bodhisattva will find himself seated upon a lotus-like throne in a splendid jewel-adorned palace and surrounded by Bodhisattvas of equal rank. Buddhas from all the Buddha-lands will gather about him and with their pure and fragrant hands resting on his forehead will give him ordination and recognition as one of themselves. Then they will assign him a Buddha-land that he may possess and perfect as his own.

The tenth stage is called the Great Truth Cloud (Dharmamegha), inconceivable, inscrutable. Only the Tathagatas can realise its perfect Imagelessness and Oneness and Solitude. It is Mahesvara, the Radiant Land, the Pure Land, the Land of Far-distances; surrounding and surpassing the lesser worlds of form and desire (karmadhatu), in which the Bodhisattva will find himself at-one-ment. Its rays of Noble Wisdom which is the self-nature of the Tathagatas, many-colored, entrancing, auspicious, are transforming the triple world as other worlds have been transformed in the past, and still other worlds will be transformed in the future. But in the Perfect Oneness of Noble Wisdom there is no gradation nor succession nor effort, The tenth stage is the first, the first is the eighth, the eighth is the fifth, the fifth is the seventh: what gradation can there be where perfect Imagelessness and Oneness prevail? And what is the reality of Noble Wisdom? It is the ineffable potency of the Dharmakaya; it has no bounds nor limits; It surpasses all the Buddha-lands, and pervades the Akanistha and the heavenly mansions of the Tushita.

Chapter 12

Tathagatahood Which Is Noble Wisdom

THEN SAID MAHAMATI to the Blessed One: it has been taught in the canonical books that the Buddhas are subject to neither birth nor destruction, and you have said that "the Unborn" is one of the names of the Tathagatas; does that mean that the Tathagata is a non-entity?

The Blessed One replied: The Tathagata is not a non-entity nor is he to be conceived as other things are as neither born nor disappearing, nor is he subject to causation, nor is he without significance; yet I refer to him as "The Un-born." There is yet another name for the Tathagata, "The Mind-appearing One" (Manomayakaya) which his Essence-body assumes at will in the transformations incident to his work of emancipation. This is beyond the understanding of common disciples and masters and even beyond the full comprehension of those Bodhisattvas who remain in the seventh stage. Yes, Mahamati, "The Un-born" is synonymous with Tathagata.

Then Mahamati said: If the Tathagatas are un-born, there does not seem to be anything to take hold of--no entity--or is there something that bears another name than entity? And what can that "something" be?

The Blessed One replied: Objects are frequently known by different names according to different aspects that they present, the god Indra is sometimes known as Shakra, and sometimes as Purandara. These different names are sometimes used interchangeably and sometimes they are discriminated, but different objects are not to be imagined because of the different names, nor are they without individuation. The same can be said of myself as I appear in this world of patience before ignorant people and where I am known by uncounted trillions of names. They address me by different names not realising that they are all names of the one Tathagata. Some recognise me as Tathagata, some as The Self-existent One, some as Gautama the Ascetic, some as Buddha. Then there are others who recognise me as Brahma, as Vishnu, as Ishvara; some see me as Sun, as Moon; some as a reincarnation of the ancient sages; some as one of "the ten powers"; some as Rama, some as Indra, and some as Varuna. Still there are others who speak of me as The Un-born, as Emptiness, as "Suchness," as Truth, as Reality, as Ultimate Principle; still there are others who see me as Dharmakaya, as Nirvana, as the Eternal; some speak of me as sameness, as non-duality, as undying, as formless; some think of me as the doctrine of Buddha-causation, or of Emancipation, or of the Noble Path; and some think of me as Divine Mind and Noble Wisdom. Thus in this world and in other worlds am I known by these uncounted names, but they all see me as the moon is seen in water. Though they all honor, praise and esteem me, they do not fully understand the meaning and significance of the words they use; not having their own self-realisation of Truth they cling to the words of their canonical books, or to what has been told them, or to what they have imagined, and fail to see that the name they are using is only one of the many names of the Tathagata. In their studies they follow the mere words of the text vainly trying to gain the true meaning, instead of having confidence in the one "text" where self-confirming Truth is revealed, that is, having confidence in the self-realisation of Noble Wisdom.

THEN SAID MAHAMATI: Pray tell us, Blessed One about the self-nature of the Tathagatas?

The Blessed One replied: If the Tathagata is to be described by such expressions as made or un-made, effect or cause, we would have to describe him as neither made, nor un-made, nor effect, nor cause; but if we so described him we would be guilty of dualistic discrimination. If the Tathagata is something made, he would be impermanent; if he is impermanent anything made would be a Tathagata. If he is something un-made, then all effort to realise Tathagatahood would be useless. That which is neither an effect nor a cause, is neither a being nor a non-being, and that which is neither a being nor a non-being is outside the four propositions. The four propositions belong to worldly usage; that which is outside them is no more than a word, like a barren-woman's child; so are all the terms concerning the Tathagata to be understood.

When it is said that all things are egoless, it means that all things are devoid of self-hood. Each thing may have its own individuality--the being of a horse is not of cow nature--it is such as it is of its own nature and is thus discriminated by the ignorant, but, nevertheless, its own nature is of the nature of a dream or a vision.

That is why the ignorant and the simple-minded, who are in the habit of discriminating appearances, fail to understand the significance of egolessness. It is not until discrimination is gotten rid of that the fact that all things are empty, un-born and without self-nature can be appreciated.

Mahamati, all these expressions as applied to the Tathagatas are without meaning, for that which is none of these is something removed from all measurement, and that which is removed from all measurement turns into a meaningless word; that which is a mere word is something un-born; that which is unborn is not subject to destruction; that which is not subject to destruction is like space and space is neither effect nor cause; that which is neither effect nor cause is something unconditioned; that which is unconditioned is beyond all reasoning; that which is beyond all reasoning,-- that is the Tathagata. The self-nature of Tathagatahood is far removed from all predicates and measurements; the self-nature of Tathagatahood is Noble Wisdom.

THEN MAHAMATI SAID to the Blessed One: Are the Tathagatas permanent or impermanent?

The Blessed One replied: The Tathagatas are neither permanent nor impermanent; if either is asserted there is error connected with it. If the Tathagata is said to be permanent then he will be connected with the creating agencies for, according to the philosophers, the creating agencies are something uncreated and permanent. But the Tathagatas are not connected with the so-called creating agencies and in that sense he is impermanent. If he is said to be impermanent then he is connected with things that are created for they also are impermanent. For these reasons the Tathagatas are neither permanent nor impermanent.

Neither can the Tathagatas he said to be permanent in the sense that space is said to be permanent, or that the horns of a hare can be said to be permanent for, being unreal, they exclude all ideas of permanency or impermanency. This does not apply to the Tathagatas because they come forth from the habit-energy of ignorance which is connected with the mind-system and the elements that make up personality. The triple world originates from the discrimination of unrealities and where discrimination takes place there is duality and the notion of permanency and impermanency, but the Tathagatas do not rise from the discrimination of unrealities. Thus, as long as there is discrimination there will be the notion of permanency and impermanency; when discrimination is done away with, Noble Wisdom, which is based on the significance of solitude, will be established.

However, there is another sense in which the Tathagatas may be said to be permanent. Transcendental Intelligence rising with the attainment of enlightenment is of a permanent nature. This Truth-essence which is discoverable in the enlightenment of all who are enlightened, is realisable as the regulative and sustaining principle of Reality, which forever abides. The Transcendental Intelligence attained intuitively by the Tathagatas by their self-realisation of Noble Wisdom, is a realisation of their own self-nature, in this sense the Tathagatas are permanent. The eternal-unthinkable of the Tathagatas is the "suchness" of Noble Wisdom realised within themselves. It is both eternal and beyond thought. It conforms to the idea of a cause and yet is beyond existence and non-existence. Because it is the exalted state of Noble-Wisdom, it has its own character. Because it is the cause of highest Reality, it is its own causation. Its eternality is not derived from reasonings based on external notions of being and non-being, nor of eternality nor non-eternality. Being classed under the same head as space, cessasion, Nirvana, it is eternal. Because it has nothing to do with existence and non-existence, it is no creator; because it has nothing to do with creation, nor with being and non-being, but is only revealed in the exalted state of Noble Wisdom, it is truly eternal.

When the twofold passions are destroyed, and the twofold hindrances are cleared away, and the twofold egolessness is fully understood, and the inconceivable transformation death of the Bodhisattva is attained--that which remains is the self-nature of the Tathagatas. When the teachings of the Dharma are fully understood and are perfectly realised by the disciples and masters, that which is realised in their deepest consciousness is their own Buddha-nature revealed as Tathagata.

In a true sense there are four kinds of sameness relating to Buddha-nature: there is sameness of letters, sameness of words, sameness of meaning, and sameness of Essence. The name Buddha is spelt: B-U-D-D-H-A; the letters are the same when used for any Buddha or Tathagata. When the Brahmans teach they use various words, and when the Tathagatas teach they use the very same words; in respect to words there is a sameness between us. In the teachings of all the Tathagatas there is a sameness of meaning. Among all the Buddhas there is a sameness of Buddha-nature. They all have the thirty-two marks of excellence and the eighty minor signs of bodily perfection; there is no distinction among them except as they manifest various transformations according to the different dispositions of beings who are to be disciplined and emancipated by various means. In the Ultimate Essence which is Dharmakaya, all the Buddhas of the past, present and future, are of one sameness.

THEN SAID MAHAMATI to the Blessed One: It has been said by the Blessed One that from the night of the Enlightenment to the night of the Parinirvana, the Tathagata has uttered no word nor ever will utter a word. In what deep meaning is this true?

The Blessed One replied: By two reasons of deepest meaning is it true: In the light of the Truth self-realised by Noble Wisdom; and in the Truth of an eternally-abiding Reality. The self-realisation of Noble Wisdom by all the Tathagatas is the same as my own self-realisation of Noble Wisdom; there is no more, no less, no difference; and all the Tathagatas bear witness that the state of self-realisation is free from words and discriminations and has nothing to do with the dualistic way of speaking, that is, all beings receive the teachings of the Tathagatas through self-realisation of Noble Wisdom, not through words of discrimination.

Again, Mahamati, there has always been an eternally-abiding Reality. The "substance" of Truth (dharmadhatu) abides forever whether a Tathagata appears in the world or not. So does the Reason of all things (dharmata) eternally abide; so does Reality (paramartha) abide and keep its order. What has been realised by myself and all other Tathagatas is this Reality (Dharmakaya), the eternally-abiding self-orderliness of Reality; the "suchness" (tathata) of things; the realness of things (bhutata); Noble Wisdom which is Truth itself. The sun radiates its splendor spontaneously on all alike and with no words of explanation; in like manner do the Tathagatas radiate the Truth of Noble Wisdom with no recourse to words and to all alike. For these reasons is it stated by me that from the night of the Enlightenment to the night of the Tathagata's Parinirvana, he has not uttered, nor ever will he utter, one word. And the same is true of all the Buddhas.

THEN SAID MAHAMATI: Blessed One, you speak of the sameness of all the Buddhas, but in other places you have spoken of Dharmata-Buddha, Nishyanda-Buddha and Nirmana-Buddha as though they were different from each other; how can they be the same and yet different?

The Blessed One replied: I speak of the different Buddhas as opposed to the views of the philosophers who base their teachings on the reality of an external world of form and who cherish discriminations and attachments arising therefrom; against the teachings of these philosophers I disclose the Nirmana-Buddha, the Buddha of Transformations. In the many transformations of the Tathagata stage, the Nirmana-Buddha establishes such matters as charity, morality, patience, thoughtfulness, and tranquillisation; by right-knowledge he teaches the true understanding of the maya-like nature of the elements that make up personality and its external world; he teaches the true nature of the mind-system as a whole and in the distinctions of its forms, functions and ways of performance. In a deeper sense, The Nirmana-Buddha symbolises the principles of differentiation and integration by reason of which all component things are distributed, all complexities simplified, all thoughts analysed; at the same time it symbolises the harmonising, unifying power of sympathy and compassion; it removes all obstacles, it harmonises all differences, it brings into perfect Oneness the discordant many. For the emancipation of all beings the Bodhisattvas and Tathagatas assume bodies of transformation and employ many skillful devices, this is the work of the Nirmana-Buddha.

For the enlightenment of the Bodhisattvas and their sustaining along the stages, the Inconceivable is made realisable. The Nishyanda-Buddha, the "Out-flowing-Buddha," through Transcendental Intelligence, reveals the true meaning and significance of appearances, discrimination, attachment; and of the power of habit-energy which is accumulated by them and conditions them; and of the un-bornness the emptiness, the egolessness of all things. Because of Transcendental Intelligence and the purification of the evil out-flowings of life, all dualistic views of existence and nonexistence are transcended and by self-realisation of Noble Wisdom the true imagelessness of Reality is made manifest. The inconceivable glory of Buddhahood is made manifest in rays of Noble Wisdom; Noble Wisdom is the self-nature of the Tathagatas. This is the work of the Nishyanda-Buddha. In a deeper sense, the Nishyanda-Buddha symbolises the emergence of the principles of intellection and compassion but as yet undifferentiated and in perfect balance, potential but unmanifest. Looked at from the in-going side of the Bodhisattvas, Nishyanda-Buddha is seen in the glorified bodies of the Tathagatas; looked at from the forth-going side of Buddhahood, Nishyanda-Buddha is seen in the radiant personalities of the Tathagatas ready and eager to manifest the inherent Love and Wisdom of the Dharmakaya.

Dharmata-Buddha is Buddhahood in its self-nature of Perfect Oneness in whom absolute tranquillity prevails. As Noble Wisdom, Dharmata-Buddha transcends all differentiated knowledge, is the goal of intuitive self-realisation, and is the self-nature of the Tathagatas. As Noble Wisdom, Dharmata-Buddha is inscrutable, ineffable, unconditioned. Dharmata-Buddha is the Ultimate Principle of Reality from which all things derive their being and truthfulness, but which in itself transcends all predicates. Dharmata-Buddha is the central sun which holds all, illumines all. Its inconceivable Essence is made manifest in the "out-flowing" glory of Nishyanda-Buddha and in the transformations of Nirmana-Buddha.

THEN SAID MAHAMATI: Pray tell us, Blessed One, more about the Dharmakaya?

The Blessed One replied: We have been speaking of it in terms of Buddhahood, but as it is inscrutable and beyond predicate we may just as well speak of it as the Truth-body, or the Truth-principle of Ultimate Reality (Paramartha). This Ultimate Principle of Reality may be considered as it is manifested under seven aspects: First, as Citta-gocara, it is the world of spiritual experience and the abode of the Tathagatas on their outgoing mission of emancipation. It is Noble Wisdom manifested as the principle of irradiancy and individuation. Second, as Jnana, it is the mind-world and its principle of intellection and consciousness. Third, as Dristi, it is the realm of dualism which is the physical world of birth and death wherein are manifested all the differentiations of thinker, thinking and thought-about and wherein are manifested the principles of sensation, perception, discrimination, desire, attachment and suffering.

Fourth, because of the greed, anger, infatuation, suffering and need of the physical world incident to discrimination and attachment, it reveals a world beyond the realm of dualism wherein it appears as the integrating principle of charity and sympathy. Fifth, in a realm still higher, which is the abode of the Bodhisattva stages, and is analogous to the mind-world, where the interests of heart transcend those of the mind, it appears as the principle of compassion and self-giving. Sixth, in the spiritual realm where the Bodhisattvas attain Buddhahood, it appears as the principle of perfect Love (Karuna). Here the last clinging to an ego-self is abandoned and the Bodhisattva enters into his self-realisation of Noble Wisdom which is the bliss of the Tathagata's perfect enjoyment of his inmost nature. Seventh, as Prajna it is the active aspect of the Ultimate Principle wherein both the forth-going and the in-coming principles are alike, implicit and potential, and wherein both Wisdom and Love are in perfect balance, harmony and Oneness.

These are the seven aspects of the Ultimate Principle of Dharmakaya, by reason of which all things are made manifest and perfected and then reintegrated, and all remaining within its inscrutable Oneness, with no signs of individuation, nor beginning, nor succession, nor ending. We speak of it as Dharmakaya, as Ultimate Principle, as Buddhahood, as Nirvana; what matters it? They are only other names for Noble Wisdom.

Mahamati, you and all the Bodhisattva-Mahasattvas should avoid the erroneous reasonings of the philosophers and seek for a self-realisation of Noble Wisdom.

Chapter 13

Nirvana

THEN SAID MAHAMATI to the Blessed One: Pray tell Us about Nirvana?

The Blessed One replied: The term, Nirvana, is used with many different meanings, by different people, but these people may be divided into four groups: There are people who are suffering, or who are afraid of suffering, and who think of Nirvana; there are the philosophers who try to discriminate Nirvana; there are the class of disciples who think of Nirvana in relation to themselves; and, finally there is the Nirvana of the Buddhas.

Those who are suffering or who fear suffering, think of Nirvana as an escape and a recompense. They imagine that Nirvana consists in the future annihilation of the senses and the sense-minds; they are not aware that Universal Mind and Nirvana are One, and that this life-and-death world and Nirvana are not to be separated. These ignorant ones, instead of meditating on the imagelessness of Nirvana, talk of different ways of emancipation. Being ignorant of, or not understanding, the teachings of the Tathagatas, they cling to the notion of Nirvana that is outside what is seen of the mind and, thus, go on rolling themselves along with the wheel of life and death.

As to the Nirvanas discriminated by the philosophers: there really are none. Some philosophers conceive Nirvana to be found where the mind-system no more operates owing to the cessation of the elements that make up personality and its world; or is found where there is utter indifference to the objective world and its impermanency. Some conceive Nirvana to be a state where there is no recollection of the past or present, just as when a lamp is extinguished, or when a seed is burnt, or when a fire goes out; because then there is the cessation of all the substrate, which is explained by the philosophers as the non-rising of discrimination. But this is not Nirvana, because Nirvana does not consist in simple annihilation and vacuity.

Again, some philosophers explain deliverance as though it was the mere stopping of discrimination, as when the wind stops blowing, or as when one by self-effort gets rid of the dualistic view of knower and known, or gets rid of the notions of permanency and impermanency; or gets rid of the notions of good and evil; or overcomes passion by means of knowledge;--to them Nirvana is deliverance. Some, seeing in "form" the bearer of pain are alarmed by the notion of "form" and look for happiness in a world of "no-form." Some conceive that in consideration of individuality and generality recognisable in all things inner and outer, that there is no destruction and that all beings maintain their being for ever and, in this eternality, see Nirvana. Others see the eternality of things in the conception of Nirvana as the absorption of the finite-soul in Supreme Atman; or who see all things as a manifestation of the vital-force of some Supreme Spirit to which all return; and some, who are especially silly, declare that there are two primary things, a primary substance and a primary soul, that react differently upon each other and thus produce all things from the transformations of qualities; some think that the world is born of action and interaction and that no other cause is necessary; others think that Ishvara is the free creator of all things; clinging to these foolish notions, there is no awakening, and they consider Nirvana to consist in the fact that there is no awakening.

Some imagine that Nirvana is where self-nature exists in its own right, unhampered by other self-natures, as the varigated feathers of a peacock, or various precious crystals, or the pointedness of a thorn. Some conceive being to be Nirvana, some non-being, while others conceive that all things and Nirvana are not to be distinguished from one another. Some, thinking that time is the creator and that as the rise of the world depends on time, they conceive that Nirvana consists in the recognition of time as Nirvana. Some think that there will be Nirvana when the "twenty-five" truths are generally accepted, or when the king observes the six virtues, and some religionists think that Nirvana is the attainment of paradise.

These views severally advanced by the philosophers with their various reasonings are not in accord with logic nor are they acceptable to the wise. They all conceive Nirvana dualistically and in some causal connection; by these discriminations philosophers imagine Nirvana, but where there is no rising and no disappearing, how can there be discrimination? Each philosopher relying on his own textbook from which he draws his understanding, sins against the truth, because truth is not where he imagines it to be. The only result is that it sets his mind to wandering about and becoming more confused as Nirvana is not to be found by mental searching, and the more his mind becomes confused the more he confuses other people.

As to the notion of Nirvana as held by disciples and masters who still cling to the notion of an ego-self, and who try to find it by going off by themselves into solitude: their notion of Nirvana is an eternity of bliss like the bliss of the Samadhis-for themselves. They recognise that the world is only a manifestation of mind and that all discriminations are of the mind, and so they forsake social relations and practise various spiritual disciplines and in solitude seek self-realisation of Noble Wisdom by self-effort. They follow the stages to the sixth and attain the bliss of the Samadhis, but as they are still clinging to egoism they do not attain the "turning-about" at the deepest seat of consciousness and, therefore, they are not free from the thinking-mind and the accumulation of its habit-energy. Clinging to the bliss of the Samadhis, they pass to their Nirvana, but it is not the Nirvana of the Tathagatas. They are of those who have "entered the stream"; they must return to this world of life and death.

THEN SAID MAHAMATI to the Blessed One: When the Bodhisattvas yield up their stock of merit for the emancipation of all beings, they become spiritually one with all animate life; they themselves may be purified, but in others there yet remain unexhausted evil and unmatured karma. Pray tell us, Blessed One, how the Bodhisattvas are given assurance of Nirvana? and what is the Nirvana of the Bodhisattvas?

The Blessed One replied: Mahamati, this assurance is not an assurance of numbers nor logic; it is not the mind that is to be assured but the heart. The Bodhisattva's assurance comes with the unfolding insight that follows passion hindrances cleared away, knowledge hindrance purified, and egolessness clearly perceived and patiently accepted. As the mortal-mind ceases to discriminate, there is no more thirst for life, no more sex-lust, no more thirst for learning, no more thirst for eternal life; with the disappearance of these fourfold thirsts, there is no more accumulation of habit-energy; with no more accumulation of habit-energy the defilements on the face of Universal Mind clear away, and the Bodhisattva attains self-realisation of Noble Wisdom that is the heart's assurance of Nirvana.

There are Bodhisattvas here and in other Buddha-lands, who are sincerely devoted to the Bodhisattva's mission and yet who cannot wholly forget the bliss of the Samadhis and the peace of Nirvana-for themselves. The teaching of Nirvana in which there is no substrate left behind, is revealed according to a hidden meaning for the sake of these disciples who still cling to thoughts of Nirvana for themselves, that they may be inspired to exert themselves in the Bodhisattva's mission of emancipation for all beings. The Transformation-Buddhas teach a doctrine of Nirvana to meet conditions as they find them, and to give encouragement to the timid and selfish. In order to turn their thoughts away from themselves and to encourage them to a deeper compassion and more earnest zeal for others, they are given assurance as to the future by the sustaining power of the Buddhas of Transformation, but not by the Dharmata-Buddha.

The Dharma which establishes the Truth of Noble Wisdom belongs to the realm of the Dharmata-Buddha. To the Bodhisattvas of the seventh and eighth stages, Transcendental Intelligence is revealed by the Dharmata-Buddha and the Path is pointed out to them which they are to follow. In the perfect self-realisation of Noble Wisdom that follows the inconceivable transformation death of the Bodhisattva's individualised will-control, he no longer lives unto himself, but the life that he lives thereafter is the Tathagata's universalised life as manifested in its transformations. In this perfect self-realisation of Noble Wisdom the Bodhisattva realises that for Buddhas there is no Nirvana.

The death of a Buddha, the great Parinirvana, is neither destruction nor death, else would it be birth and continuation. If it were destruction, it would be an effect-producing deed, which it is not. Neither is it a vanishing nor an abandonment, neither is it attainment, nor is it of no attainment; neither is it of one significance nor of no significance, for there is no Nirvana for the Buddhas.

The Tathagata's Nirvana is where it is recognised that there is nothing but what is seen of the mind itself; is where, recognising the nature of the self-mind, one no longer cherishes the dualisms of discrimination; is where there is no more thirst nor grasping; is where there is no more attachment to external things. Nirvana is where the thinking-mind with all its discriminations, attachments, aversions and egoism is forever put away; is where logical measures, as they are seen to be inert, are no longer seized upon; is where even the notion of truth is treated with indifference because of its causing bewilderment; Is where, getting rid of the four propositions, there is insight into the abode of Reality. Nirvana is where the twofold passions have subsided and the twofold hindrances are cleared away and the twofold egolessness is patiently accepted; is where, by the attainment of the "turning-about" in the deepest seat of consciousness, self-realisation of Noble Wisdom is fully entered into, that is the Nirvana of the Tathagatas.

Nirvana is where the Bodhisattva stages are passed one after another; is where the sustaining power of the Buddhas upholds the Bodhisattvas in the bliss of the Samadhis; is where compassion for others transcends all thoughts of self; is where the Tathagata stage is finally realised.

Nirvana is the realm of Dharmata-Buddha; it is where the manifestation of Noble Wisdom that is Buddhahood expresses itself in Perfect Love for all; it is where the manifestation of Perfect Love that is Tathagatahood expresses itself in Noble Wisdom for the enlightenment of all;--there, indeed, is Nirvana!

There are two classes of those who may not enter the Nirvana of the Tathagatas: there are those who have abandoned the Bodhisattva ideals, saying, they are not in conformity with the sutras, the codes of morality, nor with emancipation. Then there are the true Bodhisattvas who, on account of their original vows made for the sake of all beings, saying, "So long as they do not attain Nirvana, I will not attain it myself," voluntarily keep themselves out of Nirvana. But no beings are left outside by the will of the Tathagatas; some day each and every one will be influenced by the wisdom and love of the Tathagatas of Transformation to lay up a stock of merit and ascend the stages. But, if they only realised it, they are already in the Tathagata's Nirvana for, in Noble Wisdom, all things are in Nirvana from the beginning.

The Brahmajala Sutra (or Brahma Net Sutra)

*The name of this sutra derives from the vast net that the god Brahma hangs in his palace, and how each jewel in the net reflects the light of every other jewel.

I. Vairocana Buddha

At some point, Vairocana Buddha began speaking in general about the Mind-Ground for the benefit of the Great Assembly. What he said represents but an infinitesimal part, the tip of a hair, of His innumerable teachings -- as numerous as the grains of sand in the river Ganges.

He concluded: "The Mind-Ground has been explained, is being explained and will be explained by all the Buddhas -- past, present, and future. It is also the Dharma Door (cultivation method) that all the Bodhisattvas of the past, present, and future have studied, are studying and will study."

"I have cultivated this Mind-Ground Dharma Door for hundreds of eons. My name is Vairocana. I request all Buddhas to transmit my words to all sentient beings, so as to open this path of cultivation to all."

At that time, from his Lion's Throne in the Lotus Treasury World, Vairocana Buddha emitted rays of light. A voice among the rays is heard telling the Buddhas seated on thousands of lotus petals, "You should practice and uphold the Mind-Ground Dharma Door and transmit it to the innumerable Sakyamuni Buddhas, one after another, as well as to all sentient beings. Everyone should uphold, read, recite, and singlemindedly put its teachings into practice."

After receiving the Dharma-door of the Mind-Ground, the Buddhas seated atop the thousands of lotus flowers along with the innumerable Sakyamuni Buddhas all arose from their Lion seats, their bodies emitting innumerable rays of light. In each of these rays appeared innumerable Buddhas who simultaneously made offerings of green, yellow, red and white celestial flowers to Vairocana Buddha. They then slowly took their leave.

The Buddhas then disappeared from the Lotus Treasury World, entered the Essence-Nature Empty Space Floral Brilliance Samadhi and returned to their former places under the Bodhi-tree in this world of Jambudvipa. They then arose from their samadhi, sat on their Diamond

Thrones in Jambudvipa and the Heaven of the Four Kings, and preached the Dharma of the "Ten Oceans of Worlds."

Thereupon, they ascended to Lord Shakya's palace and expounded the "Ten Dwellings," proceeded to the Suyama Heaven and taught the "Ten Practices," proceeded further to the Fourth Heaven and taught the "Ten Dedications," proceeded further to the Transformation of Bliss Heaven and taught the "Ten Dhyana Samadhi," proceeded further to the Heaven of Comfort From Others' Emanations and taught the "Ten Grounds," proceeded further to the First Dhyana Heaven and taught the "Ten Vajra Stages," proceeded further to the Second Dhyana Heaven and taught the "Ten Patiences," and proceeded further to the Third Dhyana Heaven and taught the "Ten Vows." Finally, in the Fourth Dhyana Heaven, at Lord Brahma's Palace, they taught the "Mind-Ground Dharma-Door" chapter, which Vairocana Buddha, in eons past, expounded in the Lotus Treasury World (the cosmos).

All the other innumerable transformation Sakyamuni Buddhas did likewise in their respective worlds as the chapter "Auspicious Kalpa" has explained.

II. Sakyamuni Buddha

At that time, Sakyamuni Buddha, after first appearing in the Lotus Treasury World, proceeded to the east and appeared in the Heavenly King's palace to teach the "Demon Transforming Sutra." He then descended to Jambudvipa to be born in Kapilavastu -- his name being Siddhartha and his father's name Suddhodana. His mother was Queen Maya. He achieved Enlightenment at the age of thirty, after seven years of cultivation, under the name of Sakyamuni Buddha

The Buddha spoke in ten assemblies from the Diamond Seat at Bodhgaya to the palace of Brahma.

At that time, he contemplated the wonderful Jewel Net hung in Lord Brahma's palace and preached the Brahma Net Sutra for the Great Assembly. He said:

"The innumerable worlds in the cosmos are like the eyes of the net. Each and every world is different, its variety infinite. So too are the Dharma Doors (methods of cultivation) taught by the Buddhas.

"I have come to this world eight thousand times. Based in this Saha World, seated upon the Jeweled Diamond Seat in Bodhgaya and all the way up to the palace of the Brahma King, I have spoken in general about the Mind-Ground Dharma Door for the benefit of the great multitude.

"Thereafter, I descended from the Brahma King's palace to Jambudvipa, the Human World. I have preached the Diamond Illuminated Jeweled Precepts (the Bodhisattva precepts) from beneath the Bodhi-tree for the sake of all sentient beings on earth, however dull and ignorant they may be. These precepts were customarily recited by Vairocana Buddha when he first developed the Bodhi Mind in the causal stages. They are precisely the original source of all Buddhas and all Bodhisattvas as well as the seed of the Buddha Nature.

"All sentient beings possess this Buddha Nature. All with consciousness, form, and mind are encompassed by the precepts of the Buddha Nature. Sentient beings possess the correct cause of the Buddha Nature and therefore they will assuredly attain the ever-present Dharma Body.

For this reason, the ten Pratimoksa (Bodhisattva) precepts came into being in this world. These precepts belong to the True Dharma. They are received and upheld in utmost reverence by all sentient beings of the Three Periods of Time -- past, present and future.

"Once again, I shall preach for the Great Assembly the chapter on the Inexhaustible Precept Treasury. These are the precepts of all sentient beings, the source of the pure Self-Nature."

Now, I, Vairocana Buddha
Am sitting atop a lotus pedestal;
On a thousand flowers surrounding me
Are a thousand Sakyamuni Buddhas.
Each flower supports a hundred million worlds;
In each world a Sakyamuni Buddha appears.
All are seated beneath a Bodhi-tree,
All simultaneously attain Buddhahood.
All these innumerable Buddhas
Have Vairocana as their original body.
These countless Sakyamuni Buddhas
All bring followers along -- as numerous as motes of dust.
They all proceed to my lotus pedestal
To listen to the Buddha's precepts.
I now preach the Dharma, this exquisite nectar.
Afterward, the countless Buddhas return to

their respective worlds
And, under a Bodhi-tree, proclaim these
major and minor precepts
Of Vairocana, the Original Buddha.
The precepts are like the radiant sun and moon,
Like a shining necklace of gems,
Bodhisattvas as numerous as motes of dust
Uphold them and attain Buddhahood.
These precepts are recited by Vairocana,
These precepts I recite as well.
You novice Bodhisattvas
Should reverently accept and uphold them.
And once you have done so,
Transmit and teach them to sentient beings.
Now listen attentively as I recite
The Bodhisattva Pratimoksa -- the source of all precepts in the Buddha Dharma.
All of you in the Great Assembly should firmly believe
That you are the Buddhas of the future,
While I am a Buddha already accomplished.
If you should have such faith at all times,
Then this precept code is fulfilled.
All beings with resolve
Should accept and uphold the Buddha's precepts.
Sentient beings on receiving them
Join forthwith the ranks of Buddhas.
They are in essence equal to the Buddhas,
They are the true offspring of the Buddhas.
Therefore, Great Assembly,
Listen with utmost reverence
As I proclaim the Bodhisattva Moral Code.

III. The Buddha Reciting the Bodhisattva Precepts

At that time, when Sakyamuni Buddha first attained Supreme Enlightenment under the Bodhi tree, he explained the Bodhisattva precepts. The Buddha taught filial piety toward one's parents, Elder Masters and the Triple Jewel. Filial piety and obedience, he said, are the Ultimate Path [to Buddhahood]. Filial piety is called the precepts -- and it means restraint and cessation.

The Buddha then emitted limitless lights from his mouth. Thereupon, the whole Great Assembly, consisting of innumerable Bodhisattvas, the gods of the eighteen Brahma Heavens, the gods of the six Desire Heavens, and the rulers of the sixteen great kingdoms all joined their palms and listened singlemindedly to the Buddha recite the Mahayana precepts.

The Buddha then said to the Bodhisattvas: Twice a month I recite the precepts observed by all Buddhas. All Bodhisattvas, from those who have just developed the Bodhi Mind to the Bodhisattvas of the Ten Dwellings, the Ten Practices, the Ten Dedications, and the Ten Grounds also recite them. Therefore, this precept-light shines forth from my mouth. It does not arise without a cause. This light is neither blue, yellow, red, white, nor black. It is neither form, nor thought. It is neither existent nor nonexistent, neither cause nor effect. This precept-light is precisely the original source of all Buddhas and all members of this Great Assembly. Therefore all you disciples of the Buddha should receive and observe, read, recite and study these precepts with utmost attention.

Disciples of the Buddha, listen attentively! Whoever can understand and accept a Dharma Master's words of transmission can receive the Bodhisattva precepts and be called foremost in purity. This is true whether that person is a king, a prince, an official, a monk, a nun, or a god of the eighteen Brahma Heavens, a god of the six Desire Heavens, or a human, a eunuch, a libertine, a prostitute, a slave, or a member of the Eight Divisions of Divinities, a Vajra spirit, an animal, or even a transformation-being.

IV. The Ten Major Precepts

The Buddhas said to his disciples, "There are ten major Bodhisattva precepts. If one receives the precepts but fails to recite them, he is not a Bodhisattva, nor is he a seed of Buddhahood. I, too, recite these precepts.

"All Bodhisattvas have studied them in the past, will study in the future, and are studying them now. I have explained the main characteristics of the Bodhisattva precepts. You should study and observe them with all your heart."

The Buddha continued:

1. First Major Precept On Killing

A disciple of the Buddha shall not himself kill, encourage others to kill, kill by expedient means, praise killing, rejoice at witnessing killing, or kill through incantation or deviant mantras. He must not create the causes, conditions, methods, or karma of killing, and shall not intentionally kill any living creature.

As a Buddha's disciple, he ought to nurture a mind of compassion and filial piety, always devising expedient means to rescue and protect all beings. If instead, he fails to restrain himself and kills sentient beings without mercy, he commits a Parajika (major) offense.

2. Second Major Precept On Stealing

A disciple of the Buddha must not himself steal or encourage others to steal, steal by expedient means, steal by means of incantation or deviant mantras. He should not create the causes, conditions, methods, or karma of stealing. No valuables or possessions, even those belonging to ghosts and spirits or thieves and robbers, be they as small as a needle or blade of grass, may be stolen.

As a Buddha's disciple, he ought to have a mind of mercy, compassion, and filial piety -- always helping people earn merits and achieve happiness. If instead, he steals the possessions of others, he commits a Parajika offense.

3. Third Major Precept On Sexual Misconduct

A disciple of the Buddha must not engage in licentious acts or encourage others to do so. [As a monk] he should not have sexual relations with any female -- be she a human, animal, deity or spirit -- nor create the causes, conditions, methods, or karma of such misconduct. Indeed, he must not engage in improper sexual conduct with anyone.

A Buddha's disciple ought to have a mind of filial piety -- rescuing all sentient beings and instructing them in the Dharma of purity and chastity. If instead, he lacks compassion and encourages others to engage in sexual relations promiscuously, including with animals and even their mothers, daughters, sisters, or other close relatives, he commits a Parajika offense.

4. Fourth Major Precept On Lying and False Speech

A disciple of the Buddha must not himself use false words and speech, or encourage others to lie or lie by expedient means. He should not involve himself in the causes, conditions, methods, or karma of lying, saying that he has seen what he has not seen or vice-versa, or lying implicitly through physical or mental means.

As a Buddha's disciple, he ought to maintain Right Speech and Right Views always, and lead all others to maintain them as well. If instead, he causes wrong speech, wrong views or evil karma in others, he commits a Parajika offense.

5. Fifth Major Precept On Selling Intoxicants

A disciple of the Buddha must not trade in alcoholic beverages or encourage others to do so. He should not create the causes, conditions, methods, or karma of selling any intoxicant whatsoever, for intoxicants are the causes and conditions of all kinds of offenses.

As a Buddha's disciple, he ought to help all sentient beings achieve clear wisdom. If instead, he causes them to have upside-down, topsy-turvy thinking, he commits a Parajika offense.

6. Sixth Major Precept On Broadcasting the Faults of the Assembly

A disciple of the Buddha must not himself broadcast the misdeeds or infractions of Bodhisattva-clerics or Bodhisattva-laypersons, or of [ordinary] monks and nuns -- nor encourage others to do so. He must not create the causes, conditions, methods, or karma of discussing the offenses of the assembly.

As a Buddha's disciple, whenever he hears evil persons, externalists or followers of the Two Vehicles speak of practices contrary to the Dharma or contrary to the precepts within the Buddhist community, he should instruct them with a compassionate mind and lead them to develop wholesome faith in the Mahayana.

If instead, he discusses the faults and misdeeds that occur within the assembly, he commits a Parajika offense.

7. Seventh Major Precept On Praising Oneself and Disparaging Others

A disciple of the Buddha shall not praise himself and speak ill of others, or encourage others to do so. He must not create the causes, conditions, methods, or karma of praising himself and disparaging others.

As a disciple of the Buddha, he should be willing to stand in for all sentient beings and endure humiliation and slander -- accepting blame and letting sentient beings have all the glory. If instead, he displays his own virtues and conceals the good points of others, thus causing them to suffer slander, he commits a Parajika offense.

8. Eighth Major Precept On Stinginess and Abuse

A disciple of the Buddha must not be stingy or encourage others to be stingy. He should not create the causes, conditions, methods, or karma of stinginess. As a Bodhisattva, whenever a destitute person comes for help, he should give that person what he needs. If instead, out of anger and resentment, he denies all assistance -- refusing to help with even a penny, a needle, a blade of grass, even a single sentence or verse or a phrase of Dharma, but instead scolds and abuses that person -- he commits a Parajika offense.

9. Ninth Major Precept On Anger and Resentment

A disciple of the Buddha shall not harbor anger or encourage others to be angry. He should not create the causes, conditions, methods, or karma of anger.

As a disciple of the Buddha, he ought to be compassionate and filial, helping all sentient beings develop the good roots of non-contention. If instead, he insults and abuses sentient beings, or even transformation beings [such as deities and spirits], with harsh words, hitting them with his fists or feet, or attacking them with a knife or club -- or harbors grudges even when the victim confesses his mistakes and humbly seeks forgiveness in a soft, conciliatory voice -- the disciple commits a Parajika offense.

10. Tenth Major Precept On Slandering the Triple Jewel

A Buddha's disciple shall not himself speak ill of the Triple Jewel or encourage others to do so. He must not create the causes, conditions, methods or karma of slander. If a disciple hears but a single word of slander against the Buddha from externalists or evil beings, he experiences a pain similar to that of three hundred spears piercing his heart. How then could he possibly slander the Triple Jewel himself?

Hence, if a disciple lacks faith and filial piety towards the Triple Jewel, and even assists evil persons or those of aberrant views to slander the Triple Jewel, he commits a Parajika offense.

V. Conclusion: The Ten Major Precepts

As a disciple of the Buddha, you should study these ten parajika (major) precepts and not break any one of them in even the slightest way -- much less break all of them! Anyone guilty of doing so cannot develop the Bodhi Mind in his current life and will lose whatever high position he may have attained, be it that of an emperor, Wheel-Turning King, Bhiksu, Bhiksuni -- as well as whatever level of Bodhisattvahood he may have reached, whether the Ten Dwellings, the Ten Practices, the Ten Dedications, the Ten Grounds -- and all the fruits of the eternal Buddha Nature. He will lose all of those levels of attainment and descend into the Three Evil Realms, unable to hear the words "parents" or "Triple Jewel" for eons! Therefore, Buddha's disciples should avoid breaking any one of these major precepts. All of you Bodhisattvas should study and observe the Ten Precepts, which have been observed, are being observed, and will be observed by all Bodhisattvas. They were explained in detail in the chapter, "The Eighty Thousand Rules of Conduct."

VI. The Forty-eight Minor Precepts

Then the Buddha told the Bodhisattvas, "Now that I have explained the Ten Major Precepts, I will speak about the forty-eight secondary precepts."

1. Disrespect toward Teachers and Friends

A disciple of the Buddha who is destined to become an emperor, a Wheel-Turning King, or high official should first receive the Bodhisattva precepts. He will then be under the protection of all guardian deities and spirits, and the Buddhas will be pleased.

Once he has received the precepts, the disciple should develop a mind of filial piety and respect. Whenever he meets an Elder Master, a monk, or a fellow cultivator of like views and like conduct, he should rise and greet him with respect. He must then respectfully make offerings to the guest-monks, in accord with the Dharma. He should be willing to pledge himself, his family, as well as his kingdom, cities, jewels and other possessions.

If instead, he should develop conceit or arrogance, delusion or anger, refusing to rise and greet guest-monks and make offerings to them respectfully, in accordance with the Dharma, he commits a secondary offense.

2. On Consuming Alcoholic Beverages

A disciple of the Buddha should not intentionally consume alcoholic beverages, as they are the source of countless offenses. If he but offers a glass of wine to another person, his retribution will be to have no hands for five hundred lifetimes. How could he then consume liquor himself! Indeed, a Bodhisattva should not encourage any person or any other sentient being to consume alcohol, much less take any alcoholic beverages himself. A disciple should not drink any alcoholic beverages whatsoever. If instead, he deliberately does so or encourages others to do so, he commits a secondary offense.

3. On Eating Meat

A disciple of the Buddha must not deliberately eat meat. He should not eat the flesh of any sentient being. The meat-eater forfeits the seed of Great Compassion, severs the seed of the Buddha Nature and causes [animals and transcendental] beings to avoid him. Those who do so are guilty of countless offenses. Therefore, Bodhisattvas should not eat the flesh of any sentient beings whatsoever. If instead, he deliberately eats meat, he commits a secondary offense.

4. On Five Pungent Herbs

A disciple of the Buddha should not eat the five pungent herbs -- garlic, chives, leeks, onions, and asafoetida.This is so even if they are added as flavoring to other main dishes. Hence, if he deliberately does so, he commits a secondary offense.

5. On Not Teaching Repentance

If a disciple of the Buddha should see any being violate the Five Precepts, the Eight Precepts, the Ten Precepts, other prohibitions, or commit any of the Seven Cardinal Sins or any offense which leads to the Eight Adversities -- any violations of the precepts whatever -- he should counsel the offender to repent and reform.

Hence, if a Bodhisattva does not do so and furthermore continues to live together in the assembly with the offender, share in the offerings of the laity, participate in the same Uposatha ceremony and recite the precepts -- while failing to bring up that person's offense, enjoining him to repent -- the disciple commits a secondary offense.

6. Failing to Request the Dharma or Make Offerings

If an Elder Master, a Mahayana monk or fellow cultivator of like views and practice should come from far away to the temple, residence, city or village of a disciple of the Buddha, the disciple should respectfully welcome him and see him off. He should minister to his needs at all times, though doing so may cost as much as three taels of gold! Moreover, the disciple of the Buddha should respectfully request the guest-master to preach the Dharma three times a day by bowing to him without a single thought of resentment or weariness. He should be willing to sacrifice himself for the Dharma and never be lax in requesting it.

If he does not act in this manner, he commits a secondary offense.

7. Failing to Attend Dharma Lectures

A Bodhisattva disciple who is new to the Order should take copies of the appropriate sutras or precept codes to any place where such sutras, commentaries, or moral codes are being explained, to listen, study, and inquire about the Dharma. He should go anywhere, be it in a house, beneath a tree, in a temple, in the forests or mountains, or elsewhere. If he fails to do so, he commits a secondary offense.

8. On Turning Away from the Mahayana

If a disciple of the Buddha disavows the eternal Mahayana sutras and moral codes, declaring that they were not actually taught by the Buddha, and instead follows and observes those of the Two Vehicles and deluded externalists, he commits a secondary offense.

9. On Failure to Care for the Sick

If a disciple of the Buddha should see anyone who is sick, he should wholeheartedly provide for that person's needs just as he would for a Buddha. Of the eight Fields of Blessings, looking after the sick is the most important. A Buddha's disciple should take care of his father, mother, Dharma teacher or disciple -- regardless of whether the latter are disabled or suffering from various kinds of diseases.

If instead, he becomes angry and resentful and fails to do so, or refuses to rescue the sick or disabled in temples, cities and towns, forests and mountains, or along the road, he commits a secondary offense.

10. On Storing Deadly Weapons

A disciple of the Buddha should not store weapons such as knives, clubs, bows, arrows, spears, axes or any other weapons, nor may he keep nets, traps or any such devices used in destroying life.

As a disciple of the Buddha, he must not even avenge the death of his parents -- let alone kill sentient beings! He should not store any weapons or devices that can be used to kill sentient beings. If he deliberately does so, he commits a secondary offense.

The first ten secondary precepts have just been described. Disciples of the Buddha should study and respectfully observe them. They are explained in detail in the six chapters [now lost] following these precepts.

11. On Serving as an Emissary

A disciple of the Buddha shall not, out of personal benefit or evil intentions, act as a country's emissary to foster military confrontation and war causing the slaughter of countless sentient beings. As a disciple of the Buddha, he should not be involved in military affairs, or serve as a courier between armies, much less act as a willing catalyst for war. If he deliberately does so, he commits a secondary offense.

12. On Unlawful Business Undertakings

A disciple of the Buddha must not deliberately trade in slaves or sell anyone into servitude, nor should he trade in domestic animals, coffins or wood for caskets. He cannot engage in these types of business himself much less encourage others to do so. Otherwise, he commits a secondary offense.

13. On Slander and Libel

A disciple of the Buddha must not, without cause and with evil intentions, slander virtuous people, such as Elder Masters, monks or nuns, kings, princes or other upright persons, saying that they have committed the Seven Cardinal Sins or broken the Ten Major Bodhisattva Precepts. He should be compassionate and filial and treat all virtuous people as if they were his father, mother, siblings or other close relatives. If instead, he slanders and harms them, he commits a secondary offense.

14. On Starting Wildfires

A disciple of the Buddha shall not, out of evil intentions, start wildfires to clear forests and burn vegetation on mountains and plains, during the fourth to the ninth months of the lunar year. Such fires [are particularly injurious to animals during that period and may spread] to people's homes, towns and villages, temples and monasteries, fields and groves, as well as the [unseen] dwellings and possessions of deities and ghosts. He must not intentionally set fire to any place where there is life. If he deliberately does so, he commits a secondary offense.

15. Teaching Non-Mahayana Dharma

A disciple of the Buddha must teach one and all, from fellow disciples, relatives and spiritual friends, to externalists and evil beings, how to receive and observe the Mahayana sutras and moral codes. He should teach the Mahayana principles to them and help them develop the Bodhi Mind -- as well as the Ten Dwellings, the Ten Practices and the Ten Dedications, explaining the order and function of each of these Thirty Minds (levels).

If instead, the disciple, with evil, hateful intentions, perversely teaches them the sutras and moral codes of the Two Vehicle tradition as well as the commentaries of deluded externalists, he thereby commits a secondary offense.

16. Unsound Explanation of the Dharma

A Bodhisattva Dharma Master must first, with a wholesome mind, study the rules of deportment, as well as sutras and moral codes of the Mahayana tradition, and understand their meanings in depth. Then, whenever novices come from afar to seek instruction, he should explain, according to the Dharma, all the Bodhisattva renunciation practices, such as burning one's body, arm, or finger [as the ultimate act in the quest for Supreme Enlightenment]. If a novice is not prepared to follow these practices as an offering to the Buddhas, he is not a Bodhisattva monk. Moreover, a Bodhisattva monk should be willing to sacrifice his body and limbs for starving beasts and hungry ghosts [as the ultimate act of compassion in rescuing sentient beings].

After these explanations, the Bodhisattva Dharma Master should teach the novices in an orderly way, to awaken their minds. If instead, for personal gain, he refuses to teach or teaches in a confused manner, quoting passages out of order and context, or teaches in a manner that disparages the Triple Jewel, he commits a secondary offense.

17. On Exacting Donations

A disciple of the Buddha must not, for the sake of food, drink, money, possessions or fame, approach and befriend kings, princes, or high officials and [on the strength of such relationships], exact money, goods or other advantages. Nor may he encourage others to do so. These actions are called untoward, excessive demands and lack compassion and filial piety. Such a disciple commits a secondary offense.

18. On Serving as an Inadequate Master

A disciple of the Buddha should study the Twelve Divisions of the Dharma and recite the Bodhisattva precepts frequently. He should strictly observe these precepts in the Six Periods of the day and night and fully understand their meaning and principles as well as the essence of their Buddha Nature.

If instead, the disciple of the Buddha fails to understand even a sentence or a verse of the moral code or the causes and conditions related to the precepts, but pretends to understand them, he is deceiving both himself and others. A disciple who understands nothing of the Dharma, yet acts as a teacher transmitting the precepts, commits a secondary offense.

19. On Double-tongued Speech

A disciple of the Buddha must not, with malicious intent gossip or spread rumors and slander, create discord and disdain for virtuous people. [An example is] disparaging a monk who observes the Bodhisattva precepts, as he [makes offerings to the Buddhas by] holding an incense burner to his forehead. A disciple of the Buddha who does so commits a secondary offense.

20. Failure to Liberate Sentient Beings

A disciple of the Buddha should have a mind of compassion and cultivate the practice of liberating sentient beings. He must reflect thus: throughout the eons of time, all male sentient beings have been my father, all female sentient beings my mother. I was born of them, now I slaughter them, I would be slaughtering my parents as well as eating flesh that was once my own. This is so because all elemental earth, water, fire and air -- the four constituents of all life -- have previously been part of my body, part of my substance. I must therefore always cultivate the practice of liberating sentient beings and enjoin others to do likewise -- as sentient beings are forever reborn, again and again, lifetime after lifetime. If a Bodhisattva sees an animal on the verge of being killed, he must devise a way to rescue and protect it, helping it to escape suffering and death. The disciple should always teach the Bodhisattva precepts to rescue and deliver sentient beings.

On the day his father, mother, and siblings die, he should invite Dharma Masters to explain the Bodhisattva sutras and precepts. This will generate merits and virtues and help the deceased either to achieve rebirth in the Pure Lands and meet the Buddhas or to secure rebirth in the human or celestial realms. If instead, a disciple fails to do so, he commits a secondary offense.

You should study and respectfully observe the above ten precepts. Each of them is explained in detail in the chapter "Expiating Offenses."

21. On Violence and Vengefulness

A disciple of the Buddha must not return anger for anger, blow for blow. He should not seek revenge, even if his father, mother, siblings, or close relatives are killed -- nor should he do so if the ruler or king of his country is murdered. To take the life of one being in order to avenge the killing of another is contrary to filial piety [as we are all related through the eons of birth and rebirth].

Furthermore, he should not keep others in servitude, much less beat or abuse them, creating evil karma of mind, speech and body day after day -- particularly the offenses of speech. How much less should he deliberately commit the Seven Cardinal Sins. Therefore, if a Bodhisattva-monk lacks compassion and deliberately seeks revenge, even for an injustice done to his close relatives, he commits a secondary offense.

22. Arrogance and Failure to Request the Dharma

A disciple of the Buddha who has only recently left home and is still a novice in the Dharma should not be conceited. He must not refuse instruction on the sutras and moral codes from Dharma Masters on account of his own intelligence, worldly learning, high position, advanced age, noble lineage, vast understanding, great merits, extensive wealth and possessions, etc. Although these Masters may be of humble birth, young in age, poor, or suffering physical disabilities, they may still have genuine virtue and deep understanding of sutras and moral codes.

The novice Bodhisattva should not judge Dharma Masters on the basis of their family background and refuse to seek instructions on the Mahayana truths from them. If he does so, he commits a secondary offense.

23. On Teaching the Dharma Grudgingly

After my passing, if a disciple should, with a wholesome mind, wish to receive the Bodhisattva precepts, he may make a vow to do so before the images of Buddhas and Bodhisattvas and practice repentance before these images for seven days. If he then experiences a vision, he has received the precepts. If he does not, he should continue doing so for fourteen days, twenty-one days, or even a whole year, seeking to witness an auspicious sign. After witnessing such a sign, he could, in front of images of Buddhas and Bodhisattvas, formally receive the precepts. If he has not witnessed such a sign, although he may have accepted the precepts before the Buddha images, he has not actually received the precepts.

However, the witnessing of auspicious signs is not necessary if the disciple receives the precepts directly from a Dharma Master who has himself received the precepts. Why is this so? It is because this is a case of transmission from Master to Master and therefore all that is required is a mind of utter sincerity and respect on the part of the disciple.

If, within a radius of some three hundred fifty miles, a disciple cannot find a Master capable of conferring the Bodhisattva precepts, he may seek to receive them in front of Buddha or Bodhisattva images. However, he must witness an auspicious sign.

If a Dharma Master, on account of his extensive knowledge of sutras and Mahayana moral codes as well as his close relationship with kings, princes, and high officials, refuses to give appropriate answers to student-Bodhisattvas seeking the meaning of sutras and moral codes, or does so grudgingly, with resentment and arrogance, he commits a secondary offense.

24. Failure to Practice Mahayana Teachings

If a disciple of the Buddha fails to study Mahayana sutras and moral codes assiduously and cultivate correct views, correct nature and the correct Dharma Body, it is like abandoning the Seven Precious Jewels for [mere stones]: worldly texts and the Two-Vehicle or externalist commentaries. To do so is to create the causes and conditions that obstruct the Path to Enlightenment and cut himself off from his Buddha Nature. It is a failure to follow the Bodhisattva path. If a disciple intentionally acts in such a manner, he commits a secondary offense.

25. Unskilled Leadership of the Assembly

After my passing, if a disciple should serve as an abbot, elder Dharma Master, Precept Master, Meditation Master, or Guest Prefect, he must develop a compassionate mind and peacefully settle differences within the Assembly -- skillfully administering the resources of the Three Jewels, spending frugally and not treating them as his own property. If instead, he were to create disorder, provoke quarrels and disputes or squander the resources of the Assembly, he would commit a secondary offense.

26. Accepting Personal Offerings

Once a disciple of the Buddha has settled down in a temple, if visiting Bodhisattva Bhiksus should arrive at the temple precincts, the guest quarters established by the king, or even the summer retreat quarters, or the quarters of the Great Assembly, the disciple should welcome the visiting monks and see them off. He should provide them with such essentials as food and drink, a place to live, beds, chairs, and the like. If the host does not have the necessary means, he should be willing to pawn himself or cut off and sell his own flesh.

Whenever there are meal offerings and ceremonies at a layman's home, visiting monks should be given a fair share of the offerings. The abbot should send the monks, whether residents or guests, to the donor's place in turn [according to their sacerdotal age or merits and virtues]. If only resident monks are allowed to accept invitations and not visiting monks, the abbot is committing a grievous offense and is behaving no differently than an animal. He is unworthy of being a monk or a son of the Buddha, and is guilty of a secondary offense.

27. Accepting Discriminatory Invitations

A disciple of the Buddha must not accept personal invitations nor appropriate the offerings for himself. Such offerings rightly belong to the Sangha -- the whole community of monks and nuns of the Ten Directions. To accept personal offerings is to steal the possessions of the Sangha of the Ten Directions. It is tantamount to stealing what belongs to the Eight Fields of Blessings: Buddhas, Sages, Dharma Masters, Precept Masters, monks/nuns, mothers, fathers, the sick. Such a disciple commits a secondary offense.

28. Issuing Discriminatory Invitations

A disciple of the Buddha, be he a Bodhisattva monk, lay Bodhisattva, or other donor, should, when inviting monks or nuns to conduct a prayer session, come to the temple and inform the monk in charge. The monk will then tell him: "Inviting members of the Sangha according to the proper order is tantamount to inviting the Arhats of the Ten Directions. To offer a discriminatory special invitation to [such a worthy group as] five hundred Arhats or Bodhisattva-monks will not generate as much merit as inviting one ordinary monk, if it is his turn.

There is no provision in the teachings of the Seven Buddhas for discriminatory invitations. To do so is to follow externalist practices and to contradict filial piety [toward all sentient beings]. If a disciple deliberately issues a discriminatory invitation, he commits a secondary offense.

29. On Improper Livelihoods

A disciple of the Buddha should not, for the sake of gain or with evil intentions, engage in the business of prostitution, selling the wiles and charms of men and women. He must also not cook for himself, milling and pounding grain. Neither may he act as a fortune-teller predicting the gender of children, reading dreams and the like. Nor shall he practice sorcery, work as a trainer of falcons or hunting dogs, nor make a living concocting hundreds and thousands of poisons from deadly snakes, insects, or from gold and silver. Such occupations lack mercy, compassion, and filial piety [toward sentient beings]. Therefore, if a Bodhisattva intentionally engages in these occupations, he commits a secondary offense.

30. On Handling Business Affairs for the Laity

A disciple of the Buddha must not, with evil intentions, slander the Triple Jewel while pretending to be their close adherent -- preaching the Truth of Emptiness while his actions are in the realm of Existence. Furthermore, he must not handle worldly affairs for the laity, acting as a go-between or matchmaker -- creating the karma of attachment. Moreover, during the six days of fasting each month and the three months of fasting each year, a disciple should strictly observe all precepts, particularly against killing, stealing and the rules against breaking the fast. Otherwise, the disciple commits a secondary offense.

A Bodhisattva should respectfully study and observe the ten preceding precepts. They are explained in detail in the Chapter on "Prohibitions".

31. Rescuing Clerics Along with Sacred Objects

After my passing, in the evil periods that will follow, there will be externalists, evil persons, thieves and robbers who steal and sell statues and paintings of Buddhas, Bodhisattvas and [those to whom respect is due such as] their parents. They may even peddle copies of sutras and moral codes, or sell monks, nuns or those who follow the Bodhisattva Path or have developed the Bodhi Mind to serve as retainers or servants to officials and others.

A disciple of the Buddha, upon witnessing such pitiful events, must develop a mind of compassion and find ways to rescue and protect all persons and valuables, raising funds wherever he can for this purpose. If a Bodhisattva does not act in this manner, he commits a secondary offense.

32. On Harming Sentient Beings

A disciple of the Buddha must not sell knives, clubs, bows, arrows, other life-taking devices, nor keep altered scales or measuring devices. He should not abuse his governmental position to confiscate people's possessions, nor should he, with malice at heart, restrain or imprison others or sabotage their success. In addition, he should not raise cats, dogs, foxes, pigs and other such animals. If he intentionally does such things, he commits a secondary offense.

33. On Watching Improper Activities

A disciple of the Buddha must not, with evil intentions, watch people fighting or the battling of armies, rebels, gangs and the like, should not listen to the sounds of conch shells, drums, horns, guitars, flutes, lutes, songs or other music, nor should he be party to any form of gambling, whether dice, checkers, or the like. Furthermore, he should not practice fortune-telling or divination nor should he be an accomplice to thieves and bandits. He must not participate in any of these activities. If instead, he intentionally does so, he commits a secondary offense.

34. Temporary Abandoning of the Bodhi Mind

A disciple of the Buddha should observe the Bodhisattva precepts every day, whether walking, standing, reclining or seated -- reading and reciting them day and night. He should be resolute in keeping the precepts, as strong as a diamond, as desperate as a shipwrecked person clinging to a small log while attempting to cross the ocean, or as principled as the "Bhiksu bound by reeds". Furthermore, he should always have a wholesome faith in the teachings of the Mahayana. Conscious that sentient beings are Buddhas-to-be while the Buddhas are realized Buddhas, he should develop the Bodhi Mind and maintain it in each and every thought, without retrogression.

If a Bodhisattva has but a single thought in the direction of the Two Vehicles or externalist teachings, he commits a secondary offense.

35. Failure to Make Great Vows

A Bodhisattva must make many great vows -- to be filial to his parents and Dharma teachers, to meet good spiritual advisors, friends, and colleagues who will keep teaching him the Mahayana sutras and moral codes as well as the Stages of Bodhisattva Practice (the Ten Dwellings, the Ten Practices, the Ten Dedications, and the Ten Grounds). He should further vow to understand these teachings clearly so that he can practice according to the Dharma while resolutely keeping the precepts of the Buddhas. If necessary, he should lay down his life rather than abandon this resolve for even a single moment. If a Bodhisattva does not make such vows, he commits a secondary offense.

36. Failure to Make Resolutions

Once a Bodhisattva has made these Great Vows, he should strictly keep the precepts of the Buddhas and make the following resolutions:

1.- I would rather jump into a raging blaze, a deep abyss, or into a mountain of knives, than engage in impure actions with any woman, thus violating the sutras and moral codes of the Buddhas of the Three Periods of Time.

2.- I would rather wrap myself a thousand times with a red-hot iron net, than let this body, should it break the precepts, wear clothing provided by the faithful.

I would rather swallow red hot iron pellets and drink molten iron for hundreds of thousands of eons, than let this mouth, should it break the precepts, consume food and drink provided by the faithful.

I would rather lie on a bonfire or a burning iron net than let this body, should it break the precepts, rest on bedding, blankets and mats supplied by the faithful.

I would rather be impaled for eons by hundreds of spears, than let this body, should it break the precepts, receive medications from the faithful.

I would rather jump into a cauldron of boiling oil and roast for hundreds of thousands of eons, than let this body, should it break the precepts, receive shelter, groves, gardens, or fields from the faithful.

3.- I would rather be pulverized from head to toe by an iron sledge hammer, than let this body, should it break the precepts, accept respect and reverence from the faithful.

4.- I would rather have both eyes blinded by hundreds of thousands of swords and spears, rather than break the precepts by looking at beautiful forms. [In the same vein, I shall keep my mind from being sullied by exquisite sounds, fragrances, food and sensations.]

5.- I further vow that all sentient beings will achieve Buddhahood.

If a disciple of the Buddha does not make the preceding great resolutions, he commits a secondary offense.

37. Traveling in Dangerous Areas

[As a cleric], a disciple of the Buddha should engage in ascetic practices twice each year. He should sit in meditation, winter and summer, and observe the summer retreat. During those periods, he should always carry eighteen essentials such as a willow branch (for a toothbrush), ash-water (for soap), the traditional three clerical robes, an incense burner, a begging bowl, a sitting mat, a water filter, bedding, copies of sutras and moral codes as well as statues of Buddhas and Bodhisattvas.

When practicing austerities and when traveling, be it for thirty miles or three hundred miles, a cleric should always have the eighteen essentials with him. The two periods of austerities are from the 15th of the first lunar month to the 15th of the third month, and from the 15th of the eighth lunar month to the 15th of the tenth month. During the periods of austerities, he requires these eighteen essentials just as a bird needs its two wings.

Twice each month, the novice Bodhisattva should attend the Uposattha ceremony and recite the Ten Major and Forty-eight Secondary Precepts. Such recitations should be done before images of the Buddhas and Bodhisattvas. If only one person attends the ceremony, then he should do the reciting. If two, three, or even hundreds of thousands attend the ceremony, still only one person should recite. Everyone else should listen in silence. The one reciting should sit on a higher level than the audience, and everyone should be dressed in clerical robes. During the summer retreat, each and every activity should be managed in accordance with the Dharma.

When practicing the austerities, the Buddhist disciple should avoid dangerous areas, unstable kingdoms, countries ruled by evil kings, precipitous terrains, remote wildernesses, regions inhabited by bandits, thieves, or lions, tigers, wolves, poisonous snakes, or areas subject to hurricanes, floods and fires. The disciple should avoid all such dangerous areas when practicing the austerities and also when observing the summer retreat. Otherwise, he commits a secondary offense.

38. Order of Seating Within the Assembly

A disciple of the Buddha should sit in the proper order when in the Assembly. Those who received the Bodhisattva precepts first sit first, those who received the precepts afterwards should sit behind. Whether old or young, a Bhiksu or Bhiksuni, a person of status, a king, a prince, a eunuch, or a servant, etc., each should sit according to the order in which he received the precepts. Disciples of the Buddha should not be like externalists or deluded people who base their order on age or sit without any order at all -- in barbarian fashion. In my Dharma, the order of sitting is based on seniority of ordination.

Therefore, if a Bodhisattva does not follow the order of sitting according to the Dharma, he commits a secondary offense.

39. Failure to Cultivate Merits and Wisdom

A disciple of the Buddha should constantly counsel and teach all people to establish monasteries, temples and pagodas in mountains and forests, gardens and fields. He should also construct stupas for the Buddhas and buildings for winter and summer retreats. All facilities required for the practice of the Dharma should be established.

Moreover, a disciple of the Buddha should explain Mahayana sutras and the Bodhisattva precepts to all sentient beings. In times of sickness, national calamities, impending warfare or upon the death of one's parents, brothers and sisters, Dharma Masters and Precept Masters, a Bodhisattva should lecture and explain Mahayana sutras and the Bodhisattva precepts weekly for up to seven weeks.

The disciple should read, recite, and explain the Mahayana sutras and the Bodhisattva precepts in all prayer gatherings, in his business undertakings and during periods of calamity -- fire, flood, storms, ships lost at sea in turbulent waters or stalked by demons ... In the same vein, he should do so in order to transcend evil karma, the Three Evil Realms, the Eight Difficulties, the Seven Cardinal Sins, all forms of imprisonment, or excessive sexual desire, anger, delusion, and illness.

If a novice Bodhisattva fails to act as indicated, he commits a secondary offense.

The Bodhisattva should study and respectfully observe the nine precepts just mentioned above, as explained in the "Brahma Altar" chapter.

40. Discrimination in Conferring the Precepts

A disciple of the Buddha should not be selective and show preference in conferring the Bodhisattva precepts. Each and every person can receive the precepts -- kings, princes, high officials, Bhiksus, Bhiksunis, laymen, laywomen, libertines, prostitutes, the gods in the eighteen Brahma Heavens or the six Desire Heavens, asexual persons, bisexual persons, eunuchs, slaves, or demons and ghosts of all types. Buddhist disciples should be instructed to wear robes and sleep on cloth of a neutral color, formed by blending blue, yellow, red, black and purple dyes all together.

The clothing of monks and nuns should, in all countries, be different from those worn by ordinary persons.

Before someone is allowed to receive the Bodhisattva precepts, he should be asked: "have you committed any of the Cardinal Sins?" The Precept Master should not allow those who have committed such sins to receive the precepts.

Here are the Seven Cardinal Sins: shedding the Buddha's blood, murdering an Arhat, killing one's father, killing one's mother, murdering a Dharma Teacher, murdering a Precept Master or disrupting the harmony of the Sangha.

Except for those who have committed the Cardinal Sins, everyone can receive the Bodhisattva precepts.

The Dharma rules of the Buddhist Order prohibit monks and nuns from bowing down before rulers, parents, relatives, demons and ghosts.

Anyone who understands the explanations of the Precept Master can receive the Bodhisattva precepts. Therefore, if a person were to come from thirty to three hundred miles away seeking the Dharma and the Precept Master, out of meanness and anger, does not promptly confer these precepts, he commits a secondary offense.

41. Teaching for the Sake of Profit

If a disciple of the Buddha, when teaching others and developing their faith in the Mahayana, should discover that a particular person wishes to receive the Bodhisattva precepts, he should act as a teaching master and instruct that person to seek out two Masters, a Dharma Master and a Precept Master.

These two Masters should ask the Precept candidate whether he has committed any of the Seven Cardinal Sins in this life. If he has, he cannot receive the precepts. If not, he may receive the precepts.

If he has broken any of the Ten Major Precepts, he should be instructed to repent before the statues of Buddhas and Bodhisattvas. He should do so six times a day and recite the Ten Major and Forty-eight Minor Precepts, paying respect with utter sincerity to the Buddhas of the Three Periods of Time. He should continue in this manner until he receives an auspicious response, which could occur after seven days, fourteen days, twenty-one days, or even a year. Examples of auspicious signs include: experiencing the Buddhas rub the crown of one's head, or seeing lights, halos, flowers and other such rare phenomena.

The witnessing of an auspicious sign indicates that the candidate's karma has been dissipated. Otherwise, although he has repented, it was of no avail. He still has not received the precepts. However, the merits accrued will increase his chances of receiving the precepts in a future lifetime.

Unlike the case of a major Bodhisattva precept, if a candidate has violated any of the Forty-eight Secondary Precepts, he can confess his infraction and sincerely repent before Bodhisattva-monks or nuns. After that, his offense will be eradicated.

The officiating Master, however, must fully understand the Mahayana sutras and moral codes, the secondary as well as the major Bodhisattva precepts, what constitutes an offense and what does not, the truth of Primary Meaning, as well as the various Bodhisattva cultivation stages -- the Ten Dwellings, the Ten Practices, the Ten Dedications, the Ten Grounds, and Equal and Wonderful Enlightenment.

He should also know the type and degree of contemplation required for entering and exiting these stages and be familiar with the Ten Limbs of Enlightenment as well as a variety of other contemplations.

If he is not familiar with the above and, out of greed for fame, disciples or offerings, he makes a pretense of understanding the sutras and moral codes, he is deceiving himself as well as others. Hence, if he intentionally acts as Precept Master, transmitting the precepts to others, he commits a secondary offense.

42. Reciting the Precepts to Evil Persons

A disciple of the Buddha should not, with a greedy motive, expound the great precepts of the Buddhas before those who have not received them, externalists or persons with heterodox views. Except in the case of kings or supreme rulers, he may not expound the precepts before any such person.

Persons who hold heterodox views and do not accept the precepts of the Buddhas are untamed in nature. They will not, lifetime after lifetime, encounter the Triple Jewel. They are as mindless as trees and stones; they are no different from wooden stumps. Hence, if a disciple of the Buddha expounds the precepts of the Seven Buddhas before such persons, he commits a secondary offense.

43. Thoughts of Violating the Precepts

If a disciple of the Buddha joins the Order out of pure faith, receives the correct precepts of the Buddhas, but then develops thoughts of violating the precepts, he is unworthy of receiving any offerings from the faithful, unworthy of walking on the ground of his motherland, unworthy of drinking its water.

Five thousand guardian spirits constantly block his way, calling him "Evil thief!" These spirits always follow him into people's homes, villages and towns, sweeping away his very footprints. Everyone curses such a disciple, calling him a "Thief within the Dharma." All sentient beings avert their eyes, not wishing to see him.

A disciple of the Buddha who breaks the precepts is no different from an animal or a wooden stump. Hence, if a disciple intentionally violates the correct precepts, he commits a secondary offense.

44. Failure to Honor the Sutras and Moral Codes

A disciple of the Buddha should always singlemindedly receive, observe, read and recite the Mahayana sutras and moral codes. He should copy the sutras and moral codes onto bark, paper, fine cloth, or bamboo slats and not hesitate to use his own skin as paper, draw his own blood for ink and his marrow for ink solvent, or split his bones for use as pens. He should use precious gems, priceless incense and flowers and other precious things to make and adorn covers and cases to store the sutras and codes.

Hence, if he does not make offerings to the sutras and moral codes, in accordance with the Dharma, he commits a secondary offense.

45. Failure to Teach Sentient Beings

A disciple of the Buddha should develop a mind of Great Compassion. Whenever he enters people's homes, villages, cities or towns, and sees sentient beings, he should say aloud, "You sentient beings should all take the Three Refuges and receive the Ten [Major Bodhisattva] Precepts." Should he come across cows, pigs, horses, sheep and other kinds of animals, he should concentrate and say aloud, "You are now animals; you should develop the Bodhi Mind." A Bodhisattva, wherever he goes, be it climbing a mountain, entering a forest, crossing a river, or walking through a field should help all sentient beings develop the Bodhi Mind.

If a disciple of the Buddha does not wholeheartedly teach and rescue sentient beings in such a manner, he commits a secondary offense.

46. Preaching in an Inappropriate Manner

A disciple of the Buddha should always have a mind of Great Compassion to teach and transform sentient beings. Whether visiting wealthy and aristocratic donors or addressing Dharma gatherings, he should not remain standing while explaining the Dharma to laymen, but should occupy a raised seat in front of the lay assembly.

A Bhiksu serving as Dharma instructor must not be standing while lecturing to the Fourfold Assembly. During such lectures, the Dharma Master should sit on a raised seat amidst flowers and incense, while the Fourfold Assembly must listen from lower seats. The Assembly must respect and follow the Master like filial sons obeying their parents or Brahmans worshipping fire. If a Dharma Master does not follow these rules while preaching the Dharma, he commits a secondary offense.

47. On Regulations Against the Dharma

A disciple of the Buddha who has accepted the precepts of the Buddhas with a faithful mind, must not use his high official position (as a king, prince, official, etc.) to undermine the moral code of the Buddhas. He may not establish rules and regulations preventing the four kinds of lay disciples from joining the Zen Order and practicing the Way, nor may he prohibit the making of Buddha or Bodhisattva images, statues and stupas, or the printing and distribution of sutras and codes. Likewise, he must not establish rules and regulations placing controls on the Fourfold Assembly. If highly placed lay disciples engage in actions contrary to the Dharma, they are no different from vassals in the service of [illegitimate] rulers.

A Bodhisattva should rightfully receive respect and offerings from all. If instead, he is forced to defer to officials, this is contrary to the Dharma, contrary to the moral code.

Hence, if a king or official has received the Bodhisattva precepts with a wholesome mind, he should avoid offenses that harm the Three Jewels. If instead, he intentionally commits such acts, he is guilty of a secondary offense.

48. On Destroying the Dharma

A disciple of the Buddha who becomes a monk with wholesome intentions must not, for fame or profit, explain the precepts to kings or officials in such a way as to cause monks, nuns or laymen who have received the Bodhisattva precepts to be tied up, thrown into prison or forcefully conscripted. If a Bodhisattva acts in such a manner, he is no different from a worm in a lion's body, eating away at the lion's flesh. This is not something a worm living outside the lion can do. Likewise, only disciples of the Buddhas can bring down the Dharma -- no externalist or demon can do so.

Those who have received the precepts of the Buddha should protect and observe them just as a mother would care for her only child or a filial son his parents. They must not break the precepts.

If a Bodhisattva hears externalists or evil-minded persons speak ill of, or disparage, the precepts of the Buddhas, he should feel as though his heart were pierced by three hundred spears, or his body stabbed with a thousand knives or thrashed with a thousand clubs. He would rather suffer in the hells himself for a hundred eons than hear evil beings disparage the precepts of the Buddha. How much worse it would be if the disciple were to break the precepts himself or incite others to do so! This is indeed an unfilial mind! Hence, if he violates the precepts intentionally, he commits a secondary offense.

The preceding nine precepts should be studied and respectfully observed with utmost faith.

Conclusion

The Buddha said, "All of you disciples! These are the Forty-eight Secondary Precepts that you should observe. Bodhisattvas of the past have recited them, those of the future will recite them, those of the present are now reciting them.

"Disciples of the Buddha! You should all listen! These Ten Major and Forty-eight Secondary Precepts are recited by all Buddhas of the Three Periods of Time -- past, present, and future. I now recite them as well."

Epilogue

The Buddha continued: "Everyone in the Assembly -- kings, princes, officials, Bhiksus, Bhiksunis, laymen, laywomen and those who have received the Bodhisattva precepts -- should receive and observe, read and recite, explain and copy these precepts of the eternal Buddha Nature so that they can circulate without interruption for the edification of all sentient beings. They will then encounter the Buddhas and receive the teachings from each one in succession. Lifetime after lifetime, they will escape the Three Evil Paths and the Eight Difficulties and will always be reborn in the human and celestial realms."

I have concluded a general explanation of the precepts of the Buddhas beneath this Bodhi Tree. All in this Assembly should singlemindedly study the Pratimoksa precepts and joyfully observe them.

These precepts are explained in detail in the exhortation section of the "Markless Celestial King" chapter.

At that time, the Bodhisattvas of the Three Thousand World System (cosmos) sat listening with utmost reverence to the Buddha reciting the precepts. They then joyously received and observed them.

As Buddha Sakyamuni finished explaining the Ten Inexhaustible Precepts of the "Mind-Ground Dharma Door" chapter, (which Vairocana Buddha had previously proclaimed in the Lotus Flower Treasury World), countless other Sakyamuni Buddhas did the same.

As Sakyamuni Buddha preached in ten different places, from the Mahesvara Heaven Palace to the Bodhi Tree, for the benefit of countless Bodhisattvas and other beings, all the countless Buddhas in the infinite lands of the Lotus Treasury World did the same.

They explained the Buddha's Mind Treasury (the Thirty Minds), Ground Treasury, Precept Treasury, Infinite Actions and Vows Treasury, the Treasury of the Ever-Present Buddha Nature as Cause and Effect of

Buddhahood. Thus, all the Buddhas completed their expositions of the countless Dharma Treasuries.

All sentient beings throughout the billions of worlds gladly receive and observe these Teachings.

The characteristics of the Mind-Ground are explained in greater detail in the chapter "Seven Forms of Conduct of the Buddha Floral Brilliance King."

Verses of Praise

The sages with great samadhi and wisdom
Can observe this teaching;
Even before reaching Buddhahood
They are blessed with five benefits:
First, the Buddhas of the Ten Directions
Always keep them in mind and protect them.
Secondly, at the time of death
They hold correct views with a joyous mind.
Third, wherever they are reborn,
The Bodhisattvas are their friends.
Fourth, merits and virtues abound as
The Paramita of Precepts is accomplished.
Fifth, in this life and in succeeding ones,
Observing all precepts, they are filled with merits and wisdom.

Such disciples are sons of the Buddha.
Wise people should ponder this well.
Common beings clinging to marks and self
Cannot obtain this teaching.
Nor can followers of the Two Vehicles,
abiding in quietude,

Plant their seeds within it.
To nurture the sprouts of Bodhi,
To illuminate the world with wisdom,
You should carefully observe
The True Mark of all dharmas:
Neither born nor unborn,
Neither eternal nor extinct,
Neither the same nor different,
Neither coming nor going.
In that singleminded state
The disciple should diligently cultivate

*And adorn the Bodhisattva's practices and deeds
In sequential order.
Between the teachings of study and non-study,
One should not develop thoughts of discrimination.
This is the Foremost Path --
Also known as Mahayana.
All offenses of idle speculation and meaningless debate
Invariably disappear at this juncture;
The Buddha's omniscient wisdom
Also arises from this.
Therefore, all disciples of the Buddha
Should develop great resolve,
And strictly observe the Buddha's precepts
As though they were brilliant gems.
All Bodhisattvas of the past
Have studied these precepts;
Those of the future will also study them.
Those of the present study them as well.
This is the path walked by the Buddhas,
And praised by the Buddhas.
I have now finished explaining the precepts,
The body of immense merit and virtue.
I now transfer them all to sentient beings;
May they all attain Supreme Wisdom;
May the sentient beings who hear this Dharma
All attain Buddhahood.*

X. Verses of Dedication

*In the Lotus Treasury World,
Vairocana explained an infinitesimal part of the Mind-Ground Door,
Transmitting it to the Sakyamunis:
Major and minor precepts are clearly delineated,
All sentient beings receive immense benefits.*

Book 3

Pure Land Teachings

The Threefold Lotus Sutras

The Contemplation Sutra
Sutra on the Contemplation of Buddha Amitayus

The Infinite Life Sutra
The Larger Sukhavativyuha

The Amithaba Sutra
The Smaller Sukhavativyuha

Translated from Japanese texts

The Contemplation Sutra
Sutra on the Contemplation of Buddha Amitayus

Part 1.

1. Thus have I heard: At one time the Buddha dwelt in Rajagriha, on Vulture Peak, with a large assembly of Bhikkhus (monks) and with thirty-two thousand Bodhisattvas, with Manjushri the Dharma-Prince at the head of the assembly.

2. At that time, in the great city of Rajagriha there was a prince, the heir-apparent, named Ajatasatru. He listened to the wicked counsel of Devadatta and other friends and forcibly arrested Bimbisara his father, the king, and shut him up by himself in a room with seven walls, proclaiming to all the courtiers that no one should approach (the king). The chief consort of the king, Vaidehi by name, was true and faithful to her lord, the king. She supported him in this way: having purified herself by bathing and washing, she anointed her body with honey and ghee mixed with corn-flour, and she concealed the juice of grapes in the various garlands she wore in order to give him food without being noticed by the warder. As she stole in and made an offering to him, he was able to eat the flour and to drink the juice of grapes. Then he called for water and rinsed his mouth. That done, the king stretched forth his folded hands towards Vulture Peak and duly and respectfully made obeisance to the World-Honored One, who at that time was living there. And he uttered the following prayer:
'Mahamaudgalyayana is my friend and relative; let him, I pray, feel compassion towards me, and come and communicate to me the eight prohibitive precepts of the Buddha.' On this, Mahamaudgalyayana at once appeared before the king, coming with a speed equal to the flight of a falcon or an eagle, and communicated to him the eight precepts.

Day after day he visited the king. The World-Honored One sent also his worthy disciple Purna to preach the Dharma to the king. Thus a period of three weeks passed by. The king showed in his expression that he was happy and contented when he had an opportunity of hearing the Dharma as well as of enjoying the honey and flour.

3. At that time, Ajatasatru asked the warder of the gate whether his father was yet alive. On this, the warder answered him : 'Exalted king, the chief consort of your father brought food and presented it to him by anointing her body with honey and flour and filling her garlands with the juice of grapes, and the Sramanas, Mahamaudgalyayana and Purna, approached the king through the sky in order to preach the Dharma to him. It is impossible, king, to prevent them coming.'

When the prince heard this answer his indignation arose against his mother: 'My mother,' he cried, 'is indeed a rebel, for she was found in the company of that rebel. Wicked people are those Sramanas, and it is their art of spells causing illusion and delusion that delayed the death of that wicked king for so many days.' Instantly he brandished his sharp sword, intending to slay his mother. At that moment, there intervened a minister named Chandraprabha, who was possessed of great wisdom and intelligence, and Jiva (a famous physician). They saluted the prince and remonstrated with him, saying: 'We, ministers, Great king, heard that since the beginning of the kalpas (eons) there had been several wicked kings, even to the number of eighteen thousand, who killed their own fathers, coveting the throne of their respective kingdoms, as mentioned in the Sutra of the discourse of the Veda. Yet never have we heard of a man killing his mother, though he be void of virtue. Now, if you, king, should dare to commit such a deadly sin, you would bring a stain upon the blood of the Kshatriyas, the kingly race. We cannot even bear to hear of it. You are indeed a Chandala, the lowest race; we will not stay here with you.'

After this, the two great ministers withdrew stepping backward, each with his hand placed on his sword. Ajatasatru was then frightened and greatly afraid of them, and asked Jiva, 'Will you not be my friend?' In reply Jiva said to him, 'Do not then, O great king, by any means think of injuring your mother.' On hearing this, the prince repented and sought for mercy, and at once laid down his sword and did his mother no harm. He finally ordered the officers of the inner chambers to put the queen in a hidden palace and not to allow her to come out again.

4. When Vaidehi was thus locked up in confinement she became afflicted by sorrow and distress. She began to do homage to Buddha from afar, looking towards the Vulture Peak. She uttered the following words: 'Tathagata! World-Honored One! In former times you have constantly sent Ananda to me for enquiry and consolation. I am now in sorrow and grief. You, World-Honored One, are majestic and exalted; in no way shall I be able to see thee. Will thou, I pray you, command Mahamaudgalyayana and your honoured disciple, Ananda, to come and have an interview with me ?' After this speech, she grieved and wept, shedding tears like a shower of rain. Before she raised her head from doing homage to the distant Buddha, the World-Honored One knew what Vaidehi was wishing in her mind, though he was on the Vulture Peak. Therefore, he instantly ordered Mahamaudgalyayana and Ananda to go to her through the sky. Buddha himself disappeared from that mountain and appeared in the royal palace.

When the queen raised her head as she finished homage to Buddha, she saw before her the World-Honored Buddha Shakyamuni, whose body was purple gold in color, sitting on a lotus-flower which consists of a hundred jewels, with Mahamaudgalyayana attending on his left, and with Ananda on his right. Sakra (Indra), Brahman, and other gods that protect the world were seen in the midst of the sky, everywhere showering heavenly flowers with which they made offerings to Buddha in their obeisance. Vaidehi, at the sight of Buddha the World-Honored One, took off her garlands and prostrated herself on the ground, crying, sobbing, and speaking to Buddha: 'World-Honored One! what former sin of mine has produced such a wicked son? And again, Exalted One, from what cause and circumstances have you such an affinity (by blood and religion) with Devadatta (Buddha's wicked cousin and once his disciple)?'

5. 'My only prayer,' she continued, 'is this: World-Honored One, may you preach to me in detail of all the places where there is no sorrow or trouble, and where I ought to go to be born anew. I am not satisfied with this world of depravities, with Jambudvipa, which is full of hells, full of hungry spirits, and of the brute creatures. In this world of depravities, there are many assemblies of the wicked. May I not hear, I pray, the voice of the wicked in the future and may I not see any wicked person.

'Now I throw my limbs down to the ground before you, and seek for your mercy by confessing my sins. I pray for this only that the Sun-like Buddha may instruct me how to meditate on a world wherein all actions are pure.' At that moment, the World-Honored One flashed forth a golden ray from between his eyebrows. It extended to all the innumerable worlds of the ten quarters. On its return the ray rested on the top of the Buddha's head and transformed itself into a golden pillar just like Mount Sumeru, wherein the pure and admirable countries of the Buddhas in the ten quarters appeared simultaneously illuminated.

One was a country consisting of seven jewels, another was a country all full of lotus-flowers; one was like the palace of Mahesvara Deva (god Siva), another was like a mirror of crystal, with the countries in the ten quarters reflected therein. There were innumerable countries like these, resplendent, gorgeous, and delightful to look upon. All were meant for Vaidehi to see (and choose from).

Thereupon Vaidehi again spoke to Buddha: 'World-Honored One, although all other Buddha countries are pure and radiant with light, I should, nevertheless, wish myself to be born in the realm of Buddha Amitayus, in the world of Highest Happiness, Sukhavati. Now I simply pray you, World-

Honored One, to teach me how to concentrate my thought so as to obtain a right vision of that country.'

6. Thereupon the World-Honored One gently smiled upon her, and rays of five colors issued forth out of his mouth, each ray shining as far as the head of king Bimbisara.

At that moment, the mental vision of that exalted king was perfectly clear though he was shut up in lonely retirement, and he could see the World-Honored One from afar. As he paid homage with his head and face, he naturally increased and advanced in wisdom, whereby he attained to the fruition of an Anagamin, the third of the four grades to Nirvana.

7. Then the World-Honored One said: 'Now do you not know, Vaidehi, that Buddha Amitayus is not very far from here? You should apply your mind entirely to close meditation upon those who have already perfected the pure actions necessary for that Buddha country.

'I now proceed to fully expound them for you in many parables, and thereby afford all ordinary persons of the future who wish to cultivate these pure actions an opportunity of being born in the Land of Highest Happiness (Sukhavati) in the western quarter. Those who wish to be born in that country of Buddha have to cultivate a threefold goodness. First, they should act filially towards their parents and support them; serve and respect their teachers and elders; be of compassionate mind, abstain from doing any injury, and cultivate the ten virtuous actions". Second, they should take and observe the vow of seeking refuge with the Three jewels, fulfill all moral precepts, and not lower their dignity or neglect any ceremonial observance. Third, they should give their whole mind to the attainment of perfect wisdom, deeply believe in the principle of cause and effect, study and recite the Mahayana doctrine, and persuade and encourage others who pursue the same course as themselves.

'These three groups as enumerated are called the pure actions leading to the Buddha country.'

'Vaidehi!'Buddha continued, 'To clarify if do you not understand now: These three classes of actions are the effective cause of the pure actions taught by all the Buddhas of the past, present, and future.'

8. The Buddha then addressed Ananda as well as Vaidehi: 'Listen carefully, listen carefully! Ponder carefully on what you hear! I, Tathagata, now declare the pure actions needful for Birth in that Buddha country, for the sake of all beings hereafter that are subject to the misery inflicted by the

enemy of the passions. Well done, Vaidehi! Appropriate are the questions which you have asked! Ananda, be sure to remember these words of mine, the Buddha, and repeat them openly to many assemblies. I, Tathagata, now teach Vaidehi and also all beings hereafter in order that they may meditate on the World of Highest Happiness, Sukhavati, in the western quarter.

'It is by the power of Buddha only that one can see that pure land of Buddha as clear as one sees the image of one's face reflected in the transparent mirror held up before one.

'When one sees the state of happiness of that country in its highest excellence, one greatly rejoices in one's heart and immediately attains a spirit of resignation prepared to endure whatever consequences may yet arise.' Buddha, turning again to Vaidehi, said: 'You are but an ordinary person; the quality of your mind is weak and confused.

'You have not as yet obtained the divine eye and cannot perceive what is at a distance. All the Buddhas, Tathagatas have various means at their disposal and can therefore afford you an opportunity of seeing that Buddha country.' Then Vaidehi rejoined: 'World-Honored One, people such as I can now see that land by the power of Buddha, but how shall all those beings who are to come after Buddha's Nirvana, and who, as being depraved and devoid of good qualities, will be harassed by the five worldly sufferings - how shall they see the World of Highest Happiness of the Buddha Amitayus?'

PART II.

9. Buddha then replied: 'You and all other beings besides ought to make it your only aim, with concentrated thought, to get a perception of the western quarter. You will ask how that perception is to be formed. I will explain it now. All beings, if not blind from birth, are uniformly possessed of sight, and they all see the setting sun. You should sit down properly, looking in the western direction, and prepare your thought for a close meditation on the sun; cause your mind to be firmly fixed on it so as to have an unwavering perception by the exclusive application of your mind, and gaze upon it in particular when it is about to set and looks like a suspended drum.

'After you have thus seen the sun, let that image remain clear and fixed, whether your eyes be shut or open;-such is the perception of the sun, which is the First Meditation.

10. 'Next you should form the perception of water; gaze on the water clear and pure, and let (this image) also remain clear and fixed (afterwards); never allow your thought to be scattered and lost.

'When you have thus seen the water you should form the perception of ice. As you see the ice shining and transparent, you should imagine the appearance of lapis lazuli.

'After that has been done, you will see the ground consisting of lapis lazuli, transparent and shining both within and without. Beneath this ground of lapis lazuli there will be seen a golden banner with the seven jewels, diamonds and the rest, supporting the ground. It extends to the eight points of the compass, and thus the eight corners (of the ground) are perfectly filled up. Every side of the eight quarters consists of a hundred jewels, every jewel has a thousand rays, and every ray has eighty-four thousand colors which, when reflected in the ground of lapis lazuli, look like a thousand million suns, and. it is difficult to see them all one by one. Over the surface of that ground of lapis lazuli there are stretched golden ropes intertwined crosswise; divisions are made by means of strings of seven jewels with every part clear and distinct.

'Each jewel has rays of five hundred colors which look like flowers or like the moon and stars. Lodged high up in the open sky these rays form a tower of rays, whose stories and galleries are ten millions in number and built of a hundred jewels. Both sides of the tower have each a hundred million flowery banners furnished and decked with numberless musical instruments. Eight kinds of cool breezes proceed from the brilliant rays. When those musical instruments are played, they emit the sounds "suffering," "non-existence," "impermanence," and "non-self "; such is the perception of the water, which is the Second Meditation.

11. 'When this perception has been formed, you should meditate on its (constituents) one by one and make (the images) as clear as possible, so that they may never be scattered and lost, whether your eyes be shut or open. Except only during the time of your sleep, you should always keep this in your mind. One who has reached this (stage of) perception is said to have dimly seen the Land of Highest Happiness (Sukhavati).'

'One who has obtained the Samadhi of supernatural calm is able to see the land of that Buddha country clearly and distinctly: this state is too much to be explained fully; such is the perception of the land, and it is the Third Meditation.

'You should remember, Ananda, the Buddha words of mine, and repeat this law for attaining to the perception of the land of the Buddha country for the sake of the great mass of the people hereafter who may wish to be delivered from their sufferings. If anyone meditates on the land of that Buddha country, his sins which bind him to births and deaths during eighty million kalpas (eons) shall be expiated; after the abandonment of his present body, he will assuredly be born in the pure land in the following life. The practice of this kind of meditation is called the "right meditation." If it is of any other kind it is called "heretical meditation."'

12. Buddha then spoke to Ananda and Vaidehi: 'When the perception of the land (of that Buddha country) has been gained, you should next meditate on the jewel-trees (of that country). In meditating on the jewel-trees, you should take each by itself and form a perception of the seven rows of trees; every tree is eight hundred yojanas high, and all the jewel-trees have flowers and leaves consisting of seven jewels all perfect. All flowers and leaves have colors like the colors of various jewels -from the color of lapis lazuli there issues a golden ray; from the color of crystal, a saffron ray; from the color of agate, a diamond ray; from the color of diamond, a ray of blue pearls. Corals, amber, and all other gems are used as ornaments for illumination; nets of excellent pearls are spread over the trees, each tree is covered by seven sets of nets, and between one set and another there are five hundred million palaces built of excellent flowers, resembling the palace of the Lord Brahman; all heavenly children live there, quite naturally; every child has a garland consisting of five hundred million precious gems like those that are fastened on Sakra's (Indra's) head, the rays of which shine over a hundred yojanas, just as if a hundred million suns and moons were united together; it is difficult to explain them in detail. That (garland) is the most excellent among all, as it is the commixture of all sorts of jewels. Rows of these jewel-trees touch one another; the leaves of the trees also join one another.

'Among the dense foliage there blossom various beautiful flowers, upon which are miraculously found fruits of seven jewels. The leaves of the trees are all exactly equal in length and in breadth, measuring twenty-five yojanas each way; every leaf has a thousand colors and a hundred different pictures on it, just like a heavenly garland. There are many excellent flowers which have the color of Jambunada gold and an appearance of fire-wheels in motion, turning between the leaves in a graceful fashion. All the fruits are produced just (as easily) as if they flowed out from the pitcher of the God Sakra. There is a magnificent ray which transforms itself into numberless jewelled canopies with banners and flags. Within these jewelled canopies the works of all the Buddhas of the Great Chiliocosm appear illuminated; the Buddha countries of the ten quarters also are manifested therein. When you have seen these trees you should also meditate on them one by one in order. In meditating on the trees, trunks, branches, leaves, flowers, and fruits, let them all be distinct and clear;- such is the perception of the trees (of that Buddha country), and it is the Fourth Meditation.

13. 'Next, you should perceive the water (of that country). The perception of the water is as follows:

'In the Land of Highest Happiness there are waters in eight lakes; the water in every lake consists of seven jewels which are soft and yielding. Deriving its source from the king of jewels that fulfills every wish, the water is divided into fourteen streams; every stream has the color of seven jewels; its channel is built of gold, the bed of which consists of the sand of variegated diamonds.

'In the midst of each lake there are sixty million lotus-flowers, made of seven jewels; all the flowers are perfectly round and exactly equal (in circumference), being twelve yojanas. The water of jewels flows amidst the flowers and rises and falls by the stalks (of the lotus); the sound of the streaming water is melodious and pleasing, and propounds all the perfect virtues (Paramitas), "suffering," "non-existence," "impermanence," and "non-self;" it proclaims also the praise of the signs of perfection, and minor marks of excellence of all Buddhas. From the king of jewels that fulfills every wish, stream forth the golden-colored rays excessively beautiful, the radiance of which transforms itself into birds possessing the colors of a hundred jewels, which sing out harmonious notes, sweet and delicious, ever praising the remembrance of Buddha, the remembrance of the Dharma, and the remembrance of the Sangha -- such is the perception of the water of eight good qualities, and it is the Fifth Meditation.

14. 'Each division of that (Buddha) country, which consists of several jewels, has also jewelled stories and galleries to the number of five hundred million; within each storey and gallery there are innumerable Devas engaged in playing heavenly music. There are some musical instruments that are hung up in the open sky, like the jewelled banners of heaven; they emit musical sounds without being struck, which, while resounding variously, all propound the remembrance of Buddha, of the Dharma and of the Sangha, Bhikhus (monks), and so forth. When this perception is duly accomplished, one is said to have dimly seen the jewel-trees, jewel-ground, and jewel-lakes of that World of Highest Happiness (Sukhavati) -- such is the perception formed by meditating on the general features of that Land, and it is the Sixth Meditation.

'If one has experienced this, one has expiated the greatest sinful deeds which would otherwise lead one to Transmigration for numberless millions of kalpas; after his death he will assuredly be born in that land.

15. 'Listen carefully! listen carefully! Think over what you have heard! I, Buddha, am about to explain in detail the law of delivering one's self from trouble and torment. Commit this to your memory in order to explain it in detail before a great assembly.' While Buddha was uttering these words, Buddha Amitayus stood in the midst of the sky with Bodhisattvas Mahasthama and Avalokitesvara, attending on his right and left respectively. There was such a bright and dazzling radiance that no one could see clearly; the brilliance was a hundred thousand times greater than that of gold (Jambunada). Thereupon Vaidehi saw Buddha Amitayus and approached the World-Honored One, and made obeisance to him, touching his feet, and spoke to him as follows: 'Exalted One! I am now able, by the power of Buddha, to see Buddha Amitayus together with the two Bodhisattvas. But how shall all the beings of the future meditate on Buddha Amitayus and the two Bodhisattvas?'

16. The Buddha answered: 'Those who wish to meditate on that Buddha ought first to direct their thought as follows: form the perception of a lotus-flower on a ground of seven jewels, each leaf of that lotus exhibits the colors of a hundred jewels, and has eighty-four thousand veins, just like heavenly pictures; each vein possesses eighty-four thousand rays, of which each can be clearly seen. Every small leaf and flower is two hundred and fifty yojanas in length and the same measurement in breadth. Each lotus-flower possesses eighty-four thousand leaves, each leaf has the kingly pearls to the number of a hundred million, as ornaments for illumination; each pearl shoots out a thousand rays like bright canopies. The surface of the ground is entirely covered by a mixture of seven jewels. There is a tower built of the gems which are like those that are fastened on Sakra's head. It is inlaid and decked with eighty thousand diamonds, Kimsuka jewels, Brahma-mani and excellent pearl nets.

'On that tower there are miraculously found four posts with jewelled banners; each banner looks like a hundred thousand million Sumeru mountains.

'The jewelled veil over these banners is like that of the celestial palace of Yama, illuminated with five hundred million excellent jewels, each jewel has eighty-four thousand rays, each ray has various golden colors to the number of eighty-four thousand, each golden color covers the whole jewelled soil, it changes and is transformed at various places, every now and then exhibiting various appearances; now it becomes a diamond tower, now a pearl net, again clouds of mixed flowers, freely changing its manifestation in the ten directions it exhibits the state of Buddha -- such is the perception of the flowery throne, and it is the Seventh Meditation.'

Buddha, turning to Ananda, said: 'These excellent flowers were created originally by the power of the prayer of Bhikkhu, Dharmakara. All who wish to exercise the remembrance of that Buddha ought first to form the perception of that flowery throne. When engaged in it one ought not to perceive vaguely, but fix the mind upon each detail separately. Leaf, jewel, ray, tower, and banner should be clear and distinct, just as one sees the image of one's own face in a mirror. When one has achieved this perception, the sins which would produce births and deaths during fifty thousand kalpas are expiated, and he is one who will most assuredly be born in the World of Highest Happiness.

17. 'When you have perceived this, you should next perceive Buddha himself. Do you ask how? Every Buddha Tathagata is one whose spiritual body is the principle of nature (Darmadhatu-kaya), so that he may enter into the mind of any beings. Consequently, when you have perceived Buddha, it is indeed that mind of yours that possesses those thirty-two signs of perfection and eighty minor marks of excellence which you see in a Buddha. In conclusion, it is your mind that becomes Buddha, nay, it is your mind. that is indeed Buddha. The ocean of true and universal knowledge of all the Buddhas derives its source from one's own mind and thought. Therefore you should apply your thought with an undivided attention to a careful meditation on that Buddha Tathagata, Arhat, the Holy and Fully Enlightened One. In forming the perception of that Buddha, you should first perceive the image of that Buddha; whether, your eyes are open or shut, look at an image like Jambunada gold in color, sitting on that flower throne mentioned before.

'When you have seen the seated figure your mental vision will become clear, and you will be able to see clearly and distinctly the adornment of that Buddha country, the jewelled ground, and so forth. In seeing these things, let them be clear and fixed just as you see the palms of your hands. When you have passed through this experience, you should further form a perception of another great lotus-flower which is on the left side of Buddha, and is exactly equal in every way to the above-mentioned lotus-flower of Buddha. Still further, you should form (a perception of) another lotus-flower which is on the right side of Buddha. Perceive that an image of Bodhisattva Avalokitesvara is sitting on the left-hand flowery throne, shooting forth golden rays exactly like those of Buddha. Perceive then that an image of Bodhisattva Mahasthama is sitting on the right-hand flowery throne.

'When these perceptions are gained the images of Buddha and the Bodhisattvas will all send forth brilliant rays, clearly lighting up all the jewel-trees with golden color. Under every tree there are also three lotus-flowers. On every lotus-flower there is an image, either of Buddha or of a Bodhisattva; thus (the images of the Bodhisattvas and of Buddha) are found everywhere in that country. When this perception has been gained, the devotee should hear the excellent Dharma preached by means of a stream of water, a brilliant ray of light, several jewel-trees, ducks, geese, and swans. Whether he be wrapped in meditation or whether he has ceased from it, he should ever hear the excellent Dharma. What the devotee hears must be kept in memory and not be lost, when he ceases from that meditation; and it should agree with the Sutras, for if it does not agree with the Sutras, it is called an illusory perception, whereas if it does agree, it is called the rough perception of the World of Highest Happiness;-such is the perception of the images, and it is the Eighth Meditation.

'He who has practiced this meditation is freed from the sins (which otherwise involve him in) births and deaths for innumerable million kalpas, and during this present life he obtains the Samadhi due to the remembrance of Buddha.

18. 'Further, when this perception is gained, you should next proceed to meditate on the bodily marks and the light of Buddha Amitayus.

'You should know, Ananda, that the body of Buddha Amitayus is a hundred thousand million times as bright as the color of the Jambunada gold of the heavenly abode of Yama; the height of that Buddha is six hundred thousand nayutas of kotis of yojanas innumerable as are the sands of the river Ganges.

'The white twist of hair between the eyebrows all turning to the right is just like the five Sumeru mountains.

'The eyes of Buddha are like the water of the four great oceans; the blue and the white are quite distinct.

'All the roots of hair of his body issue forth brilliant rays which are also like the Sumeru mountains.

'The halo of that Buddha is like a hundred million Great Chiliocosms; in that halo there are Buddhas miraculously created, to the number of a million nayutas of kotis innumerable as the sands of the Ganges; each of these

Buddhas has for attendants a great assembly of numberless Bodhisattvas who are also miraculously created.

'Buddha Amitayus has eighty-four thousand signs of perfection, each sign is possessed of eighty-four minor marks of excellence, each mark has eighty-four thousand rays, each ray extends so far as to shine over the worlds of the ten quarters, whereby Buddha embraces and protects all the beings who think upon him and does not exclude any one of them. His rays, signs, and so forth are difficult to be explained in detail. But in simple meditation let the mind's eye dwell upon them.

'If you pass through this experience, you will at the same time see all the Buddhas of the ten quarters. Since you see all the Buddhas it is called the Samadhi of the remembrance of the Buddhas.

'Those who have practiced this meditation are said to have contemplated the bodies of all the Buddhas. Since they have meditated on Buddha's body, they will also see Buddha's mind. It is great compassion that is called Buddha's mind. It is by his absolute compassion that he receives all beings.

'Those who have practiced this meditation will, when they die, be born in the presence of the Buddhas in another life, and obtain a spirit of resignation wherewith to face all the consequences which shall hereafter arise.

'Therefore, those who have wisdom should direct their thought to the careful meditation upon that Buddha Amitayus. Let those who meditate on Buddha Amitayus begin with one single sign or mark -- let them first meditate on the white twist of hair between the eyebrows as clearly as possible; when they have done this, the eighty-four thousand signs and marks will naturally appear before their eyes. Those who see Amitayus will also see all the innumerable Buddhas of the ten quarters. Since they have seen all the innumerable Buddhas, they will receive the prophecy of their future destiny to become Buddha in the presence of all the Buddhas -- Such is the perception gained by a complete meditation on all forms and bodies of Buddha, and it is the Ninth Meditation.

19. 'When you have seen Buddha Amitayus distinctly, you should then further meditate upon Bodhisattva Avalokitesvara, whose height is eight hundred thousand nayutas of yojanas; the color of his body is purple gold, his head has a turban at the back of which there is a halo; the circumference of his face is a hundred thousand yojanas. In that halo, there are five hundred Buddhas miraculously transformed just like those of Shakyamuni Buddha; each transformed Buddha is attended by five

hundred transformed Bodhisattvas who are also attended by numberless gods. Within the circle of light emanating from his whole body appear illuminated the various forms and marks of all beings that live in the five paths of existence.

'On the top of his head Is a heavenly crown of gems like those that are fastened (on Indra's head), in which crown there is a transformed Buddha standing, twenty-five yojanas high.

'The face of Bodhisattva Avalokitesvara In, like Jambunada gold in color.

'The soft hair between the eyebrows has all the colors of the seven jewels, from which eighty-four kinds of rays flow out, each ray has innumerable transformed Buddhas, each of whom is attended by numberless transformed Bodhisattvas; freely changing their manifestations they fill up the worlds of the ten quarters; (the appearance) can be compared with the color of the red lotus-flower.

'He wears a garland consisting of eight thousand rays, in which is seen fully reflected a state of perfect beauty. The palm of his hand has a mixed color of five hundred lotus-flowers. His hands have ten tips of fingers, each tip has eighty-four thousand pictures, which are like signet-marks, each picture has eighty-four thousand colors, each color has eighty-four thousand rays which are soft and mild and shine over all things that exist. With these jewel hands he draws and embraces all beings. When he lifts up his feet, the soles of his feet are seen to be marked with a wheel of a thousand spokes which miraculously transform themselves into five hundred million pillars of rays. When he puts his feet down to the ground, the flowers of diamonds and jewels are scattered about, and all things are simply covered by them. All the other signs of his body and the minor marks of excellence are perfect, and not at all different from those of Buddha, except the signs of having the turban on his head and the top of his head invisible, which two signs of him are inferior to those of the World-Honored One -- such is the perception of the real form and body of Bodhisattva Avalokitesvara, and it is the Tenth Meditation.'

The Buddha, especially addressing Ananda, said: 'Whosoever wishes to meditate on Bodhisattva Avalokitesvara must do so in the way I have explained. Those who practice this meditation will not suffer any calamity; they will utterly remove the obstacle that is raised by karma, and will expiate the sins which would involve them in births-and deaths for numberless kalpas. Even the hearing of the name of this Bodhisattva will enable one to obtain immeasurable happiness. How much more, then, will the diligent contemplation of him!

'Whosoever will meditate on Bodhisattva Avalokitesvara should first meditate on the turban of his head and then on his heavenly crown.

'All the other signs should also be meditated on according to their order, and they should be clear and distinct just as one sees the palms of one's hands.

'Next you should meditate on Bodhisattva Mahasthama, whose bodily signs, height and size are equal to those of Avalokitesvara; the circumference of his halo is one hundred and twenty-five yojanas, and it shines as far as two hundred and fifty yojanas. The rays of his whole body shine over the countries of the ten quarters, they are purple gold in color, and can be seen by all beings that are in favorable circumstances. If one but sees the ray that issues from a single root of the hair of this Bodhisattva, he will at the same time see the pure and excellent rays of all the innumerable Buddhas of the ten quarters.

'For this reason this Bodhisattva is named the Unlimited Light; it is with this light of wisdom that he shines over all beings and causes them to be removed from the three paths of existence, and to obtain the highest power. For the same reason this Bodhisattva is called the Bodhisattva of Great Strength (Mahasthama). His heavenly crown has five hundred jewel-flowers; each jewel-flower has five hundred jewel-towers, in each tower are seen manifested all the pure and excellent features of the far-stretching Buddha countries in the ten quarters. The turban on his head is like a lotus-flower; on the top of the turban there is a jewel pitcher, which is filled with various brilliant rays fully manifesting the state of Buddha. All his other bodily signs are quite equal to those of Avalokitesvara. When this Bodhisattva walks about, all the regions of the ten quarters tremble and quake. Wherever the earth quakes there appear five hundred million jewel-flowers; each jewel-flower with its splendid dazzling beauty looks like the World of Highest Happiness (Sukhavati).

'When this Bodhisattva sits down, all the countries of seven jewels at once tremble and quake: all the incarnate, divided Amitayuses - innumerable as the dust of the earth - and all the incarnate Bodhisattvas - Avalokitesvara and Mahasthamaprapta - who dwell in the middlemost Buddha countries situated between the Buddha country of the lower region presided over by Buddha "Golden Light," and the country of the upper region presided over by Buddha "King of Light" -- all these assemble in the World of Highest Happiness (Sukhavati) like gathering clouds, sit on their thrones of lotus-flowers which fill the whole sky, and preach the excellent Dharma in order to deliver all the beings that are immersed in suffering -- such is the perception of the form and body of Bodhisattva Mahasthamaprapta, and it is the Eleventh Meditation.

'Those who practice this meditation are freed from the sins which would otherwise trap them in births-and-deaths for innumerable asamkhya kalpas (eons).

'Those who have practiced this meditation do not live in an embryo state but obtain free access to the excellent and admirable countries of Buddhas. Those who have experienced this are said to have perfectly meditated upon the two Bodhisattvas Avalokitesvara and Mahasthamaprapta.

20. 'After you have had this perception, you should imagine yourself to be born in the World of Highest Happiness in the western quarter, and to be seated, cross-legged, on a lotus-flower there. Then imagine that the flower has shut you in and has afterwards unfolded; when the flower has thus unfolded, five hundred colored rays will shine over your body, your eyes will be opened so as to see the Buddhas and Bodhisattvas who fill the whole sky; you will hear the sounds of waters and trees, the notes of birds, and the voices of many Buddhas preaching the excellent Dharma, in accordance with the twelve divisions of the scriptures. When you have ceased from that meditation you must remember the experience ever after.

'If you have passed through this experience you are said to have seen the World of Highest Happiness in the realm of the Buddha Amitayus -- this is the perception obtained by a complete meditation on that Buddha country, and is called the Twelfth Meditation.

'The innumerable incarnate bodies of Amitayus, together with those of Avalokitesvara and Mahasthamaprapta, constantly come and appear before such devotees as above mentioned.'

21. Buddha then spoke to Ananda and Vaidehi: 'Those who wish, by means of their serene thoughts, to be born in the western land, should first meditate on an image of the Buddha, who is sixteen cubits high, seated on a lotus-flower in the water of the lake. As it was stated before, the real body and its measurement are unlimited, incomprehensible to the ordinary mind.

'But by the efficacy of the ancient prayer of that Tathagata, those who think of and remember him shall certainly be able to accomplish their aim.

'Even the mere perceiving of the image of that Buddha brings to one immeasurable blessings. How much more, then, will the meditating upon all the complete bodily signs of that Buddha! Buddha Amitayus has supernatural power; since everything is at his disposal, he freely transforms himself in the regions of the ten quarters. At one time he shows himself as possessing a magnificent body, which fills the whole sky, at another he makes his body appear small, the height being only sixteen or eighteen cubits. The body he manifests is always pure gold in color; his halo - bright with transformed Buddhas - and his jewel lotus-flowers are as mentioned above. The bodies of the two Bodhisattvas are the same always.

'All beings can recognize either of the two Bodhisattvas by simply glancing at the marks of their heads. These two Bodhisattvas assist Amitayus in his work of universal salvation -- such is the meditation that forms a joint perception of the Buddha and Bodhisattvas, and it is the Thirteenth Meditation.'

PART III.

22. Buddha then spoke to Ananda and Vaidehi: 'The beings who will be born in the highest form of the highest grade (i. e. to Buddhahood) are those, whoever they may be, who wish to be born in that country and cherish the threefold thought whereby they are at once destined to be born there. What is the threefold thought, you may ask. First, the True Thought; second, the Deep Believing Thought; third, the Desire to be born in that Pure Land by bringing one's own stock of merit to maturity. Those who have this threefold thought in perfection shall most assuredly be born into that country.

'There are also three classes of beings who are able to be born in that country. What, you may ask, are the three classes of beings? First, those who are possessed of a compassionate mind, who do no injury to any beings, and accomplish all virtuous actions according to Buddha's precepts; second, those who study and recite the Sutras of the Mahayana doctrine, for instance, the Vaipulya Sutras; third, those who practice the sixfold remembrance. These three classes of beings who wish to be born in that country by bringing (their respective stocks of merit) to maturity, will become destined to be born there if they have accomplished any of those meritorious deeds for one day or even for seven days.

'When one who has practiced (these merits) is about to be born in that country, Buddha Amitayus, together with the two Bodhisattvas Avalokitesvara and Mahasthamaprapta, also numberless created Buddhas, and a hundred thousand Bhikkhus and Sravakas (disciples), with their whole retinue, and innumerable gods, together with the palaces of seven jewels, will appear before him out of regard for his diligence and courage;

Avalokitesvara together with Mahasthamaprapta, will offer a diamond seat to him; thereupon Amitayus himself will send forth magnificent rays of light to shine over the dying person's body. He and many Bodhisattvas will offer their hands and welcome him, when Avalokitesvara, Mahasthamaprapta, and all the other Bodhisattvas will praise the glory of the man who practiced the meritorious deeds, and convey an exhortation to his mind. When the new-comer, having seen these, rejoicing and leaping for joy, looks at himself, he will find his own body seated on that diamond throne; and as he follows behind Buddha he will be born into that country, in a moment When he has been born there, he will see Buddha's form and body with every sign of perfection complete, and also the perfect forms and signs of all the Bodhisattvas; he will also see brilliant rays and jewel forests and hear them propounding the excellent Dharma, and instantly be conscious of a spirit of resignation to whatever consequences may hereafter arise. Before long he will serve every one of the Buddhas who live in the regions of the ten quarters. In the presence of each of those Buddhas he will obtain successively a prophecy of his future destiny. On his return to his own land Sukhavati, in which he has just been born he will obtain countless hundreds of thousand Dharanis -- such are those who are to be born in the highest form of the highest grade to Buddhahood.

23. 'Next, the beings who will be born in the middle form of the highest grade are those who do not necessarily learn, remember, study, or recite those Vaipulya Sutras, but fully understand the meaning of the truth contained in them, and having a firm grasp of the highest truth do not speak evil of the Mahayana doctrine, but deeply believe in (the principle of) cause and effect; who by bringing these good qualities to maturity seek to be born in that Country of Highest Happiness. When one who has acquired these qualities is about to die, Amitayus, surrounded by the two Bodhisattvas Avalokitesvara and Mahasthamaprapta, and an innumerable retinue of dependents, will bring a seat of purple gold and approach him with words of praise, saying: "O my son in the Dharma! you have practiced the Mahayana doctrine; you have understood and believed the highest truth; therefore I now come to meet and welcome you." He and the thousand created Buddhas extend their hands all at once.

'When that man looks at his own body, he will find himself seated on that purple gold seat; he will, then, stretching forth his folded hands, praise and eulogize all the Buddhas. As quick as thought he will be born in the lake of seven jewels of that country. That purple gold seat on which he sits is like a magnificent jewel-flower, and will open after a night; the new-comer's body becomes purple gold in color, and he will also find under his feet a lotus-flower consisting of seven jewels. Buddha and the Bodhisattvas at the same time will send forth brilliant rays to shine over the body of that person whose eyes will instantaneously be opened and become clear. According to his former usage (in the human world) he will hear all the voices that are there, preaching primary truths of the deepest significance.

'Then he will descend from that golden seat and make obeisance to the Buddha with folded hands, praising and eulogizing the World-Honored One. After seven days, he will immediately attain to the state of the highest perfect knowledge, anuttarasamyaksambodhi, from which he will never fall away; next he will fly to all the ten regions and successively serve all the Buddhas therein; he will practice many a Samadhi in the presence of those Buddhas. After the lapse of a lesser kalpa he will attain a spirit of resignation to whatever consequences may hereafter arise, and he will also obtain a prophecy of his future destiny in the presence of Buddhas.

24. 'Next are those who are to be born in the lowest form of the highest grade: this class of beings also believes in the principle of cause and effect, and without slandering the Mahayana doctrine, simply cherishes the thought of obtaining the highest Bodhi and by bringing this good quality to maturity seeks to be born in that Country of Highest Happiness. When a devotee of this class dies, Amitayus, with Avalokitesvara, Mahasthamaprapta and all the dependents, will offer him a golden lotus-flower; he will also miraculously create five hundred Buddhas in order to send for and meet him. These five hundred created Buddhas will all at once extend their hands and praise him, saying: "O my son in the Dharma! you are pure now; as you have cherished the thought of obtaining the highest Bodhi, we come to meet you." When he has seen them, he will find himself seated on that golden lotus-flower. Soon the flower will close upon him; following behind the World-Honored One he will go to be born in the lake of seven jewels. After one day and one night the lotus-flower will unfold itself. Within seven days he may see Buddha's body, though his mind is not as yet clear enough to perceive all the signs and marks of the Buddha, which he will be able to see clearly after three weeks; then he will hear many sounds and voices preaching the excellent Dharma, and he himself, travelling through all the ten quarters, will make obeisance to all the Buddhas, from whom he will learn the deepest significance of the Dharma. After three lesser kalpas (eons) he will gain entrance to the knowledge of a hundred divisions of nature and become settled in the first joyful stage of Bodhisattva. The perception of these three classes of beings is called the meditation upon the superior class of beings, and is the Fourteenth Meditation.

25. 'The beings who will be born in the highest form of the middle grade are those who observe the five prohibitive precepts, the eight prohibitive precepts and the fasting, and practice all the moral precepts; who do not commit the five deadly sins, and who bring no blame or trouble upon any

being; and who by bringing these good qualities to maturity seek to be born in the World of Highest Happiness in the western quarter. On the eve of such a person's departure from this life, Amitayus, surrounded by Bhikkhus and dependents, will appear before him, flashing forth rays of golden color, and will preach the Dharma of suffering, non-existence, impermanence, and non-self. He will also praise the virtue of homelessness that can liberate one from all sufferings. At the sight of Buddha, that believer will excessively rejoice in his heart; he will soon find himself seated on a lotus-flower. Kneeling down on the ground and stretching forth his folded hands he will pay homage to Buddha. Before he raises his head he will reach that Country of Highest Happiness and be born there. Soon the lotus-flower will unfold, when he will hear sounds and voices praising and glorifying the Four Noble Truths of suffering. He will immediately attain to the fruition of Arhatship, gain the threefold knowledge and the six supernatural faculties, and complete the eightfold emancipation.

26. 'The beings who will be born in the middle form of the middle grade are those who either observe the eight prohibitive precepts, and the fasting for one day and one night, or observe the prohibitive precept for Sramanera for the same period, or observe the perfect moral precepts, not lowering their dignity nor neglecting any ceremonial observance for one day and one night, and by bringing their respective merits to maturity seek to be born in the Country of Highest Happiness. On the eve of departure from this life, such a believer who is possessed of this moral virtue, which he has made fragrant by cultivation during his life, will see Amitayus, followed by all his retinue; flashing forth rays of golden color, this Buddha will come before him and offer a lotus-flower of seven jewels.

'He will hear a voice in the sky, praising him and saying: "O son of a noble family, you are indeed an excellent man. Out of regard for your obedience to the teachings of all the Buddhas of the three worlds, I now come and meet you." Then the newcomer will see himself seated on that lotus-flower. Soon the lotus-flower will fold around him, and being in this he will be born in the jewel-lake of the World of Highest Happiness in the western quarter.

'After seven days that flower will unfold again, when the believer will open his eyes, and praise the World-Honored One, stretching forth his folded hands. Having heard the Dharma, he will rejoice and obtain the fruition of a Srotapanna.

'In the lapse of half a kalpa he will become an Arhat.

27. 'Next are the beings who will be born in the lowest form of the middle grade to Buddhahood. If there are sons or daughters of a noble family who are filial to their parents and support them, besides exercising benevolence and compassion in the world, at their departure from this life such persons will meet a good and learned teacher who will fully describe to them the state of happiness in that Buddha country of Amitayus, and will also explain the forty-eight prayers of the Bhikkhu Dharmakara. As soon as any such person has heard these details, his life will come to an end. In a brief moment he will be born in the World of Highest Happiness in the western quarter.

'After seven days he will meet Avalokitesvara and Mahasthamaprapta, from whom he will learn the Dharma and rejoice. After the lapse of a lesser kalpa he will attain to the fruition of an Arhat. The perception of these three sorts of beings is called the Fifteenth Meditation.

28. 'Next are the beings who will be born in the highest form of the lowest grade. If there be any one who commits many evil deeds, provided that he does not speak evil of the Mahayana Sutras, he, though himself a very stupid man, and neither ashamed nor sorry for all the evil actions that he has done, yet, while dying, may meet a good and learned teacher who will recite and laud the headings and titles of the twelve divisions of the Mahayana scriptures. Having thus heard the names of all the Sutras, he will be freed from the greatest sins which would involve him in births and deaths during a thousand kalpas.

'A wise man also will teach him to stretch forth his folded hands and to say, "Adoration to Buddha Amitayus" (Namo Amitabhaya Buddhaya, or Namu Amida Butsu). Having uttered the name of the Buddha, he will be freed from the sins which would otherwise involve him in births and deaths for fifty million kalpas. Thereupon the Buddha will send a created Buddha, and the created Bodhisattvas Avalokitesvara and Mahasthamaprapta, to approach that person with words of praise, saying: "O son of a noble family, as you have uttered the name of that Buddha, all your sins have, been destroyed and expiated, and therefore we now come to meet you." After this speech the devotee will observe the rays of that created Buddha flooding his chamber with light, and while rejoicing at the sight he will depart this life. Seated on a lotus-flower he will follow that created Buddha and go to be born in the jewel-lake.

'After the lapse of seven weeks, the lotus-flower will unfold, when the great compassionate Bodhisattvas Avalokitesvara and Mahasthamaprapta will stand before him, flashing forth magnificent rays, and will preach to him the deepest meaning of the twelve divisions of the scriptures. Having heard this, he will understand and believe it, and cherish the thought of attaining the highest Bodhi. In a period of ten lesser kalpas he will gain entrance to the knowledge of the hundred divisions of nature and be able to enter upon the first joyful stage of Bodhisattva. Those who have had an opportunity of hearing the name of Buddha, the name of the Dharma, and the name of the Sangha - the names of the Three jewels - can also be born in that country.'

29. Buddha continued: 'Next are the beings who will be born in the middle form of the lowest grade. If there is anyone who transgresses the five and the eight prohibitive precepts, and also all the perfect moral precepts; he, being himself so stupid as to steal things that belong to the whole community or things that belong to a particular Bhikkhu and not be ashamed nor sorry for his impure preaching of the Dharma (in case of preacher), but magnify and glorify himself with many wicked deeds - such a sinful person deserves to fall into hell in consequence of those sins. At the time of his death, when the fires of hell approach him from all sides, he will meet a good and learned teacher who will, out of great compassion, preach the power and virtue of the ten faculties of Amitayus and fully explain the supernatural powers and brilliant rays of that Buddha; and will further praise moral virtue, meditation, wisdom, emancipation, and the thorough knowledge that follows emancipation. After having heard this, he will be freed from his sins, which would involve him in births and deaths during eighty million kalpas; thereupon those violent fires of hell will transform themselves into a pure and cool wind blowing about heavenly flowers. On each of these flowers will stand a created Buddha or Bodhisattva to meet and receive that person. In a moment he will be born in a lotus-flower growing in the lake of seven jewels. After six kalpas the lotus-flower will open, when Avalokitesvara and Mahasthama will soothe and encourage him with their Brahma-voices, and preach to him the Mahayana Sutras of the deepest significance.

'Having heard this Dharma, he will instantaneously direct his thought toward the attainment of the highest Bodhi.

30. 'Finally, there are the beings who will be born in the lowest form of the lowest grade. If there is anyone who commits evil deeds, and even completes the ten wicked actions, the five deadly sins and the like; that man, being himself stupid and guilty of many crimes, deserves to fall into a miserable path of existence and suffer endless pains during many kalpas. On the eve of death he will meet a good and learned teacher who will, soothing and encouraging him in various ways, preach to him the excellent Dharma and teach him the remembrance of Buddha, but, being harassed by pains, he will have no time to think of Buddha. Some good friend will

then say to him: "Even if you cannot exercise the remembrance of Buddha, you may, at least, utter the name, "Buddha Amitayus." Let him do so serenely with his voice uninterrupted; let him be (continually) thinking of Buddha until he has completed ten times the thought, repeating the formula, "Adoration to Buddha Amitayus" (Namah Amitabha Buddhayah, Namu Amida Butsu). On the strength of his merit of uttering that Buddha's name he will, during every repetition, expiate the sins which involved him in births and deaths during eighty million kalpas. He will, while dying, see a golden lotus-flower like the disk of the sun appearing before his eyes; in a moment he will be born in the World of Highest Happiness. After twelve greater kalpas the lotus-flower will unfold; thereupon the Bodhisattvas Avalokitesvara and Mahasthamaprapta, raising their voices in great compassion, will preach to him in detail the real state of all the elements of nature and the law of the expiation of sins. On hearing them he will rejoice and will immediately direct his thought toward the attainment of the Bodhi - - such are the beings who are to be born in the lowest form of the lowest grade to Buddhahood. The perception of the above three is called the meditation of the inferior class of beings, and is the Sixteenth Meditation.'

PART IV.

31. When Buddha had finished this speech, Vaidehi, together with her five hundred female attendants, could see, as guided by the Buddha's words, the scene of the far-stretching World of the Highest Happiness, and could also see the body of Buddha and the bodies of the two Bodhisattvas. With her mind filled with joy she praised them, saying: 'Never have I seen such a wonder!' Instantaneously she became wholly and fully enlightened, and attained a spirit of resignation, prepared to endure whatever consequences might yet arise. Her five hundred female attendants too cherished the thought of obtaining the highest perfect knowledge, and sought to be born in that Buddha country.

32. The World-Honored One predicted that they would all be born in that Buddha country and be able to obtain the Samadhi (the supernatural calm) of the presence of many Buddhas. All the innumerable Devas (gods) also directed their thought toward the attainment of the highest Bodhi.

Thereupon Ananda rose from his seat, approached Buddha, and spoke thus: 'World-Honored One, what should we call this Sutra? And how should we receive and remember it in the future?'

Buddha said in his reply to Ananda: 'Ananda, this Sutra should be called 'The Meditation on the Land of Sukhavati, on Buddha Amitayus, Bodhisattva Avalokitesvara, Bodhisattva Mahasthamaprapta,' or otherwise be called

'The Sutra on the entire removal of the obstacle of Karma, the means of being born in the realm of the Buddhas.' You should take and hold it, not forgetting nor losing it. Those who practice the Samadhi in accordance with this Sutra will be able to see, in the present life, Buddha Amitayus and the two great Bodhisattvas.

'In case of a son or a daughter of a noble family, the mere hearing of the names of the Buddha and the two Bodhisattvas will expiate the sins which would involve them in births and deaths during innumerable kalpas (eons). How much more will the remembrance of that Buddha and the Bodhisattvas!

'Know that the one who remembers that Buddha is the White Lotus among people, whom the Bodhisattvas Avalokitesvara and Mahasthama consider an excellent friend. Such a person will, sitting in the Bodhi-mandala, be born in the abode of Buddhas.'

The Buddha further spoke to Ananda: 'You should carefully remember these words. To remember these words is to remember the name of Buddha Amitayus. When Buddha concluded these words, the worthy disciples Mahamaudgalyayana, and Ananda, Vaidehi and the others were all enraptured with boundless joy.

33. Thereupon the World-Honored One came back, walking through the open sky to Vulture Peak. Ananda soon after spoke before a great assembly of all the occurrences as stated above. On hearing this, all the innumerable Devas, Nagas and Yakshas were inspired with great joy; and having made obeisance to the Buddha they went their way.

The Infinite Life Sutra
The Larger Sukhavativyuha

Om.
Adoration to the Three Treasures!
Om.
Adoration to all the glorious Buddhas and Bodhisattvas!
Adoration to all Buddhas, Bodhisattvas, Aryas, Sravakas, and Pratyekabuddhas, past, present, and to come, who dwell in the unlimited and endless world systems of the ten quarters!
Adoration to Amitabha!
Adoration to him whose soul is endowed with incomprehensible virtues!
Adoration to Amitabha, to the Jina, to thee, O Sage!
I go to Sukhavati through thy compassion also;
To Sukhavati, with its groves, resplendent with gold,
The delightful, adorned with the sons of Sugata,--
I go to it, which is full of many jewels and treasures;
And the refuge of thee, the famous and wise.

1. Thus it was heard by me. At one time the Bhagavat dwelt in Rajagriha, on the mountain Gridhrakuta, with a large assembly of Bhikkhus, with thirty-two thousands of Bhikkhus, all arhats, free from frailties and cares, who had performed their religious duties, whose thoughts had been thoroughly freed through perfect knowledge, with inquiring thoughts, who had broken the fetters of existence, who had obtained their desires, who had conquered, who had achieved the highest self restraint, whose thoughts and whose knowledge were unfettered, great heroes, possessed of the six kinds of knowledge, self-controlled, meditating on the eight kinds of salvation, possessed of the powers, wise in wisdom, elders, great disciples, that is, Ajnatakaundinya, Asvajit, Vashpa, Mahanaman, Bhadrajit, Yasodeva, Vimala, Subahu, Purna Maitrayaniputra, Uruvilva-kasyapa, Nadi-kasyapa, Gaya-kasyapa, Kumara-kasyapa, Maha-kasyapa, Shariputra, Mahamaudgalyayana, Mahakaushthilya, Mahakaphila, Mahakunda, Aniruddha, Nandika, Kampila, Subhuti, Revata, Khadiravanika, Vakula, Svagata, Amogharaja, Parayanika, Patka, Kullapatka, Nanda, Rahula, and the blessed *Ananda*--with these and with other elders, and great disciples, who were wise in wisdom, with the exception of one person who had still to be advanced on the path of the disciples, that is, the blessed Ananda--and with many noble-minded Bodhisattvas, led by Maitreya.

2. Then the blessed Ananda, having risen from his seat, having put his cloak on one shoulder, and knelt on the earth with his right knee, making obeisance with folded hands in the direction of the Bhagavat, spoke thus to

the Bhagavat: 'Thy organs of sense, O Bhagavat, are serene, the color of thy skin is clear, the color of thy face bright and yellowish. As an autumn cloud is pale, clear, bright and yellowish, thus the organs of sense of the Bhagavat are serene, the color of his face is clear, the color of his skin bright and yellowish. And as, O Bhagavat, a piece of gold coming from the Jambu river, having been thrown into a furnace by a clever smith or by his apprentice, and well fashioned, when thrown on a pale cloth, looks extremely clear, bright and yellowish, thus the organs of sense of the Bhagavat are serene, the color of his face is clear, and the color of his skin bright and yellowish. Moreover, I do not know, O Bhagavat, that I have ever seen the organs of sense of the Tathagata so serene, the color of his face so clear and the color of his skin so bright and yellowish before now. This thought occurs to me, O Bhagavat: probably, the Tathagata dwells to-day in the state of a Buddha, probably the Tathagata dwells to-day in the state of a Jina, in the state of omniscience, in the state of a Mahanaga; and he contemplates the holy and fully enlightened Tathagatas of the past, future, and present.'

After these words, the Bhagavat thus spoke to the blessed Ananda: 'Well said! well said! Ananda. Did the gods suggest this matter to you? or the blessed Buddhas? Or do you know this through the philosophical knowledge which you possess?'

After these words the blessed Ananda spoke thus to the Bhagavat: 'The gods, O Bhagavat, do not suggest this matter to me, nor the blessed Buddhas, but this thought occurs to me by my own philosophy alone, that is, that probably the Tathagata dwells to-day in the state of a Buddha, probably the Tathagata dwells to-day in the state of a Jina, in the state of omniscience, in the state of a Mahanaga; or he contemplates the venerable Buddhas of the past, future, and present.'

After these words the Bhagavat spoke thus to the blessed Ananda: 'Well said! well said! Ananda; excellent indeed is your question, good your philosophy, and beautiful your understanding! You, O Ananda, have arrived for the benefit and happiness of many people, out of compassion for the world, for the sake of the great body of men, for the benefit and happiness of gods and men, as you think it right to ask the Tathagata this matter: Thus, indeed, Ananda, might pile up intellectual knowledge under immeasurable and innumerable blessed, holy, and fully enlightened Tathagatas, and yet the knowledge of the Tathagata would not be exceeded thereby. And why? Because, O Ananda, one who possesses the knowledge of a Tathagata possesses an intellectual knowledge of causes that cannot be exceeded.

'If the Tathagata wished O Ananda, he could live for a whole kalpa on one alms-gift, or for a hundred kalpas, or for a thousand kalpas, or for a hundred thousand kalpas, to a hundred thousand nayutas of kotis of kalpas, nay, he could live beyond, and yet the organs of nature of the Tathagata would not perish, the color of his face would not be altered, nor would the color of his skin be injured. And why? Because, O Ananda, the Tathagata has so fully obtained the perfections which arise from Samadhi.

'The appearance of fully enlightened Buddhas is very difficult to be obtained in this world, O Ananda. As the appearance of Audumbara-flowers is very difficult to be obtained in this world; thus, O Ananda, the appearance of Tathagatas who desire welfare, wish for what is beneficial, are compassionate, and have arrived at the highest compassion, is very difficult to be obtained. But, O Ananda, it is owing to the grace of the Tathagata himself that you think that the Tathagata should be asked this question, so that there may arise in this world beings who can be teachers of all the world, for the sake of noble-minded Bodhisattvas. Therefore, O Ananda, listen, and take it well and rightly to heart! I shall tell you.'

'Yes, O Bhagavat,' so did the blessed Ananda answer the Bhagavat.

3. The Bhagavat then spoke to Ananda: 'At the time, O Ananda, which was long ago in the past, in an innumerable and more than innumerable, enormous, immeasurable, and incomprehensible kalpa before now--at that time, and at that moment, there arose in the world a holy and fully enlightened Tathagata called Dipankara. Following after Dipankara, O Ananda, there was a Tathagata Pratapavat, and after him, Prabhakara, Kandanagandha, Sumerukalpa, Kandana, Vimalanana, Anupalipta, Vimalaprabha, Nagabhibhu, Suryodana, Giririjaghosha, Merukuta, Suvarnaprabha, Gyotishprabha, Vaiduryanirbhasa, Brahmaghosha, Kandabhibho, Turyaghosha, Muktakusumapratimanditaprabha, Srikuta, Sagaravarabuddhivikriditabhijna, Varaprabha, Mahagandhajanirbhasa, Vyapagatakhilamalapratighosha, Surakuta, Rananjaha, Mahagunadharabuddhipraptibhijna, Chandrasuryajihmikarana, Uttaptavaiduryanirbhasa, Chittadharabuddhisankusumitabhyudgata, Pushpavativanarajasankusumitabhijna, Pushpakara, Udakakandra, Avidyandhakaravidhvamsanakara, Lokendra, Muktakkhatrapravatasadrisa, Tishya, Dharmamativinanditaraja, Simhasigarakutavinanditaraja, Sagaramerukandra, Brahmasvaranadabhinandita, Kusumasambhava, Praptasena, Kandrabhanu, Merukuta, Chandraprabha, Vimalanetra, Girirajaghoshesvara, Kusumaprabha, Kusumavrishtyabhiprakirna, Ratnakandra, Padmabimbyupasobhita, Chandanagandha, Ratnabhibhasa, Nimi, Mahivyuha, Vyapagatakhiladosha, Brahmaghosha,

Saptaratnabhivrishta, Mahijunadhara,
Mahatamalapatrakandanakardama, Kusumabhijna, Ajnavidhvamsana,
Kesarin, Muktakkhatra, Suvarnagarbha, Vaiduryagarbha, Mahaketu,
Dharmaketu, Ratnaketu, Ratnasri, Lokendra, Narendra, Karunika,
Lokasundara, Brahmaketu, Dharmamati, Simha, and Simhamati.

'After Simhamati, a holy and fully enlightened Tathagata arose in the
world, Lokesvararaja by name, perfect in knowledge and conduct, a
Sugata, knowing the world, without a superior, charioteer of men whose
passions have to be tamed, teacher of gods and men, a Buddha, a
Bhagavat. And again during the time of the preaching of this holy and fully
enlightened Tathagata Lokesvararaja, O Ananda, there was a Bhikkhu,
Dharmakara by name, richly endowed with memory, with understanding,
prudence, and wisdom, richly endowed with vigor, and of noble character.

4. 'Then, O Ananda, that Bhikkhu Dharmakara, having risen from his seat,
having put his cloak on one shoulder, and knelt on the earth with his right
knee, stretching forth his folded hands to where the Bhagavat Tathagata
Lokesvararaja was, and, after worshipping the Bhagavat, he, at that very
time, praised him in his presence with these Gathas:

"O thou of immeasurable light, whose knowledge is endless and
incomparable; not any other light can shine here where thou art! The rays
of the moon of Siva and of the jewel of the sun, were not bright here in the
whole world, (1)

"The form also is infinite in the best of beings; thus also the voice of Buddha
is of infinite sound; his virtue likewise, with meditation, knowledge, strength;
like unto thee there is no one in this world. (2)

"The Dharma is deep, wide, and subtle; the best of Buddhas is
incomprehensible, like the ocean; therefore there is no further exaltation of
the teacher; having left all faults, he is gone to the other shore. (3)

"Then the best of Buddhas, of endless light, lights up all regions, he the king
of kings; and I, having become Buddha, and a master of the Dharma, may I
deliver mankind from old age and death! (4)

"And I, on the strength of generosity, equanimity, virtue, forbearance,
power, meditation and absorption, undertake here the first and best duties,
and shall become a Buddha, the savior of all beings. (5)

"And I, seeking for the knowledge of the best of the Blessed Ones, shall always worship many hundred thousands of kotis of Buddhas, endless like the sand of the Ganges, the incomparable lords. (6)

"Whatever worlds there are, similar in number to the sand of the Ganges, and the endless countries which exist besides, there everywhere I shall send out light, because I have attained such power. (7)

"My land is to be noble, the first and the best; the Bodhi-tree excellent in this world. There is incomparable happiness arising from Nirvana, and this also I shall explain as vain. (8)

"Beings come hither from the ten quarters; having arrived there they quickly show my happiness. May Buddha there teach me the truth, I form a desire full of true strength and vigor. (9)

"I, knowing the worlds of the ten quarters, possessed of absolute knowledge--they also always proclaim my thought! May I, gone to Avichi hell, always abide there, but I shall never cease to practise the power of prayer! " (10)

5. 'Then, O Ananda, that Bhikkhu Dharmakara, having praised the Bhagavat, the Tathagata Lokesvararaja, in his presence, with those Gathas, spoke thus: "O Bhagavat, I wish to know the highest perfect knowledge. Again and again I raise and incline my thoughts towards the highest perfect knowledge. May therefore the Bhagavat, as a teacher, thus teach me the Dharma, that I may quickly know the highest perfect knowledge. May I become in the world a Tathagata, equal to the unequalled. And may the Bhagavat proclaim those signs by which I may comprehend the perfection of all good qualities of a Buddha country."

'After this, O Ananda, the Bhagavat Lokesvararaja, the Tathagata, thus spoke to that Bhikkhu: "Do you by yourself, O Bhikkhu, know the perfection of all excellences and good qualities of a Buddha country?

' He said: "O Bhagavat, I could not do this, but the Bhagavat alone. Explain the perfection of the excellences and all the good qualities of Buddha countries of the other Tathagatas, after hearing which we may fulfil every one of their signs."

'Then, O Ananda, the Tathagata Lokesvararaja, holy and fully enlightened, knowing the good disposition of that Bhikkhu, taught for a full koti of years the perfection of all the excellences and good qualities of Buddha countries belonging to eighty-one hundred thousand nayutas of kotis of Buddhas, together with the signs, indication, and description, desiring welfare, wishing for benefits, compassionate, full of compassion, so that there might never be an end of Buddha countries, having conceived great pity for all beings. The measure of life of that Tathagata was full forty kalpas.

6. 'Then, O Ananda, that Bhikkhu Dharmakara, taking the perfections of all the excellences and good qualities of those Buddha countries, of those eighty-one hundred thousand nayutas of kotis of Buddhas, and concentrating them all on one Buddha country, worshipped with his head the feet of the Bhagavat Lokesvararaja, the Tathagata, turned respectfully round him to the right, and walked away from the presence of this Bhagavat. And afterwards, for the space of five kalpas, he thus concentrated the perfection of all the excellences and good qualities of the Buddha countries, such as had never been known before in the ten quarters of the whole world, more excellent, and more perfect than any, and composed the most excellent prayer.

7. 'Thus, O Ananda, that Bhikkhu concentrated in his mind a perfection of a Buddha country eighty-one times more immeasurable, noble, and excellent than the perfection of the eighty-one hundred thousand nayutas of kotis of Buddha countries that had been told him by the Bhagavat Lokesvararaja, the Tathagata. And then, proceeding to where the Tathagata was, he worshipped the feet of the Bhagavat with his head, and said: "O Bhagavat, the perfection of all the excellences and good qualities of the Buddha countries has been concentrated by me."

'After this, O Ananda, the Tathagata Lokesvararaja thus spoke to the Bhikkhu: "Preach then, O Bhikkhu; the Tathagata allows it. Now is the proper time, O Bhikshu. Delight the assembly, produce joy, let the lion's voice be heard, so that now and hereafter, noble-minded Bodhisattvas, hearing it, may comprehend the different subjects of the prayers for the perfection of the good qualities of a Buddha country."

'Then, O Ananda, that Bhikkhu Dharmakara thus spoke at that time to the Bhagavat: "May the Bhagavat thus listen to me, to what my own prayers are, and how, after I shall have obtained the highest perfect knowledge, my own Buddha country will then be endowed with all inconceivable excellences and good qualities.

8. 1. "O Bhagavat, if in that Buddha country of mine there should be either hell, animals, the realm of departed spirits, or the body of fighting spirits, then may I not obtain the highest perfect knowledge.

2. "O Bhagavat, if in that Buddha country of mine the beings who are born there should die and fall into hell, the animal realm, the realm of departed spirits, or into the body of fighting spirits, then may I not obtain the highest perfect knowledge.

3. "O Bhagavat, if in that Buddha country of mine the beings who are born there should not all be of one color, that is, a golden color, then may I not obtain the highest perfect knowledge.

4. "O Bhagavat, If in that Buddha country of mine there should be perceived any difference between gods and men, except when people count and tell, saying: 'These are gods and men, but only in ordinary and imperfect parlance,' then may I not obtain the highest perfect knowledge.

5. "O Bhagavat, if in that Buddha country of mine the beings who are born there should not be possessed of the highest perfections of miraculous power and self-control, so that they could at least in the shortest moment of one thought step over a hundred thousand nayutas of kotis of Buddha countries, then may I not obtain the highest perfect knowledge.

6. "O Bhagavat, if in that Buddha country of mine the beings who are born there should not all be possessed of the recollection of their former births, so as at least to remember a hundred thousand nayutas of kotis of kalpas, then may I not the highest perfect knowledge.

7. "O Bhagavat, if in that Buddha country of mine the beings who are born there should not all acquire the divine eye, so as at least to be able to see a hundred thousand nayutas of kotis (infinite numbers) of worlds, then may I not obtain the highest perfect knowledge.

8. "O Bhagavat, if in that Buddha country of mine the beings who are born there should not all acquire the divine ear, so as at least to be able to hear at the same time the good Dharma from a hundred thousand nayutas of kotis of Buddha countries, then may I not obtain the highest perfect knowledge.

9. "O Bhagavat, if in that Buddha country of mine the beings who are born there should not all be skilled in the knowledge of the thoughts of other people, so as at least to be able to know the deeds and thoughts of beings belonging to a hundred thousand nayutas of kotis of Buddha countries, then may I not obtain the highest perfect knowledge.

10. "O Bhagavat, if in that Buddha country of mine the beings who are born there should form any idea of property, even with regard to their own body, then may I not obtain the highest perfect knowledge.

11. "O Bhagavat, if in that Buddha country of mine the beings who are born there should not all be firmly established, that is, in absolute truth, till they have reached Mahaparinirvana, then may I not obtain the highest perfect knowledge.

12. "O Bhagavat, if any being should be able to count the pupils belonging to me after I have obtained the highest perfect knowledge in that Buddha country of mine, even if all beings who are contained in those three millions of spheres of worlds, after having become Pratyekabuddhas, should be counting for a hundred thousand nayutas of kotis (infinite numbers) of kalpas, then may I not obtain the highest perfect knowledge.

13. "O Bhagavat, if, after I have obtained the highest perfect knowledge, my light should be liable to be measured in this Buddha country of mine, even by the measure of a hundred thousand nayutas of kotis of Buddha countries, then may I not obtain the highest perfect knowledge.

14 "O Bhagavat, if the measure of the life of the beings in that Buddha country of mine, after I have obtained the highest perfect knowledge, should be liable to be measured, excepting always by their own power of prayer, then may I not obtain the highest perfect knowledge.

15. "O Bhagavat, if the measure of my life after I have obtained Bodhi should be limited, even by numbering a hundred thousand nayutas of kotis of kalpas, then may I not obtain the highest perfect knowledge.

16. "O Bhagavat, if, for the beings in this Buddha country of mine, after I have obtained Bodhi, even the name of sin should exist, then may I not obtain the highest perfect knowledge.

17. "O Bhagavat, if immeasurable and innumerable blessed Buddhas in immeasurable Buddha countries do not glorify my name, after I have obtained Bodhi; if they do not preach my fame and proclaim my praise, and utter it together, then may I not obtain the highest perfect knowledge.

18. "O Bhagavat, if those beings who have directed their thought towards the highest perfect knowledge in other worlds, and who, after having heard my name, when I have obtained Bodhi , have meditated on me with serene thoughts; if at the moment of their death, after having approached them, surrounded by an assembly of Bhikkhus, I should not stand before

them, worshipped by them, that is, so that their thoughts should not be troubled, then may I not obtain the highest perfect knowledge.

19. "O Bhagavat, if those beings who in immeasurable and innumerable Buddha countries, after they have heard my name, when I shall have obtained Bodhi, should direct their thought to be born in that Buddha country of mine, and should for that purpose bring their stock of merit to maturity, if these should not be born in that Buddha country, even those who have only ten times repeated the thought of that Buddha country, barring always those beings who have committed the five deadly sins, and who have caused an obstruction and abuse of the good Law, then may I not obtain the highest perfect knowledge.

20. "O Bhagavat, if those beings who have been born in that Buddha country of mine, after I have obtained Bodhi, should not all be bound to one birth only, before reaching the highest perfect knowledge, barring always the special prayers of those very noble-minded Bodhisattvas who have put on the whole armor (of the Dharma), who understand the welfare of all beings, who are devoted, to all beings, who work for the attainment of Nirvana of all beings, who wish to perform the duty of a Bodhisattva in all worlds, who wish to serve all Buddhas, and to bring beings, in number like grains of sand of the river Ganges, to the highest perfect knowledge, and who besides are turned towards the higher practice and perfect in the practice of Samantabhadra's discipline, then may I not obtain the highest perfect knowledge.

21. "O Bhagavat, if the Bodhisattvas who are born in that Buddha country of mine, after I have obtained Bodhi, should not all be able, after having gone to other Buddha countries, after their one morning-meal, to worship many hundreds of Buddhas, many thousands of Buddhas, many hundred thousands of Buddhas, many kotis of Buddhas, and so forth, till up to many hundred thousand nayutas of kotis of Buddhas, with objects which give every kind of pleasure, and this through the grace of the Buddha, then may I not obtain the highest perfect knowledge.

22. "O Bhagavat, if those Bodhisattvas in that Buddha country of mine, after I have obtained Bodhi, should wish their stock of merit to grow in the following shapes, that is, either in gold, in silver, in jewels, in pearls, in beryls, in shells, in stones, in corals, in crystal, in amber, in red pearls, in diamond, and so forth, or in any one of the other jewels; or in all kinds of perfumes, in flowers, in garlands, anointment, in incense-powder, in cloaks, in umbrellas, in flags, in banners, or in lamps; or in all kinds of dancing, singing, and music; and if such gifts should not appear for them, from being

produced as soon as thought of, then may I not obtain the highest perfect knowledge.

23. "O Bhagavat, if those beings who are born in that Buddha country of mine, after I have obtained Bodhi, should not all recite the story of the Dharma which is accompanied by omniscience, then may I not obtain the highest perfect knowledge.

24. "O Bhagavat, if the Bodhisattvas in that Buddha country of mine, after I have obtained Bodhi, should think thus: May we, remaining in this world, honor revere, esteem, and worship the blessed Buddhas in immeasurable and innumerable Buddha countries, that is, with cloaks, alms-bowls, beds, stools, refreshments, medicines, utensils, with flowers, incense, lamps, perfumes, garlands, ointment, powder, cloaks, umbrellas, flags, banners, with different kinds of dancing singing, and music, and with showers of jewels, and if the blessed Buddhas should not accept them, when they are produced as soon as thought of, that is, from compassion, then may I not obtain the highest perfect knowledge.

25. "O Bhagavat, if the Bodhisattvas who are born in that Buddha country of mine, after I have obtained Bodhi, should not all be in possession of strength of body as strong as the diamond of Narayana, then may I not obtain the highest perfect knowledge.

26. "O Bhagavat, if any being in that Buddha country of mine, after I have obtained Bodhi, should learn the limit of the beauty of its ornament, even if he be possessed of the divine eye, and should know its various beauty, saying: 'That Buddha country possesses so much beauty and so much magnificence,' then may I not obtain the highest perfect knowledge.

27. "O Bhagavat, if in that Buddha country of mine, after I have obtained Bodhi, a Bodhisattva possessed even of a very small stock of merit, should not perceive the Bodhi-tree of noble beauty, at least a hundred yojanas in height, then may I not obtain the highest perfect knowledge.

28. "O Bhagavat, if in that Buddha country of mine, after I have obtained Bodhi, either teaching or learning should have to be made by any being, and they should not all be in possession of the perfect knowledge, then may I not obtain the highest perfect knowledge.

29. "O Bhagavat, if that Buddha country of mine, after I have obtained Bodhi, should not be so brilliant, that in it could be seen on all sides immeasurable, innumerable, inconceivable, incomparable, immense Buddha

countries, as a round face is seen in a highly burnished round mirror, then may I not obtain the highest perfect knowledge.

30. "O Bhagavat, if in that Buddha country of mine, after I have obtained Bodhi, there should not be a hundred thousand of vases full of different sweet perfumes, made of all kinds of jewels, always smoking with incense, fit for the worship of Bodhisattvas and Tathagatas, rising into the sky beyond gods, men, and all things, then may I not obtain the highest perfect knowledge.

31. "O Bhagavat, if in that Buddha country of mine, after I have obtained Bodhi, there should not be showers of sweet jewel-flowers, always pouring down, and if there should not be sweet-sounding music-clouds, always playing, then may I not obtain the highest perfect knowledge.

32. "O Bhagavat, if the beings belonging to me, after I have obtained Bodhi, who are visible by their splendor, in immeasurable, innumerable, inconceivable, incomparable worlds, should not all be filled with pleasure, far beyond gods and men, then may I not obtain the highest perfect knowledge.

33. "O Bhagavat, if, after I have obtained Bodhi, the noble-minded Bodhisattvas in immeasurable, inconceivable, incomparable, immense Buddha countries on all sides, after having heard my name, should not be delivered from birth, through the merit arising from that hearing, and should not be strong in the knowledge of dharanis, until they have obtained the very throne of Bodhi, then may I not obtain the highest perfect knowledge.

34. "O Bhagavat, if, after I have obtained Bodhi, women in immeasurable, innumerable, inconceivable, incomparable, immense Buddha countries on all sides, after having heard my name, should allow carelessness to arise, should not turn their thoughts towards Bodhi, should, when they are free from birth, not despise their female nature; and if they, being born again, should assume a second female nature, then may I not obtain the highest perfect knowledge.

35. "O Bhagavat, if, after I have obtained Bodhi, the Bodhisattvas who in immeasurable, innumerable, inconceivable, incomparable, immense Buddha countries round about in the ten quarters having heard my name, and having fallen down, shall worship me with prostrate reverence, should not, when performing the duty of Bodhisattvas, be honored by the world and by the gods, then may I not obtain the highest perfect knowledge.

36. "O Bhagavat, if, after I have obtained Bodhi, the work of dyeing, sewing, drying, washing ot his cloaks should have to be performed by any Bodhisattva, and they should not perceive themselves, as quick as thought, covered by newly-produced excellent cloaks, granted to them by the Tathagata, then may I not obtain the highest perfect knowledge.

37. "O Bhagavat, if the beings who are born at the same time in that Buddha country, after I have obtained Bodhi, should not obtain such happiness as that of the holy Bhikkhu who is free from pain and has obtained the third meditation, then may I not obtain the highest perfect knowledge.

38. "O Bhagavat, if those Bodhisattvas who are born in that Buddha country of mine, after I have obtained Bodhi, should not produce from different jewel-trees such a mass of excellent ornaments in that Buddha country, as they should wish for, then may I not obtain the highest perfect knowledge.

39. "O Bhagavat, if the Bodhisattvas who are born in other Buddha countries, when they have heard my name, after I shall have obtained Bodhi, should suffer any diminution in the strength of their senses, then may I not obtain the highest perfect knowledge.

40. "O Bhagavat, if, after I have obtained Bodhi (Nirvana), the Bodhisattvas, from hearing my name in a place of a different Buddha country, should not obtain the Samadhi in which the Bodhisattvas will see immeasurable, innumerable, inconceivable, incomparable, immense, blessed Buddhas one moment after another; and if that Samadhi of theirs should come to an end meanwhile, then may I not obtain the highest perfect knowledge.

41. "O Bhagavat, if, after I have obtained Bodhi, beings, having heard my name in Buddha countries different from this, should not, through the stock of merit which follows on that hearing, obtain birth in a noble family, till they arrive at Bodhi, then may I not obtain the highest perfect knowledge.

42. "O Bhagavat, if, after I have obtained Bodhi, the Bodhisattvas who live in other Buddha countries, after hearing my name, till they have reached Bodhi by the stock of merit which follows on that hearing, should not all obtain a combination of their stock of merit with the joy and gladness of their Bodhisattva life, then may I not obtain the highest perfect knowledge.

43. "O Bhagavat, if, after I have obtained Bodhi, the Bodhisattvas, as soon as they have heard my name, in other worlds, should not obtain the

Samadhi called Samantanugata, in which Bodhisattvas honor one moment after another immeasurable, innumerable, inconceivable, incomparable, immense, blessed Buddhas, and if that Samadhi of theirs should come to an end before they have reached the throne of Bodhi, then may I not obtain the highest perfect knowledge.

44. "O Bhagavat, if the beings who are born in that Buddha country of mine, after I have obtained Bodhi, should not hear, as quick as thought, such a teaching of the Dharma as they wish to hear, then may I not obtain the highest perfect knowledge.

45 "O Bhagavat, if, after I have obtained Bodhi, the Bodhisattvas in this and other Buddha countries, as soon as they have heard my name, should ever turn back from the highest perfect knowledge, then may I not obtain the highest perfect knowledge.

46. "O Bhagavat, if, after I have obtained Bodhi, and have become a Buddha-teacher, the Bodhisattvas who hear my name in Buddha countries, and obtain the first, the second, and the third degrees of endurance, as soon as they have heard my name, should turn away again from Buddha, the Dharma, and the Sangha, then may I not obtain the highest perfect knowledge.

9. 'And again, O Ananda, when he had spoken such prayers, that Bhikkhu Dharmakara, at that time, through the grace of Buddha spoke these verses:

1. "If, when I have obtained Bodhi, there should not be for me an excellent Pranidhana of such a character, then, O Prince, O Best of beings, may I not be endowed with the ten powers, incomparable, worthy of offerings.

2. "If there should not be for me such a country, endowed with many and various mighty and divine endowments, I should gladly go to hell, suffering pain, and not be a King of treasures.

3. "If, when I have approached the Bodhi throne, my name should not quickly reach the ten quarters, the broad and many endless Buddha countries, may I not be a lord of the world, endowed with power.

4. "If indeed I should delight in the enjoyments of love, being deprived of zeal, understanding and prudence, even after having reached the incomparable and blessed Bodhi, may I not be a teacher in the world, endowed with power.

5. "The lord of vast light, incomparable and infinite, has illuminated all Buddha countries in all the quarters, he has quieted passions, all sins and errors, he has quieted the fire in the walk of hell.

6. "After making his broad eye lustrous, after driving away the darkness from all men, after removing all untimely misfortunes, he led hither those who dwell in heaven and who shine with endless light.

7. "The splendor of sun and moon does not shine in heaven, nor the fiery splendor of the maze of jewels of the gods; the Lord overcomes all splendor, he, the bright one, who has performed his former discipline.

8. "He is the best of men, the treasure of all who suffer; there is no one like him in all the quarters. Having completed a hundred thousand good works, he, in his assembly, raised the lion-voice of Buddha.

9. "After having worshipped former self-existing Jinas, after having performed immeasurable kotis of vows and penances, he became in this, his best of spiritual existences, the best of beings, possessed of the full power of prayers.

10. "As the Bhagavat, the Lord, who is possessed of unlimited light of knowledge, knows the three kinds of knowledge in the world, may I also be worthy of equal offerings, the best of sages, the leader of men.

11. "If, O Lord, this my prayer succeeds, after I have obtained Bodhi, may this sphere of a thousand worlds tremble, and may a shower of flowers descend on the hosts of gods."

12. 'Then the earth trembled, flowers were showered down, hundreds of instruments resounded in the sky, powder of heavenly sweet sandal-wood was scattered, and there was a voice saying: "Thou wilt be a Buddha in the world."

10. 'That Bhikkhu Dharmakara, the nobleminded Bodhisattva, O Ananda, was possessed of this perfection of prayers. And a few Bodhisattvas only, O Ananda, are possessed of such a perfection of prayers. There is on this earth an appearance of a few only of such prayers. Of a few, however, existence cannot be denied.

'Then again, O Ananda, this Bhikkhu Dharmakara having recited these prayers before the Bhagavat Lokesvararaja, the Tathagata, and before the world including gods, Mara, and Brahman, and before people consisting of Sramanas and Brahmanas with gods, men, and fighting spirits, was established in the attainment of the true promise. And proclaiming this purity of the Buddha country, this greatness and excellency of the Buddha country, and performing the duty of a Bodhisattva, he never conceived the remotest thoughts of lust, malevolence, and cruelty, during a hundred thousand nayutas of kotis of years, immeasurable, innumerable, inconceivable, incomparable, measureless, immense, inexpressible; and he never conceived the idea of lust, malevolence, and cruelty, nay, he never conceived the idea of form, sound, smell, taste, and touch. He was gentle, charming indeed, and compassionate; pleasant to live with, agreeable, amiable, content, of few wishes, satisfied, retired, not evil, not foolish, not suspicious, not crooked, not wicked, not deceitful, tender, kindly speaking, always zealous, docile in searching after the pure Dharma. And for the good of all beings, he recited the great prayer, showing respect to friends, teachers, masters, the Sangha, the Dharma, and Buddha, always girded for the performance of the duties of the Bodhisattva, righteous, gentle, not deceitful, not flattering, virtuous, a leader for the sake of rousing others to perform all good laws, producing by his activity the ideas of emptiness, causelessness, and purposelessness, and he was well guarded in his speech.

'Then, performing the duties of a Bodhisattva, after having given up all speaking which, when spoken, serves to injure one's self or others or both, he employed only such speech as served the pleasure and benefit of himself, others, or both. And he was so wise that, when entering into capitals, kingdoms, countries, towns, cities, and villages, he was always perfectly restrained with regard to all objects of sense. Performing himself the duties of the Bodhisattva without interruption, he walked himself in the highest perfection of liberality, and he also roused others to walk in the same. And himself walking in the highest perfections of knowledge, meditation, strength, patience, and virtue, he roused others also to walk in the same. And he has collected so large a stock of merit that, wherever he is born, there arise for him many hundreds of thousands of nayutas of kotis of treasures from out the earth.

'By him, while he was thus performing the duties of a Bodhisattva, immeasurable and innumerable hundreds of thousands of nayutas of kotis of beings were established in perfect enlightenment, of whom it is not easy to know the limit by means of speech. So many immeasurable and innumerable holy Buddhas were honored, revered, esteemed, and worshipped, and enabled to touch whatever causes pleasure, such as cloaks, alms-bowls, couches, seats, refreshments, medicines, and other furniture. It is not easy to know the limit by pointing it out in words, as to how many beings were established by him in the noble families of Brahmanas, Kshatriyas, ministers, householders, and merchants. In the same manner they were established in the sovereignty of Jambudvipa, and they were established in the character of Chakravartins, Lokapalas, Sakras, Suyamas, Sutushitas, Sunirmitas, Vasavartins, Devaragas, and Mahabrahmans. So many immeasurable and innumerable Buddhas were honored, revered, esteemed, and worshipped and requested to turn the wheel of the Dharma, of whom it is not easy to know the limit by means of words.

'And he collected such virtue, that out of his mouth, while performing the duties of a Bodhisattva, during immeasurable, innumerable, inconceivable, incomparable, immense, measureless, inexpressible kotis of kalpas, there breathed a sweet and more than heavenly smell of sandal-wood. From all the pores of his hair there arose the smell of lotus, and he was pleasing to everybody, gracious and beautiful, endowed with the fullness of the best bright color. As his body was adorned with all the good signs and marks, there arose from the pores and from the palms of his hands all sorts of precious ornaments in the shape of all kinds of cloaks and vestments, in the shape of all kinds of flowers, incense, scents, garlands, ointments, umbrellas, flags, and banners, and in the shape of all kinds of instrumental music. And there appeared also, streaming forth from the palms of his hands, all kinds of viands and drink, food, hard and soft, and sweetmeats, and all kinds of enjoyments and pleasures. Thus then that Bhikshu Dharmakara, O Ananda, had obtained the command of all necessaries, after performing the duties of a Bodhisattva.'

11. After this, the blessed Ananda thus spoke to the Bhagavat: "O Bhagavat, has that Bhikkhu Dharmakara, the noble-minded Bodhisattva, after having obtained the highest perfect knowledge, passed away, having entered Nirvana, or has he not yet been enlightened, or is he now living and enlightened, and does he dwell now, remain, support himself, and teach the Dharma?'

The Bhagavat said: 'Not indeed, O Ananda, has that Tathagata passed away, nor has he not yet come, but the Tathagata, the holy, after having obtained the highest perfect knowledge, dwells now, remains, supports himself, and teaches the Dharma, in the western quarter, in the Buddha country, distant from this world by a hundred thousand nayutas of kotis of Buddha countries, in the world which is called Sukhavati, being called Amitabha, the Tathagata, holy and fully enlightened. He is surrounded by innumerable Bodhisattvas, and worshipped by endless Sravakas (disciples), and in possession of the endless perfection of his Buddha country.

12. 'And his light is immeasurable, so that it is not easy to know the limit of its measure, saying, he stands illuminating so many hundreds of Buddha countries, so many thousands of Buddha countries, so many hundred

thousands of Buddha countries, so many kotis of Buddha countries, so many hundred kotis of Buddha countries, so many thousand kotis of Buddha countries, so many hundred thousands of kotis of Buddha countries, so many hundred thousands of nayutas of kotis of Buddha countries. But indeed, O Ananda, to put it briefly, a hundred thousand nayutas of kotis of Buddha countries, equal to the sands of the river Ganges, are always lighted up, in the eastern quarter, by the light of that Bhagavat Amitabha. Thus on every side in the southern, western, northern quarter, in the zenith and nadir, in every one of these quarters, there are a hundred thousand nayutas of kotis of Buddha countries, like the sands of the river Ganges, always lighted up by the light of that Bhagavat Amitabha, excepting the Buddhas, the Bhagavats, who, through the practice of their former prayers, have lighted up the world by their own light, which is a fathom in length, or by their light which is one, two, three, four, five, ten, twenty, thirty, forty, or fifty yojanas in length, or a hundred or thousand or hundred thousand yojanas in length, until their brightness reaches many hundred thousand nayutas of kotis of yojanas in length. There is not, O Ananda, any case of likeness, by which the extent of the light of that Tathagata Amitabha could be understood. Hence, O Ananda, for that reason that Tathagata is called Amitabha, possessed of infinite light, possessed of infinite splendor, possessed of infinite brilliancy, whose light is never finished, whose light is not conditioned, whose light proceeds from flames of light, whose light is that of heavenly jewels, whose light has the color of unimpeded rays, possessed of beautiful light, possessed of lovely light, possessed of delightful light, possessed of attractive light, possessed of pleasant light, possessed of light that cannot be stopped, possessed of extremely powerful light, possessed of incomparable light, possessed of light greater than that of the lords of men, nay, the lords of the three worlds, possessed of light which bends the full moon and the sun, possessed of light which bends all the conquered gods, Mahesvara, the Suddhavasas, Brahman, Sakra, and the Lokapalas.

'This splendor of the Arya is pure, great, producing bodily pleasure, happiness of mind, producing happiness, delight, and joy for men and not-men, Kinnaras, Mahoragas, Garudas, Gandharvas, Yakshas, Nagas, Asuras (power greedy deities), and Devas; and producing the pleasure of beings of good disposition.

'And in this manner, O Ananda, the Tathagata might speak for a whole kalpa on the work of the Tathagata Amitabha, beginning with his light, and yet he would not be able to reach the end of the virtues of that light of that Tathagata, neither would there be any failure of the self-confidence in the Tathagata himself. And why? Because, O Ananda, both these things are immeasurable, innumerable, inconceivable, and endless, that is, first, the greatness of the excellence of the light of that Tathagata Amitabha, the

Bhagavat, and secondly, the unsurpassed light of the knowledge possessed by myself.

13. 'And, O Ananda, the assembly of the hearers of that Tathagata Amitabha is immeasurable, so that it is not easy to learn its measure, so as to be able to say, there are so many kotis of the hearers, so many hundreds, thousands, hundred-thousands, kankaras, vimbaras, nayutas, ayutas, akshobhyas, vivahas, srotas, ogas, so many periods, called immeasurable, innumerable, countless, incomparable, inconceivable. Now, for instance, O Ananda, the Bhikshu Maudgalyayana having obtained miraculous power, might, if he wished, count in one day and night, how many kinds of stars there are in the universal world. Then, let there be a hundred thousand nayutas of kotis of such men, endowed with miraculous powers, and let them do nothing else but count the first company only of the hearers of the Tathagata Amitabha, during a hundred thousand nayutas of kotis of years, and yet by them thus counting even the hundredth part would not be counted, even the thousandth, even the hundred thousandth nay, not even so far as the minutest part, or likeness, or approach towards it would have been counted.

'Thus for instance, O Ananda, a man might throw out from the great ocean, which is not to be measured across by less than eighty-four thousand yojanas, one single drop of water by the sharp end of hair, which is divided a hundred times. What do you think then, Ananda, which would be greater, one drop of water which has been thrown up by the sharp pointed hair divided a hundred times, or the mass of water left in the great ocean?'

Ananda said: 'Even a thousand yojanas, O Bhagavat, would be a small portion of the great ocean, how much more than one drop of water thrown out by the sharp pointed hair divided a hundred times!'

Bhagavat said: 'As that one drop of water, so small in proportion, was the first company of the hearers. And let there be reckoning made by those Bhikkhus, who are like Maudgalyayana, counting for a hundred thousand nayutas of kotis of years, and yet, as to the mass of water left in the great ocean, it would even then have to be considered as not counted. How much more with regard to the second, third, and the rest of the companies of the hearers! Therefore the mass of hearers of the Bhagavat is endless and boundless, and receives the name of "immeasurable and innumerable."

14. 'And, O Ananda, the length of the life of that Bhagavat Amitabha, the Tathagata, is immeasurable, so that it is not easy to know its length, so as to be able to say that it comprises so many hundreds of kalpas, so many thousands of kalpas, so many hundred thousands of kalpas, so many kotis

of kalpas, so many hundreds of kotis of kalpas, so many thousands of kotis of kalpas, so many hundred thousands of kotis of kalpas, so many hundred thousands of nayutas of kotis of kalpas. Therefore, O Ananda, the limit of the measure of the life of that Bhagavat is immeasurable indeed. Therefore that Tathagata is called Amitayus.

'And as, O Ananda, the rule of making known the reckoning of kalpas exists here in this world, ten kalpas have passed now since Bhagavat Amitayus, the Tathagata, arose and awoke to the highest perfect knowledge.

15. 'And, O Ananda, the world called Sukhavati belonging to that Bhagavat Amitabha is prosperous, rich, good to live in, fertile, lovely, and filled with many gods and men. Then, O Ananda, in that world there are neither hells, nor the animals nor the realm of departed spirits, nor bodies of fighting spirits, nor untimely births. And there do not appear in this world such gems as are known in the world Sukhavati.

16. 'Now, O Ananda, that world Sukhavati is fragrant with several sweet-smelling scents, rich in manifold flowers and fruits. adorned with gem trees, and frequented by tribes of manifold sweet-voiced birds, which have been made by the Tathagata on purpose. And, O Ananda, those gem trees are of several colors, of many colors, and of many hundred thousand colors. There are gem trees there of golden-color, and made of gold. There are those of silver-color, and made of silver. There are those of beryl-color, and made of beryl. There are those of crystal-color, and made of crystal. There are those of coral-color, and made of coral. There are those of red pearl-color, and made of red pearls. There are those of diamond-color, and made of diamonds.

'There are some trees of two gems, that is, gold and silver. There are some of three gems, that is, gold, silver, and beryl. There are some of four gems, that is, gold, silver, beryl, and crystal. There are some of five gems, that is, gold, silver, beryl, crystal, and coral. There are some of six gems, that is, gold, silver, beryl, crystal, coral, and red pearls. There are some of seven gems, that is, gold, silver, beryl, crystal, coral, red pearls, and diamonds as the seventh.

'And there, O Ananda, of the trees made of gold, the flowers, leaves, small branches, branches, trunks, and roots are made of gold, and the fruits are made of silver. Of trees made of silver, the flowers, leaves, small branches, branches, trunks, and roots are made of silver only, and the fruits are made of beryl. Of trees made of beryl, the flowers, leaves, small branches, branches, trunks, and roots are made of beryl, and the fruits are made of crystal. Of trees made of crystal, the flowers, leaves, small branches, branches, trunks, and roots are made of crystal only, and the fruits are made of coral. Of trees made of coral, the flowers, leaves, small branches, branches, trunks, and roots are made of coral only, and the fruits are made of red pearls. Of trees made of red pearls, the flowers, leaves, small branches, branches, trunks, and roots are made of red pearls only, and the fruits are made of diamonds. Of trees made of diamonds, the flowers, leaves, small branches, branches, trunks, and roots are made of diamonds only, and the fruits are made of gold.

'Of some trees, O Ananda, the roots are made of gold, the trunks of silver, the branches of beryl, the small branches of crystal, the leaves of coral, the flowers of red pearls, and the fruits of diamonds. Of some trees, O Ananda, the roots are made of silver, the trunks of beryl, the branches of crystal, the small branches of coral, the leaves of red pearls, the flowers of diamonds, and the fruits of gold. Of some trees, O Ananda, the roots are made of beryl, the trunks of crystal, the branches of coral, the small branches of red pearls, the leaves of diamonds, the flowers of gold, and the fruits of silver. Of some trees, O Ananda, the roots are made of crystal, the trunks of coral, the branches of red pearls, the small branches of diamonds, the leaves of gold, the flowers of silver, and the fruits of beryl. Of some trees, O Ananda, the roots are made of coral, the trunks of red pearls, the branches of diamonds, the small branches of gold, the leaves of silver, the flowers of beryl, and the fruits of crystal. Of some trees, O Ananda, the roots are made of red pearls, the trunks of diamonds, the branches of gold, the small branches of silver, the leaves of beryl, the flowers of crystal, and the fruits of coral. Of some trees, O Ananda, the roots are made of diamonds, the trunks of gold, the branches of silver, the small branches of beryl, the leaves of crystal, the flowers of coral, and the fruits of red pearls. Of some trees, O Ananda, the roots are made of the seven gems, the trunks of the seven gems, the branches of the seven gems, the small branches of the seven gems, the leaves of the seven gems, the flowers of the seven gems, and the fruits of the seven gems. And, O Ananda, the roots, trunks, branches, small branches, leaves, flowers, and fruits of all those trees are pleasant to touch, and fragrant. And, when those trees are moved by the wind, a sweet and delightful sound proceeds from them, never tiring, and never disagreeable to hear. That Buddha country, O Ananda, is always on every side surrounded by such trees made of the seven gems, by masses of Kadali trees, and rows of palm-trees made of the seven gems, and entirely surrounded with golden nets, and wholly covered with lotus flowers, made of all kinds of gems.

'There are lotus flowers there, half a yojana in circumference. There are others, one yojana in circumference; and others, two, three, four, or five yojanas in circumference; nay, there are some, as much as ten yojanas in circumference. And from each gem-lotus there proceed thirty-six hundred thousand kotis of rays of light. And from each ray of light there proceed thirty-six hundred thousand kotis of Buddhas, with bodies of golden color, possessed of the thirty-two marks of great men, who go and teach the Dharma to beings in the immeasurable and innumerable worlds in the eastern quarter. Thus also in the southern, western, and northern quarters, above and below, in the cardinal and intermediate points, they go their way to the immeasurable and innumerable worlds and teach the Dharma to beings in the whole world.

17. 'And again, O Ananda, there are no black mountains anywhere in that Buddha country, nor anywhere jewel mountains, nor anywhere Sumerus, kings of mountains, nor anywhere Chakravadas, great Chakravadas, kings of mountains. And that Buddha country is level on every side, lovely, like the palm of the hand, with districts full of jewels and treasures of every kind.'

After this, the blessed Ananda spoke thus to the Bhagavat: 'But in that case, O Bhagavat, where do the gods consisting of the companies of the four Maharajas who dwell on the side of the Sumeru, and where do the Triyastrimsa gods who dwell on the top of the Sumeru, find their place?'

Bhagavat said: 'What do you think, O Ananda, where do these other beings find their place, who in this world dwell above the king of mountains, Sumeru, namely, the Yamadevas, Tushitas, Nirmanaratis, Paranirmitavasavartins, Brahmakayikas, Brahmapurohitas, Mahabrahmans, as far as the Akanishthas?'

Ananda replied: 'O Bhagavat the result of works and the outcome of works are inconceivable.'

Bhagavat said: 'Here, you see, the result of works and the outcome of works are inconceivable. But to the blessed Buddhas the position of Buddhas is not inconceivable, while to thee the holy and miraculous power of virtuous beings, whose stock of merit has become ripened, seems inconceivable.'

Ananda said: 'I had no doubt on this, no difference of opinion, or hesitation; on the contrary, I ask only the Tathagata about this matter in order to destroy the doubts, the differences of opinion, and the hesitations of future beings.'

Bhagavat said: 'All right, Ananda, this is what you ought to do.

18. ' In that world Sukhavati, O Ananda, there flow different kinds of rivers; there are great rivers there, one yojana in breadth; there are rivers up to twenty, thirty, forty, fifty yojanas in breadth, and up to twelve yojanas in depth. All these rivers are delightful, carrying water of different sweet odor, carrying bunches of flowers adorned with various gems, resounding with sweet voices. And, O Ananda, there proceeds from an instrument which consists of hundred thousand kotis of parts, which embodies heavenly music and is played by clever people, the same delightful sound which proceeds from those great rivers, the sound which is deep, unknown, incomprehensible, clear, pleasant to the ear, touching the heart, beloved, sweet, delightful, never tiring, never disagreeable, pleasant to hear, as if it always said, "Non-eternal, peaceful, unreal." Such a sound comes to be heard by these beings.

'And again, O Ananda, the borders of those great rivers on both sides are filled with jewel trees of various scents, from which bunches of flowers, leaves, and branches of all kinds hang down. And if the beings, who are on the borders of those rivers, wish to enjoy sport full of heavenly delights, the water rises to the ankle only after they have stepped into the rivers, if they wish it to be so; or if they wish it, the water rises to their knees, to their hips, to their sides, and to their ears. And heavenly pleasures arise. Again, if the beings then wish the water to be cold, it is cold; if they wish it to be hot, it is hot; if they wish it to be hot and cold, it is hot and cold, according to their pleasure.

'And those great rivers flow along, full of water scented with the best perfumes of the Uragasara sandal-wood, of Tagaras, dark, fragrant sandal-wood trees, Agarus, and heavenly Tamalapattras; covered with flowers of the white waterlilies, and heavenly Utpalas, Padmas, Kumudas, and Pundarikas; full of delightful sounds of peacocks, sparrows, kunalas, cuckoos, sarikas, parrots, ducks, geese, herons, cranes, swans and others; with small islands inhabited by flocks of birds, created by the Tathagata; adorned with fields, full of metals; with fords on which it is easy to drink, free from mud, and covered with gold dust. And when these beings there desire, thinking what kind of wishes should be fulfilled for them, then exactly such wishes are fulfilled for them according to the Dharma.

'And, O Ananda, the sound which rises from that water is delightful, and the whole Buddha country is aroused by it. And if beings, who stand on the borders of the river, wish that the sound should not come within their ear-shot, then it does not come within their ear-shot, even if they are possessed of the heavenly ear. And whatever sound a man wishes to hear, exactly that delightful sound he hears, as for instance, the sound "Buddha, Dharma,

Sangha, the perfections, the stages, the powers, perfections, freedom from attachment, consciousness; emptiness, unconditioned, free from desire, not made, not born, without origin, not being, and cessation; peace; great love, great pity, great rejoicing, and great forgiveness; resignation to consequences which have not yet arisen, and attainment of the royal stage.

'And having heard these sounds, everybody feels the highest delight and pleasure accompanied by retirement, passionlessness, quiet, cessation, law, and a stock of merit leading to the perfect knowledge.

'And O Ananda, there is nowhere in that Sukhavati world any sound of sin, obstacle, misfortune, distress, and destruction; there is nowhere any sound of pain, even the sound of perceiving what is neither pain nor pleasure is not there, O Ananda, how much less the sound of pain. For that reason, O Ananda, that world is called Sukhavati, in brief, but not in full. For, O Ananda, the whole kalpa would come to an end, while the different causes of the pleasure of the world Sukhavati are being praised, and even then the end of those causes of happiness could not be reached.

19. 'And again, O Ananda, the beings, who have been and will be born in that world Sukhavati, will be endowed with such color, strength, vigor, height and breadth, dominion, accumulation of virtue; with such enjoyments of dress, ornaments, gardens, palaces, and pavilions; and such enjoyments of touch, taste, smell, and sound; in fac, with all enjoyments and pleasures, exactly like the Paranirmitavasavartin gods.

'And again, O Ananda, in that world Sukhavati, beings do not take food consisting of gross materials of gravy or molasses; but whatever food they desire, such food they perceive, as if it were taken, and become delighted in body and mind. Yet they need not put it into their mouth.

'And if, after they are satisfied, they wish different kinds of perfumes, then with these very heavenly kinds of perfumes the whole Buddha country is scented. And whosoever wishes to perceive there such perfume, every perfume of every scent of the Gandharvaraja does always reach his nose.

'And in the same manner, if they desire musical instruments, banners, flags, umbrellas, cloaks, powders, ointments, garlands, and scents, then the whole Buddha country shines with such things. If they desire cloaks of different colors and many hundred thousand colors, then with these very best cloaks the whole Buddha country shines. And the people feel themselves covered with them.

'And if they desire such ornaments, as for instance, head-ornaments, ear-ornaments, neck-ornaments, hand and foot ornaments, namely, diadems, earrings, bracelets, armlets, necklaces, chains, ear jewels, seals, gold strings, girdles, gold nets, pearl nets, jewel nets, nets of bells made of gold and jewels, then they see that Buddha country shining with such ornaments adorned with many hundred thousand jewels, that are fastened to ornament-trees. And they perceive themselves to be adorned with these ornaments.

'And if they desire a palace, with colors and emblems of such and such height and width, adorned with hundred thousand gates made with different jewels, covered with different heavenly flowers, full of couches strewn with beautiful cushions, then exactly such a palace appears before them. And in these delightful palaces they dwell, play, sport, walk about, being honored, and surrounded by seven times seven thousands of Apsarases.

20. 'And in that world, there is no difference between gods and men, except when they are spoken of in ordinary and imperfect parlance as gods and men. And, O Ananda, as a low man and powerless man, before the face of the mighty king, is neither bright, nor warm, nor brilliant, nor is he self-confident and radiant, thus Sakra, king of the Devas, if before the face of the Paranirmitavasavartin gods, is neither bright, nor warm, nor brilliant, namely, with regard to his gardens, palaces, dresses, ornaments, his dominion, his perfection, his miraculous power, or his supremacy, his comprehension of the Dharma, and his full enjoyment of the Dharma. And, O Ananda, as the Paranirmitavasavartin gods are there, thus men must be considered in the world Sukhavati.

21. 'And again, O Ananda, in that world Sukhavati, when the time of forenoon has come, the winds are greatly agitated and blowing everywhere in the four quarters. And they shake and drive many beautiful, graceful, and many-colored stalks of the gem trees, which are perfumed with sweet heavenly scents, so that many hundred beautiful flowers of delightful scent fall down on the great earth, which is all full of jewels. And with these flowers that Buddha country is adorned on every side seven fathoms deep. As a clever man might spread out a flower-bed on the earth and make it even with both his hands, beautiful and charming, even thus with those flowers of various scents and colors that Buddha country is shining on every side seven fathoms deep. And these many flowers are soft, pleasant to touch, if one may use a comparison, like Kakilindika. If one puts one's foot on them, they sink down four inches; if one raises one's foot, they rise again four inches. When the time of the forenoon has gone again, those flowers vanish without leaving anything behind. Then that Buddha

country is again clean, pleasant, beautiful, and without fading flowers. The winds blow again everywhere in the four quarters, and scatter down fresh flowers as before. And as it is in the forenoon, so it is at noon, at twilight, in the first, middle, and last watch of the night. And the beings, if touched by those winds which blow perfume with various scents, are as full of happiness as a Bhikkhu who has obtained Nirvana.

22. 'And in that Buddha country, O Ananda, no mention is ever made of the names of fire, sun, moon, planets, constellations, and stars, or of blinding darkness. There is no mention even of day and night, except in the conversation of the Tathagata. Nor is there any idea of predial property belonging to monasteries.

23. 'And again, O Ananda, in that world Sukhavati at the proper time clouds full of heavenly perfumed water pour down heavenly flowers of all colors; heavenly seven jewels, heavenly sandalwood-powder, and heavenly umbrellas, flags, and banners are poured down. And in the sky, the heavenly flowers of all colors, and heavenly canopies are held, likewise heavenly excellent umbrellas and all kinds of ornaments, heavenly musical instruments are played, and heavenly Apsarases dance.

24. 'And again, O Ananda, in that Buddha country whatever beings have been born, and are being born, and will be born, are always constant in absolute truth, till they have reached Nirvana. And why is that? Because there is no room or mention there of the other two divisions, such as beings not constant or constant in falsehood.

'On this wise, O Ananda, that world is briefly called Sukhavati, not at full length. Even a kalpa, O Ananda, would come to an end, while the causes of happiness which exist in that world Sukhavati are being praised, and yet it would be impossible to reach the end of them.'

25. Then the Bhagavat at that time spoke the following verses:

'Thus, O Ananda, the world Sukhavati is endowed with immeasurable good qualities and excellences.

26. 'And again, O Ananda, in the ten quarters, and in each of them, in all the Buddha countries equal in number to the sand of the Ganges, the blessed Buddhas equal in number to the sand of the Ganges, glorify the name of the blessed Amitabha, the Tathagata, they preach his fame, they proclaim his glory, they extol his virtue. And why? Because all beings who hear the name of the blessed Amitabha, and having heard it, raise their

thought with joyful longing, even for once only, will not turn away again from the highest perfect knowledge.

27. 'And before the eyes of those beings, O Ananda, who again and again think of the Tathagata reverently and who make the great and unmeasured stock of good works grow, turning their thought towards Bodhi, and who pray to be born in that world, Amitabha, the Tathagata, holy and fully enlightened, when the time of their death has approached, will appear, surrounded by many companies of Bhikkhus and honored by them. And then these beings, having seen the Bhagavat, their thoughts filled with joy, will, when they have died, be born in that world of Sukhavati. And if, O Ananda, any son or daughter of a good family should wish, "How then may I see that Tathagata Amitabha visibly?" then he must raise his thought on to the highest perfect knowledge, he must direct his thought with perseverance and excessive desire towards that Buddha country, and direct the stock of his good works towards being born there.

28. ' But before the eyes of those who do not care much about the Tathagata Amitabha, and who do not vigorously increase the great and unmeasured stock of their good works, the Tathagata Amitabha, holy and fully enlightened, will appear, at the time of death, with the company of Bhikkhus, in breadth and height and form and beauty, very like the former, and very like the real Tathagata, but only created by thought. And they, through their meditation that dwells on perceiving the sight of the Tathagata, and with unfailing memory, will, when they have died, be born in the same Buddha country.

29. 'And again, O Ananda, those beings who meditate on the Tathagata by giving him ten thoughts, and who will direct their desire towards that Buddha country, and who will feel satisfaction when the profound doctrines are being preached, and who will not fall off, nor despair, nor fail, but will meditate on that Tathagata, if it were by one thought only, and will direct their desire toward that Buddha country, they also will see the Tathagata Amitabha, while they are in a dream, they will be born in the world Sukhavati, and will never turn away from the highest perfect knowledge.

30. 'And, O Ananda, after thus seeing the cause and effect, the Tathagatas of the ten quarters, in immeasurable and innumerable worlds, glorify the name of the Tathagata Amitabha, preach his fame, and proclaim his praise. And again, O Ananda, in that Buddha country, Bodhisattvas equal in number to the sand of the Ganges approach, from the ten quarters, and in each quarter towards that Tathagata Amitabha, in order to see him, to bow before him, to worship him, to consult him, and likewise in order to see that company of Bodhisattvas, and the different

kinds of perfection in the multitude of ornaments and excellences belonging to that Buddha country.'

31. Then at that time, the Bhagavat, in order to illustrate this matter in fuller measure, recited these verses:

1. 'As there are Buddha countries equal to the sand of the river Ganges in the eastern quarter, whence all the Bodhisattvas come to worship the Buddha, the lord Amitayu;

2. 'And they having taken many bunches of flowers of different colors, sweetly-scented and delightful, shower them down on the best leader of men, on Amitayu, worshipped by gods and men;

3. 'In the same manner there are as many Buddha countries in the southern, western, and northern quarters, whence they come with the Bodhisattvas to worship the Buddha, the lord Amitayus.

4. 'And they having taken many handfulls of scents of different colors, sweetly scented and delightful, shower them down on the best leader of men, on Amitayus, worshipped by gods and men.

5. 'These many Bodhisattvas having worshipped and revered the feet of Amitaprabha, and having walked round him respectfully, speak thus: "Oh, the country of Buddha shines wonderfully! "

6. 'And they cover him again with handfulls of flowers, with thoughts jubilant, with incomparable joy, and proclaim their wish before that lord: "May our country also be such as this."

7. 'And what was thrown there as handfuls of flowers arose in the form of an umbrella extending over a hundred yojanas, and the beautiful country shines and is well adorned, and flowers cover the whole body of Buddha.

8. 'These Bodhisattvas having thus honored him, how do they act? Delighted they pronounce this speech: "Gains by those people are well gained, by whom the name of the best man has been heard.

9. '"By us also all the gain has been well gained, because we have come to this Buddha country. See this dream-like country, how beautiful it is, which was made by the teacher during a hundred thousand kalpas.

10. '"Look, the Buddha possessed of a mass of the best virtues shines, surrounded by Bodhisattvas. Endless is his splendor, and endless the light, and endless the life, and endless the assembly."

11. 'And the lord Amitayus makes a smile of thirty-six nayutas of kotis of rays, which rays having issued from the circle of his mouth light up the thousand kotis of Buddha countries.

12. 'And all these rays having returned there again settle on the head of the lord; gods and men perceive the delight, because they have seen there this light of him.

13. 'There rises the Buddha-son, glorious, he indeed the mighty Avalokitesvara, and says: "What is the reason there, O Bhagavat, what is the cause, that thou smilest, O lord of the world ?

14. '"Explain this, for thou knowest the sense, and art full of kind compassion, the deliverer of many living beings. All beings will be filled with joyful thoughts, when they have thus heard this excellent and delightful speech.

15. '"And the Bodhisattvas who have come from many worlds to Sukhavati in order to see the Buddha, having heard it and having perceived the great joy, will quickly inspect this country.

16. '"And beings, come to this noble country, (quickly) obtain miraculous power, divine eye and divine ear, they remember their former births, and know the highest wisdom."

17. 'Then Buddha Amitayus preaches: "This prayer was mine formerly, so that beings having in any way whatever heard my name should for ever go to my country.

18. '"And this my excellent prayer has been fulfilled, and beings having quickly come here from many worlds into my presence, never return from here, not even for one birth."

19. 'If a Bodhisattva wishes here that his country should be such as this, and that he also should deliver many beings, through his name, through his preaching, and through his sight,

20. 'Let him quickly and with speed go to the world Sukhavati, and having gone near Amitaprabha, let him worship a thousand kotis of Buddhas.

21. 'Having worshipped many kotis of Buddhas, and having gone to many countries by means of their miraculous power, and having performed adoration in the presence of the Sugatas, they will go to Sukhavati with devotion.

32. 'And again, O Ananda, there is a Bodhi-tree belonging to Amitayus, the Tathagata, holy and fully enlightened. That Bodhi-tree is ten hundred yojanas in height, having petals, leaves, and branches spread over eight hundred yojanas, having a circumference near the base of the root of five hundred yojanas, always in leaf, always in flower, always in fruit, of different colors, of many hundred thousand colors, of different leaves, of different flowers, of different fruits, adorned with many beautiful ornaments, shining with precious jewels, bright like the moon, beautified with precious jewels such as are fastened on Sakra's head, strewn with Kintamani jewels, well adorned with the best jewels of the sea, more than heavenly, hung with golden strings, adorned with hundreds of gold chains, jewel-garlands, necklaces, bracelets, strings of red pearls and blue pearls, Simhalata, girdles, bunches, strings of jewels, and all kinds of jewels, covered with nets of bells, nets of all kinds of jewels, nets of pearls, and nets of gold, adorned with the emblems of the dolphin, the Svastika, the Nandyavarta, and the moon, adorned with nets of jewels and of bells, and with ornaments of gold and of all kinds of jewels, in fact adorned according to the desires of beings whatever their wishes may be.

'And again, O Ananda, the sound and noise of that Bodhi-tree, when it is moved by the wind, reaches immeasurable worlds. And, O Ananda, for those beings whose hearing that Bodhi-tree reaches, no disease of the ear is to be feared until they reach Bodhi. And for those immeasurable, innumerable, inconceivable, incomparable, measureless, immense, and inexpressible beings, whose sight that Bodhi-tree reaches, no disease of the eye is to be feared until they reach Bodhi. And again, O Ananda, for those beings who smell the scent of that Bodhi-tree, no disease of the nose is to be feared until they reach Bodhi. For those beings who taste the fruits of that Bodhi-tree, no disease of the tongue is to be feared until they reach Bodhi. For those beings who are lighted up by the light of that Bodhi-tree, no disease of the body is to be feared until they reach Bodhi. And again, O Ananda, for those beings who meditate on that Bodhi-tree according to the Dharma, henceforward until they reach the Bodhi, no perplexity of their thought is to be feared. And all those beings, through the seeing of that Bodhi-tree, never turn away, namely, from the highest perfect knowledge. And they obtain three kinds of resignation, namely, Ghoshanuga, resignation to natural consequences, and (resignation to consequences which have not yet arisen, through the power of the former prayers of that same Tathagata Amitayus, through the service rendered by them to the former

Jinas, and through the performance of the former prayers, to be well accomplished, and to be well conceived, without failure or without flaw.

33. 'And again, O Aranda, those Bodhisattvas who have been born, are being born, or will be born there, are all bound to one birth only, and will thence indeed obtain the highest perfect knowledge; barring always the power of prayers, as in the case of those Bodhisattvas who are preaching with the voice of lions, who are girded with the noble armor of the Dharma, and who are devoted to the work of helping all people to attain Paranirvana.

34. 'And again, O Ananda, in that Buddha country, those who are Sravakas are possessed of the light of a fathom, and those who are Bodhisattvas are possessed of the light of a hundred thousand kotis of yojanas; barring always the two Bodhisattvas, by whose light that world is everywhere shining with eternal splendor.'

Then the blessed Ananda said this to the Bhagavat: 'What are the names, O Bhagavat, of those two noble-minded Bodhisattvas?

The Bhagavat said: 'One of them, O Ananda, is the noble-minded Bodhisattva Avalokitesvara, and the second is Mahasthamaprapta by name. And, O Ananda, these two were born there, having left this Buddha country here'.

35. 'And, O Ananda, those Bodhisattvas who have been born in that Buddha country are all endowed with the thirty-two marks of a great man, possessed of perfect members, skilled in meditation and wisdom, clever in all kinds of wisdom, having sharp organs, having well-restrained organs, having organs of sense capable of thorough knowledge, not mean, possessed of the five kinds of strength, of patience under censure, and of endless and boundless good qualities.

36. 'And again, O Ananda, all those Bodhisattvas who have been born in that Buddha country are not deprived of the sight of Buddha, nor liable to fall down to the evil states, until they reach the Bodhi. Henceforward they all will never be forgetful of their former births; barring always those who are devoted to their former place, during the disturbances of the kalpas, and while the five kinds of corruption prevail, when there is the appearance of blessed Buddhas in the world, as for instance, that of me at present.

37. 'And again, O Ananda, all the Bodhisattvas who have been bom in that Buddha country, having gone during one morning meal to the other

world, worship many hundred thousand nayutas of kotis of Buddhas, as many as they like, through the favor of Buddha. They consider in many ways that they should worship Buddhas with such and such flowers, incense, lamps, scents, garlands, ointments, powder, cloaks, umbrellas, flags, banners, ensigns, music, concerts, and musical instruments; and, as soon as they have considered this, there arise also on their hands exactly such materials for every kind of worship. And while performing worship for those blessed Buddhas with those materials, beginning with flowers and ending with musical instruments, they lay up for themselves much immeasurable and innumerable merit. Again, if they wish that such handfuls of flowers should be produced on their hands, then such handfuls of heavenly flowers, of different colors, of many colors, of different scents, are produced on their hands as soon as thought of. They shower again and again such handfulls of flowers upon those blessed Buddhas. And the very smallest handfull of flowers, being thrown on high, appears above in the sky as an umbrella of flowers ten yojanas in circumference. And when the second has been thrown after it, the first does not fall down on the earth. There are handfuls of flowers there, which having been thrown up, appear in the sky as umbrellas of flowers twenty yojanas in circumference.

'There appear in the sky some flower-umbrellas, thirty, forty, or fifty yojanas in circumference, as far as a hundred thousand yojanas in circumference. Those Bodhisattvas there who perceive the noble pleasure and joy, and obtain the noble strength of thought, having caused a great and immeasurable and innumerable stock of good works to ripen, and having worshipped many hundred thousand nayutas of kotis of Buddhas, turn again to the world Sukhavati in one morning, through the favor of practising the former prayers of the same Tathagata Amitayus, owing to the hearing of the Dharma formerly given, owing to the stock of good works produced under former Jinas, owing to the perfect completion in the success of former prayers, owing to the well-ordered state of mind.

38. 'And again, O Ananda, all those beings who have been born in that Buddha country recite the story of the Dharma, which is accompanied by omniscience. And for the beings in that Buddha country there exists no idea of property whatever. And all those going and walking through that Buddha country feel neither pleasure nor pain; stepping forward they have no desire, and with desire they do not step forward. They give no thought to any beings. And again, O Ananda, for those beings who have been born in that world Sukhavati, there is no idea of others, no idea of self, no idea of inequality, no strife, no dispute, no opposition. Full of equanimity, of benevolent thought, of tender thought, of affectionate thought, of useful thought, of serene thought, of firm thought, of unbiassed thought, of undisturbed thought, of unagitated thought, of thought fixed on the practice

of discipline and transcendent wisdom, having entered on knowledge which is a firm support to all thoughts, equal to the ocean in wisdom, equal to the mountain Meru in knowledge, rich in many good qualities, delighting in the music of the Bodhyangas, devoted to the music of Buddha, they discard the eye of flesh, and assume the heavenly eye.

'And having approached the eye of wisdom, having reached the eye of the Dharma, producing the eye of Buddha, showing it, lighting it, and fully exhibiting it, they attain perfect wisdom. And being bent on the equilibrium of the three elements, having subdued and calmed their thoughts endowed with a perception of the causes of all things, clever in explanation of causes, endowed with the power of explaining the Dharma or things such as they really are, clever in taking and refusing, clever in leading and not leading, clever in resting, they, being regardless of worldly stories, derive true pleasures from stories transcending the world. They are clever in examining all things, familiar with the knowledge of the cessation of the working of all things, perceiving even what cannot be seen, caring for nothing, attached to nothing, without cares, without pain, free without clinging to anything, free from impurity, of blameless behavior, not clinging to anything, intent on the deep or profound laws, they do not sink, elevated to the entrance into the knowledge of Buddha difficult to comprehend, having obtained the path of one vehicles, free from doubt, beyond the reach of questionings, knowing the thoughts of others, free from self-confidence.

'Being elevated in knowledge, they are like Mount Sumeru; being imperturbable in thought, they are like the ocean; they surpass the light of the sun and moon, by the light of wisdom, and by the whiteness, brilliancy, purity, and beauty of their knowledge; by their light and splendor, they are like the color of molten gold; by their patiently bearing the good and evil deeds of all beings, they are like the earth; by their cleaning and carrying off the taint of all sins, they are like water; by their burning the evil of pride in anything, they are like the king of fire ; by not clinging to anything, they are like the wind; by pervading all things and yet not caring for anything, they are like the ether; by not being tainted by the whole world, they are like lotuses; by their shouting forth the Dharma, they are like the great cloud at the rainy season; by showering down the whole ocean of the Dharma, they are like the great rain; by overpowering great troops, they are like bulls; by the highest restraint of their thoughts, they are like great elephants; by being well trained, they are like noble horses; by their fearlessness, confidence, and heroism, they are like the lion, the king of beasts; by affording protection to all beings, they are like the fig-tree, the king of trees; by not being shaken by any calumniators, they are like the Sumeru, the king of mountains; by their feeling of unlimited love, they are like the sky; by their precedence, owing to their command of the Dharma, and their stock of all merit, they are like the great Brahman; by their not dwelling in what they have accumulated, they are like birds; by their scattering all calumniators, they are like Garuda, king of birds; by their not being averse to our obtaining difficult things, they are like the Udumbara flowers; calm like elephants, because their senses are neither crooked nor shaken; clever in decision, full of the sweet flavor of patience; without envy, because they do not hanker after the happiness of others; wise, because in their search after the Dharma, never tired of discussions on the Dharma; like the precious beryl, through their value; like jewel-mines, by their sacred knowledge; sweet-sounding by the noise of the great drum of the Dharma, striking the great kettledrum of the Dharma, blowing the great trumpet-shell of the Dharma, raising the great banner of the Dharma, lighting the torch of the Dharma, looking for wisdom, not foolish, faultless, passionless, pure, refined, not greedy, fond of distributing, generous, open-handed, fond of distributing gifts, not stingy in giving instruction and food, not attached, without fear, without desires, wise, patient, energetic, bashful, orderly, fearless, full of knowledge, happy, Pleasant to live with, obliging, enlightening the world, free from sorrow, free from taint, having left off the winking of the eye, possessing lightly acquired knowledge, strong in reasoning, strong in prayer, not crooked, not perverse; then, having accumulated a hundred thousand nayutas of kotis of lakshas of virtue, delivered from the thorns of pride, free from illusion, hatred, and passion; pure, devoted to what is pure, famous by the Jina-power, learned in the world, elevated by their purified knowledge, sons of the Jina, endowed with the vigor of thought, heroes, firm, unselfish, free from faults, unequalled, free from anger, collected, noble, heroes, bashful, energetic, possessed of memory, understanding, and prudence; sending forth the weapons of knowledge, possessed of purity, shining, free from faults and taints, endowed with memory, resting on serene knowledge. And such, O Ananda, are the beings in that Buddha country, stated briefly. But if the Tathagatas should describe them fully, even in a length of life that should last for a hundred thousand nayutas of kotis of kalpas, yet the end of the virtues of those good people would not be reached, and yet there would be no failure of the self-confidence of the Tathagata. And why? Because, O Ananda, both are indeed inconceivable and incomparable, that is, first, the virtues of those Bodhisattvas, and secondly, the unsurpassed light of knowledge of the Tathagata.

39. 'And now, O Ananda, stand up, facing westward, and having taken a handful of flowers, fall down. This is the quarter where that Bhagavat Amitabha, the Tathagata, holy and fully enlightened, dwells, remains, supports himself, and teaches the Dharma, whose spotless and pure name, famed in every quarter of the whole world with its ten quarters, the blessed

Buddhas, equal to the grains of the sand of the river Ganges, speaking and answering again and again without stopping, extol, praise, and eulogize.'

After this, the blessed Ananda said this to the Bhagavat: 'I wish, O Bhagavat, to see that Amitabha, Amitaprabha, Amitayus, the Tathagata, holy and fully enlightened, and those noble-minded Bodhisattvas, who are possessed of a stock of merit amassed under many hundred thousand nayutas of kotis of Buddhas.'

At that moment this speech was spoken by the blessed Ananda, and immediately that Amitabha, the Tathagata, holy and fully enlightened, let such a ray of light go out of the palm of his own hand, that even the most distant Buddha country was shining with the great splendor. And again at that time, whatever black mountains, or jewel-mountains, or Merus, great Merus, Mukilindas, great Mukilindas, Chakravadas, great Chakravadas, or erections, or pillars, trees, woods, gardens, palaces, belonging to the gods and men, exist everywhere in hundred thousand kotis of Buddha countries; all these were pervaded and overcome by the light of that Tathagata.

And as a man, followed by another at a distance of a fathom only, would see the other man, when the sun has risen, exactly in the same manner the Bhikkhus, Bhikkhunis, Upasakas, Upasikas, gods, Nagas, Yakshas, Rakshasas, Gandharvas, Asuras, Garudas, Kinnaras, Mahoragas, men and not-men, in this Buddha country, saw at that time that Amitabha, the Tathagata, holy and fully enlightened, like the Sumeru, the king of mountains, elevated above all countries, surpassing all quarters, shining, warming, glittering, blazing; and they saw that great mass of Bodhisattvas, and that company of Bhikshus, that is, by the grace of Buddha, from the pureness of that light.

And as this great earth might be, when all covered with water, so that no trees, no mountains, no islands, no grasses, bushes, herbs, large trees, no rivers, chasms, water-falls, would be seen, but only the one great earth which had all become an ocean, in exactly the same manner there is neither mark nor sign whatever to be seen in that Buddha country, except Sravakas, spreading their light over a fathom, and those Bodhisattvas, spreading their light over a hundred thousand kotis of yojanas.

And that Bhagavat Amitabha, the Tathagata, holy and fully enlightened, overshadowing that mass of Sravakas and that mass of Bodhisattvas, is seen, illuminating all quarters. Again at that time all those Bodhisattvas, Srivakas, gods and men in that world Sukhavati, saw this world Saha and Shakyamuni, the Tathagata, holy and fully enlightened, surrounded by a holy company of Bhikshus, teaching the Dharma.

40. Then, the Bhagavat addressed the nobleminded Bodhisattva Ajita, and said: 'Do you see, O Ajita, the perfection of the array of ornaments and good qualities in that Buddha country; and above in the sky places with charming parks, charming gardens, charming rivers and lotus lakes, scattered with many precious Padmas, Utpalas, Kumudas, and Pundarikas; and below, from the earth to the abode of the Akanishthas, the surface of the sky, covered with flowers, ornamented with wreaths of flowers, shining on the rows of many precious columns, frequented by flocks of all kinds of birds created by the Tathagata?'

The Bodhisattva Ajita said: 'I see, O Bhagavat.'

The Bhagavat said: 'Do you see again, O Ajita, those flocks of immortal birds, making the whole Buddha country resound with the voice of Buddha, so that those Bodhisattvas are never without meditating on Buddha?'

Ajita said: 'I see, O Bhagavat.'

The Bhagavat said: 'Do you see again, O Ajita, those beings, who have ascended to the palaces which extend over a hundred thousand yojanas in the sky, walking about respectfully?'

Ajita said: 'I see, O Bhagavat.'

The Bhagavat said: 'What do you think, O Ajita, is there any difference between the gods called Paranirmitavasavartins, and men in the world Sukhavati?'

Ajita said: 'I do not, O Bhagavat, perceive even one difference, so far as the men in that world of Sukhavati are endowed with great supernatural powers.'

The Bhagavat said: 'Do you see again, O Ajita, those men dwelling within the calyx of excellent lotus-flowers in that world Sukhavati?'

He said: 'As gods called Trayastrimsas or Yamas, having entered into palaces of fifty or hundred or five hundred yojanas in extent, are playing, sporting, walking about, exactly in the same manner I see, O Bhagavat, these men dwelling within the calyx of excellent lotus-flowers in the world Sukhavati.

41. 'Again there are, O Bhagavat, beings who, being born miraculously, appear sitting cross-legged in the lotus-flowers. What is there, O

Bhagavat, the cause, what the reason, that some dwell within the calyx, while others, being born miraculously, appear sitting cross-legged in the lotus-flowers?'

The Bhagavat said: 'Those Bodhisattvas, O Ajita, who, living in other Buddha countries, entertain doubt about being born in the world Sukhavati, and with that thought amass a stock of merit, for them there is the dwelling within the calyx. Those, on the contrary, who are filled with faith, and being free from doubt, amass a stock of merit in order to be born in the world Sukhavati, and conceive, believe, and trust in the perfect knowledge of the blessed Buddhas, they, being born miraculously, appear sitting cross-legged in the flowers of the lotus. And those noble-minded Bodhisattvas, O Ajita, who, living in other Buddha countries, raise their thought in order to see Amitabha, the Tathagata, holy and fully enlightened, who never entertain a doubt, believe in the perfect knowledge of Buddha and in their own stock of merit, for them, being born miraculously, and appearing cross-legged, there is in one minute, such a body as that of other beings who have been born there long before. See, O Ajita, the excellent, immeasurable, unfailing, unlimited wisdom, that namely for their own benefit they are deprived during five hundred years of seeing Buddhas, seeing Bodhisattvas, hearing the Dharma, speaking about the Dharma with others, and thus collecting a stock of merit; they are indeed deprived of the successful attainment of every stock of merit, and that, through their forming ideas tainted with doubt.

'And, O Ajita, there might be a dungeon belonging to an anointed Kshatriya king, inlaid entirely with gold and beryl, in which cushions, garlands, wreaths and strings are fixed, having canopies of different colors and kind, covered with silk cushions, scattered over with various flowers and blossoms, scented with excellent scents, adorned with arches, courts, windows, pinnacles, fire-places, and terraces, covered with nets of bells of the seven kinds of gems, having four angles, four pillars, four doors, four stairs; and the son of that king having been thrown into the dungeon for some misdeed is there, bound with a chain made of the Jambunada gold. And suppose there is a couch prepared for him, covered with many woollen cloths, spread over with cotton and feather cushions, having Kalinga coverings, and carpets, together with coverlids, red on both sides, beautiful and charming. There he might be then either sitting or resting. And there might be brought to him much food and drink, of various kinds, pure and well prepared. What do you think, O Ajita, would the enjoyment be great for that prince?'

Ajita said: 'Yes, it would be great, O Bhagavat.'

The Bhagavat said: 'What do you think, O Ajita, would he even taste it there, and notice it, or would he feel any satisfaction from it?'

He said: 'Not indeed, O Bhagavat; but on the contrary, when he had been led away by the king and thrown into the dungeon, he would only wish for deliverance from there. He would seek for the nobles, princes, ministers, women, elders (rich merchants), householders, and lords of castles, who might deliver him from that dungeon. Moreover, O Bhagavat, there is no pleasure for that prince in that dungeon, nor is he liberated, until the king shows him favor.'

The Bhagavat said: 'Thus, O Ajita, it is with those Bodhisattvas who, having fallen into doubt, amass a stock of merit, but doubt the knowledge of Buddha. They are born in that world Sukhavati, through the hearing of Buddha's name, and through the serenity of thought only; they do not, however, appear sitting cross-legged in the flowers of the lotus, being born miraculously, but dwell only in the calyx of the lotus-flowers. Moreover for them there exist ideas of palaces and gardens. There is no discharge, there is no phlegm or mucus, there is nothing disagreeable to the mind. But they are deprived of seeing Buddhas, hearing the Dharma, seeing Bodhisattvas, speaking about and ascertaining the Dharma, gathering any new stock of merit, and practicing the Dharma, during five hundred years. Moreover they do not rejoice there or perceive satisfaction. But they wish to remove one another, and then they step out behind. And it is not known whether their exit takes place above, below, or across.

'See, O Ajita, there might be worshippings of many hundred thousand nayutas of kotis of Buddhas during those five hundred years, and also many, immense, innumerable, immeasurable stocks of merit to be amassed. But all this they destroy by the fault of doubt. See, O Ajita, to how great an injury the doubt of the Bodhisattvas leads. Therefore now, O Ajita, after the Bodhisattvas without doubting have quickly raised their thoughts towards Bodhi, in order to obtain power of conferring happiness for the benefit of all creatures, their stock of merit should be turned towards their being born in the world Sukhavati, where the blessed Amitabha, the Tathagata, holy and fully enlightened, dwells.'

42. After these words, the Bodhisattva Ajita thus spoke to the Bhagavat: 'O Bhagavat, will the Bodhisattvas, who have gone away from this Buddha country, or from the side of other blessed Buddhas, be born in the world Sukhavati?'

The Bhagavat said: 'Indeed, O Ajita, seventy-two nayutas of kotis of Bodhisattvas are gone away from this Buddha country, who will be born in the world Sukhavati; Bodhisattvas, who will never return, thanks to the stock of merit, which they have accumulated under many hundred thousand nayutas of kotis of Buddhas. What then shall be said of those with smaller stocks of merit?

1. Eighteen hundred nayutas of kotis of Bodhisattvas will be born in the world Sukhavati from the place of the Tathagata Dushprasaha.

2. There lives in the Eastern quarter the Tathagata named Ratnakara. From his place ninety kotis of Bodhisattvas will be born in the world Sukhavati.

3. Twenty-two kotis of Bodhisattvas will be born in the world Sukhavati from the place of the Tathagata Jyotishprabha.

4. Twenty-five kotis of Bodhisattvas will be born in the world Sukhavati from the place of the Tathagata Amitaprabha.

5. Sixty kotis of Bodhisattvas will be born in the world Sukhavati from the place of the Tathagata Lokapradipa.

6. Sixty-four kotis of Bodhisattvas will be born in the world Sukhavati from the place of the Tathagata Nagabhibhu.

7. Twenty-five kotis of Bodhisattvas will be born in the world Sukhavati from the place of the Tathagata Virajaprabha.

8. Sixteen kotis of Bodhisattvas will be born in the world Sukhavati from the place of the Tathagata Simha.

9. Eighteen thousand Bodhisattvas will be born in the world Sukhavati from the place of the Tathagata Simha.

10. Eighty-one nayutas of kotis of Bodhisattvas will be born in the world Sukhavati from the place of the Tathagata Srikuta.

11. Ten nayutas of kotis of Bodhisattvas will be born in the world Sukhavati from the place of the Tathagata Narendraraja.

12. Twelve thousand Bodhisattvas will be born in the world Sukhavati from the place of the Tathagata Balabhijna.

13. Twenty-five kotis of Bodhisattvas, who have obtained strength, having gone to one place in one week of eight days, and having turned to the West during ninety hundred thousand nayutas of kotis of kalpas, will be

born in the world Sukhavati from the place of the Tathagata Pushpadhvaga.

14. Twelve kotis of Bodhisattvas will be born in the world Sukhavati from the place of the Tathagata Jvalanadhipati.

15. From the place of the Tathagata Vaisaradyaprapta, sixty-nine kotis of Bodhisattvas will be born in the world Sukhavati, in order to see the Tathagata Amitabha, to bow before him, to worship him, to ask questions of him, and to consult him.

'For this reason, O Ajita, I might proclaim during a full nayuta of kotis of kalpas the names of those Tathagatas, from whom the Bodhisattvas proceed in order to see that Tathagata Amitabha in the world Sukhavati, to bow before him, and to worship him, and yet the end could not be reached.

43. 'See, O Ajita, what easy gains are gained by those beings who will hear the name of the Tathagata Amitabha, holy and fully enlightened. Nor will those beings be of little faith, who will obtain at least one joyful thought of that Tathagata and of this treatise of the Dharma. Therefore now, O Ajita, I invite you, and command you to proclaim this treatise of the Dharma, before the world together with the gods. Having plunged into the vast universe full of fire, no one ought to turn back, if he has but once conceived the thought of going across. And why? Because kotis of Bodhisattvas indeed, O Ajita, return from the highest perfect knowledge, on account of not hearing such treatises of the Dharma as this. Therefore, from a wish for this treatise of the Dharma, a great effort should be made to hear, learn, and remember it, and to study it for the sake of fully grasping it and widely making it known. A good copy of it should be kept, after it has been copied in a book, if only during one night and day, or even during the time necessary for milking a cow.

'The name of Master should be given to a teacher who desires to conduct quickly innumerable beings to the state of never returning from the highest perfect knowledge, namely, in order that they may see the Buddha country of that blessed Amitabha, the Tathagata, and to acquire the excellent perfection of the array of good qualities peculiar to his own Buddha country.

'And, O Ajita, such beings will have easily gained their gains who, having amassed a stock of merit, having performed service under former Jinas, and having been guided by Buddhas, shall hear in future, until the destruction of the good Dharma, such-like excellent treatises of the Dharma, treatises which are praised, eulogized, and approved of by all Buddhas, and convey quickly the great knowledge of omniscience. And those also who, when they have heard it, shall obtain excellent delight and pleasure, and will learn, retain, recite and grasp, and wisely preach it to others, and be delighted by its study, or, having copied it at least, will worship it, will certainly produce much good work, so that it is difficult to count it.

'Thus indeed, O Ajita, I have done what a Tathagata ought to do. It is now for you to devote yourself to it without any doubt. Do not doubt the perfect and unfailing knowledge of Buddha. Do not enter into the dungeon made of gems built up in every way. For indeed, the birth of a Buddha, O Ajita, is difficult to be met with, so is the instruction in the Dharma, and also a timely birth. O Ajita, the way to gain the perfection of all stocks of merit has been proclaimed by me. Do now exert yourselves and move forward. O Ajita, I grant indeed a great favor to this treatise of the Dharma. Be valiant so that the laws of Buddhas may not perish or disappear. Do not break the command of the Tathagata.'

44. Then at that time, the Bhagavat spoke these verses:

1. 'Such hearings of me will not be for people who have not done good; but those who are heroes and perfect, they will hear this speech.

2. 'And those by whom the Lord of the world, the enlightened and the light-giver, has been seen, and the law been heard reverentially, will obtain the highest joy.

3. 'Low people of slothful minds cannot find any delight in the laws of Buddha; those who have worshipped in the Buddha countries learn the service of the Lords of the three worlds.

4. 'As a blind man in darkness does not know the way, and much less can show it, so also he who is only a Sravaka in the knowledge of Buddha; how then should beings who are ignorant!

5. 'The Buddha only knows the virtues of a Buddha; but not gods, Nagas, Asuras, Yakshas, and Sravakas; even for Anekabuddhas there is no such way, as when the knowledge of a Buddha is being manifested.

6. 'If all beings had attained bliss, knowing the highest meaning in pure wisdom, they would not in kotis of kalpas or even in a longer time tell all the virtues of one Buddha.

7. 'Thereupon they would attain Nirvana, preaching for many kotis of kalpas (eons), and yet the measure of the knowledge of a Buddha would not be reached, for such is the wonderfulness of the knowledge of the Jinas.

8. 'Therefore a learned man of an intelligent race who believes my words, after having perceived all paths of the knowledge of the Jinas, should utter speech, saying, "Buddha is wise."

9. 'Now and then a man is found, now and then a Buddha appears, knowledge of the object of faith is acquired after a long time; therefore one should strive to acquire the knowledge of the object of faith.'

45. And while this treatise of the Dharma was being delivered, twelve kotis of nayutas of beings obtained the pure and spotless eye of the Dharma with regard to Dharmas. Twenty-four hundred thousand nayutas of kotis of beings obtained the Anagamin reward. Eight hundred Bhikshus had their thoughts delivered from faults so as to cling no more to anything. Twenty-five kotis of Bodhisattvas obtained resignation to things to come. And by forty hundred thousand nayutas of kotis of the human and divine race, thoughts such as had never risen before were turned toward the highest perfect knowledge, and their stocks of merit were made to grow toward their being born in the world Sukhavati, from a desire to see the Tathagata, the blessed Amitabha. And all of them having been born there, will in proper order be born in other worlds, as Tathagatas, called Manjusvara (sweet-voiced). And eighty kotis of nayutas having acquired resignation under the Tathagata Dipankara, never turning back again from the highest perfect knowledge, rendered perfect by the Tathagata Amitayus, practising the duties of former Bodhisattvas, will carry out, after they are born in the world Sukhavati, the duties enjoined in the former prayers.

46. At that time this universe, the three millions of worlds, trembled in six ways. And various miracles were seen. On earth everything was perfect, and human and divine instruments were played, and the shout of joy was heard as far as the world of the Akanishthas.

47. Thus spoke the Bhagavat enraptured, and the noble-minded Bodhisattva Ajita, and the blessed Ananda, the whole Assembly, and the world, with gods, men, spirits, mighty birds, and fairies, applauded the speech of the Bhagavat. The praise of the beauty of the excellences of Sukhavati, the country of the blessed Amitabha, the Tathagata, the entry of the Bodhisattva on the stage of never returning, the story of Amitabha, the Mahayanasutra of the Description of Sukhavati is finished.

The Amitabha Sutra
The Smaller Sukhavativyuha
or
Buddha Pronounces the Sutra of Amitabha Buddha

Thus I have heard:

At one time the Buddha was staying in the Anathapindika Garden of Jetavana Park in the city kingdom of Sravasti, together with 1,250 great bhiksus, who all were great Arhats as recognized by the multitudes. Such great disciples included the Elder Sariputra, Mahamaudgalyayana, Mahakasuapa, Mahakatyayana, Mahakausthila, Revata, Suddhipanthaka, Nanda, Ananda, Rahula, Gavampati, Pindola-Bharadvaja, Kalodayin, Mahakapphina, Vakkula, Aniruddha, and others. Also present were Bodhisattva-Mahasattvas, such as Manjusri the Dharma Prince, Ajita Bodhisattva, Gandhahastin Bodhisattva, and Persistent Energetic Progress Bodhisattva. Along with great Bodhisattvas such as these, in attendance as well were the god-king Sakro-Devanam-Indra and an innumerable multitude of gods.

At that time the Buddha told the Elder Sariputra, "West of here, beyond 100,000 koti Buddha Lands, is a land called Ultimate Bliss. In that land is a Buddha called Amitabha, who is now expounding the Dharma. Sariputra, why is that land called Ultimate Bliss? Sentient beings of that land have no suffering but only experience myriad joys. Therefore, that land is called Ultimate Bliss. Moreover, Sariputra, the Land of Ultimate Bliss is surrounded by seven rows of railings, seven layers of nets, and seven lines of trees, all made of the four treasures. Therefore, that land is called Ultimate Bliss.

"Also, Sariputra, in the Land of Ultimate Bliss are ponds made of the seven treasures, filled with water with the eight virtues. Covering the bed of each pond is gold dust. The stairs and walkways on the four sides of each pond are made of gold, silver, aquamarine, and crystal. Standing majestically are lofty towers, all adorned with gold, silver, aquamarine, crystal, conch shell, ruby, and emerald. The lotus flowers in the ponds are as large as carriage wheels. The blue colors gleam with blue light; the yellow colors, yellow light; the red colors, red light; the white colors, white light. They are wonderful, fragrant, and pure. Sariputra, the Land of Ultimate Bliss is formed with such virtues as its adornments!

"Also, Sariputra, celestial music is always playing in that Buddha Land, and its ground is made of yellow gold. Day and night in the six periods, māndarāva flowers rain down from the sky. At dawn, sentient beings of that land fill their robes with wonderful flowers to make offerings to 100,000 koti Buddhas [in lands] in other directions. At mealtime, they return to their own land to eat and do walking meditation. Sariputra, the Land of Ultimate Bliss is formed with such virtues as its adornments!

In addition, Sariputra, in that land are various kinds of unusual, wonderful birds of diverse colors, such as white cranes, peacocks, parrots, saris, kalavinkas, and jivajivas. Day and night in the six periods, these birds sing harmonious, exquisite tones. These tones pronounce Dharmas, such as the Five Roots, the Five Powers, the Seven Bodhi Factors, and the Eightfold Right Path. Sentient beings that hear these tones all think of the Buddha, think of the Dharma, and think of the Sangha. Sariputra, do not say that these birds are born as a form of requital for sins [in their past lives]. Why not? Sariputra, that Buddha Land does not have the three evil life-paths. Sariputra, even the names of the three evil life-paths do not exist in that Buddha Land, much less the actual paths. These birds are all magically manifested by Amitabha Buddha to have the Dharma tones flow everywhere.

"Sariputra, as breezes blow in that Buddha Land, the jeweled trees in lines and the jeweled nets [with bells1] make wonderful music, like 100,000 melodies playing at the same time. Those who hear these tones spontaneously think of the Buddha, think of the Dharma, and think of the Sangha. Sariputra, that Buddha Land is formed with such virtues as its adornments!

"Sariputra, what is your opinion? Why is that Buddha called Amitabha? Sariputra, that Buddha's radiance is infinite, illuminating lands in the ten directions, hindrance free. Therefore, He is called Amitabha. Moreover, Sariputra, the lifespan of that Buddha and His people is measureless, limitless asaṁkhyeya kalpas. Therefore, He is called Amitāyus. Sariputra, it has been ten kalpas since Amitabha Buddha attained Buddhahood. In addition, Sariputra, that Buddha has innumerable, countless voice-hearer disciples. All of them are Arhats, their numbers unknowable by calculation. Equally unknowable is the size of the multitude of Bodhisattvas. Sariputra, that Buddha Land is formed with such virtues as its adornments!

"Furthermore, Sariputra, sentient beings reborn in the Land of Ultimate Bliss are at the spiritual level of avinivartaniya. Many among them are in the holy position of waiting to attain Buddhahood in their next life. Their numbers are so large that they are unknowable by calculation, and can be reckoned only in terms of measureless, limitless asamkhyeyas. Sariputra, sentient beings that have heard [of that land] should resolve to be reborn in that land. Why? To be in the same place together with people of superior virtues. Sariputra, no one with the condition of few roots of goodness and a meager store of merits can be reborn in that land.

"Sariputra, if, among good men and good women, there are those who, having heard of Amitabha Buddha, single-mindedly uphold His name for one day, two days, three days, four days, five days, six days, or seven days, without being distracted, then upon their dying, Amitabha Buddha, together with a multitude of holy beings, will appear before them. When these people die, their minds will not be demented and they will be reborn in Amitabha Buddha's Land of Ultimate Bliss. Sariputra, I see this benefit, so I speak these words. If there are sentient beings that hear what I say, they should resolve to be reborn in that land.

"Sariputra, as I now praise Amitabha Buddha's inconceivable merit, so too do Buddhas in worlds in the east, such as Aksobhya Buddha, Meru Banner Buddha, Great Meru Buddha, Meru Light Buddha, and Wonderful Tone Buddha. Buddhas such as these are as numerous as the sands of the Ganges. Each Buddha in His own land extends His wide-ranging, far-reaching tongue, completely covering the Three-Thousand Large Thousandfold World, and speaks these truthful words: 'You sentient beings should praise His inconceivable merit and believe in this sutra, which is protected and remembered by all Buddhas.'

"Sariputra, in worlds in the south are Sun-Moon Lamp Buddha, Renown Light Buddha, Great Flame Aggregate Buddha, 2 Meru Lamp Buddha, and Infinite Energetic Progress Buddha. Buddhas such as these are as numerous as the sands of the Ganges. Each Buddha in His own land extends His wide-ranging, far-reaching tongue, completely covering the Three-Thousand Large Thousandfold World, and speaks these truthful words: 'You sentient beings should praise His inconceivable merit and believe in this sutra, which is protected and remembered by all Buddhas.'

"Sariputra, in worlds in the west are Infinite Life Buddha, Infinite Aggregate Buddha, Infinite Banner Buddha, Great Light Buddha, Great Radiance Buddha, Jewel Brilliance Buddha, and Pure Light Buddha. Buddhas such as these are as numerous as the sands of the Ganges. Each Buddha in His own land extends His wide-ranging, far-reaching tongue, completely covering the Three-Thousand Large Thousandfold World, and speaks these truthful words: 'You sentient beings should praise His inconceivable merit and believe in this sutra, which is protected and remembered by all Buddhas.'

"Sariputra, in worlds in the north are Flame Aggregate Buddha, Supreme Tone Buddha, Hard-to-Vanquish Buddha, Sun Birth Buddha, Web-of-Radiance Buddha. Buddhas such as these are as numerous as the sands of the Ganges. Each Buddha in His own land extends His wide-ranging, far-reaching tongue, completely covering the Three-Thousand Large Thousandfold World, and speaks these truthful words: 'You sentient beings should praise His inconceivable merit and believe in this sutra, which is protected and remembered by all Buddhas.'

"Sariputra, in worlds toward the nadir are Lion Buddha, Renown Buddha, Renown Light Buddha, Dharma Buddha, Dharma Banner Buddha, and Dharma Upholder Buddha. Buddhas such as these are as numerous as the sands of the Ganges. Each Buddha in His own land extends His wide-ranging, far-reaching tongue, completely covering the Three-Thousand Large Thousandfold World, and speaks these truthful words: 'You sentient beings should praise His inconceivable merit and believe in this sutra, which is protected and remembered by all Buddhas.'

"Sariputra, in worlds toward the zenith are Brahma Tone Buddha, Constellation King Buddha, Fragrance Superior Buddha, Fragrant Light Buddha, Great Flame Aggregate Buddha, Adorned with Jeweled Flowers in Diverse Colors Buddha, Salendra King Buddha, Jeweled Lotus Flower Splendor Buddha, Seeing All Meaning Buddha, and Sumeru Likeness Buddha. Buddhas such as these are as numerous as the sands of the Ganges. Each Buddha in His own land extends His wide-ranging, far-reaching tongue, completely covering the Three-Thousand Large Thousandfold World, and speaks these truthful words: 'You sentient beings should praise His inconceivable merit and believe in this sutra, which is protected and remembered by all Buddhas.'

"Sariputra, what is your opinion? Why is this sutra called a sutra, protected and remembered by all Buddhas? Sariputra, if there are good men and good women who have heard and upheld this sutra, and have heard Buddhas' names, they are protected and remembered by all Buddhas. They will never regress from their resolve to attain anuttara-samyak-sambodhi. Therefore, Sariputra, you all should believe and accept my words and other Buddhas' words. If there are those who have resolved, are now resolving, or will resolve to be reborn in Amitabha Buddha's land, those people will never regress from their resolve to attain anuttara-samyak-sambodhi, whether they have already been reborn, are now being reborn, or will be reborn in that land. Therefore, Sariputra, if, among good men and good women, there are those who believe [my words], they should resolve to be reborn in that land.

"Sariputra, as I now praise Buddhas' inconceivable merit, 3 likewise those Buddhas praise my inconceivable merit, saying these words: 'Sakyamuni Buddha can do the extremely difficult, extraordinary thing in the Saha World during the evil times of the five turbidities—the turbidity of a kalpa, the turbidity of views, the turbidity of afflictions, the turbidity of sentient beings, and the turbidity of their lifespan—attaining anuttara-samyak-sambodhi. For the sake of sentient beings, He expounds the Dharma, which the entire world finds hard to believe.'

"Sariputra, know that, in the evil times of the five turbidities, I have done this difficult thing, attaining anuttara-samyak-sambodhi. For the sake of the entire world, I expound the hard-to-believe Dharma. It is extremely difficult!"

After the Buddha pronounced this sutra, Sariputra and other Bhikkhus, as well as gods, humans, asuras, and others in the entire world, having heard the Buddha's words, rejoiced, believed in, and accepted the teachings. They made obeisance and departed.